LON
CHANEY

THE MAN BEHIND
THE THOUSAND FACES

LON CHANEY

THE MAN BEHIND
THE THOUSAND FACES

Michael F. Blake

The Vestal Press, Ltd.
Vestal, New York

The Vestal Press, Ltd.
P.O. Box 97
Vestal, NY 13851-0097

99 98 97 96 95 94 93   1 2 3 4 5 6 7 8 9 10

Cover design by Don Bell

Library of Congress Cataloging-in-Publication Data

Blake, Michael F. (Michael Francis), 1957–
        Lon Chaney : the man behind the thousand faces / by
Michael F. Blake.
            p.   cm.
        Includes bibliographical references.
        ISBN 1-879511-08-8. – ISBN 1-879511-09-6 (pbk.)
        1. Chaney, Lon, 1883-1930.   I. Title.
PN2287.C48B58   1993
791.43'028'092–dc20   93-20212
                                                 CIP

TO THE MEMORY
OF

LAMAR D. TABB

The First Lon Chaney Fan

and a good friend.

Lon Chaney, The Man of a Thousand Faces

Table of Contents

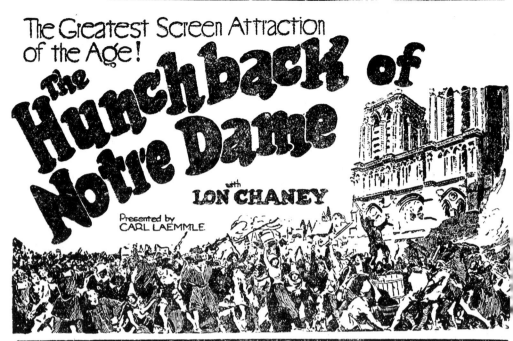

The Greatest Screen Attraction of the Age!

The Hunchback of Notre Dame

with LON CHANEY

Presented by
CARL LAEMMLE

Beginning
Wednesday

**Strongheart
the Wonder Dog**

—IN—

"THE LOVE MASTER"
WITH
LILLIAN RICH

Preface

It is difficult for today's generation to imagine what a tremendous impact motion pictures had on the public of the 'teens and 1920's. Long before cable networks, video tapes and television, which brought movie stars right into the living room of the moviegoer, the experience of a motion picture was magical, and going to a grand movie palace was a glamorous event. Theatres gave the audience their money's worth when they came to buy a ticket. Unlike today, theatres were large, clean, and staffed by a bevy of well-groomed, courteous ushers and usherettes. Some theatres even had a children's nursery! The usual bill at a movie theatre consisted of a newsreel (showing what was happening in the country and the world); then a cartoon (featuring the likes of Felix the Cat, "Out of the Inkwell" series, or a Walt Disney "Laugh-O-Gram"); then a popular serial of the day or a Mack Sennett or Hal Roach comedy starring Our Gang, Charlie Chase, or Laurel and Hardy. Sometimes vaudeville acts were on the bill as well, and then the featured film was screened. All of this entertainment was accompanied by either a huge WurliTzer organ, or in theatres of larger cities, a complete orchestra. A movie star set new trends in clothing or hair styles, and many a fan wanted to be just like his or her favorite actor or actress in his or her latest picture. Most stars had loyal followers, and theatre owners counted on fans to guarantee business whenever a picture featuring one of these stars played at their theatres. One such star was Lon Chaney.

Lon Chaney was one of those rare performers who, no matter how poor the script or how bad the direction, dominated his role. For the most part, he appealed to the male movie-going audience. A story told to me by an old friend shows how Chaney's screen presence charmed and made a fan out of one young man.

Lamar D. Tabb, like many of his school chums in the mid 1920's, regularly attended the comedies, serials, and westerns that played at local theatres in Dayton, Ohio. The chance two years earlier to see that "boring medieval picture" (as he called it), *The Hunchback of Notre Dame*, held no interest for him or his friends. One day at school, in 1925, he observed some of his friends at play — walking up to each other and bowing gracefully, while holding a long imaginary cigarette holder. Questioning his friends' strange behavior, they told him they were acting like "this guy Lon Chaney in *The Monster*." *The Monster* was admittedly not one of Lon Chaney's better films, but nonetheless, Lamar Tabb went to see the film and immediately became a loyal Chaney fan. From that point on, he never missed a Lon Chaney picture, including a revival of the *Hunchback of Notre Dame* in 1928.

What Lamar D. Tabb, and others since, have wondered is, what was Lon Chaney the man really like, and how did he create his characters and their famous faces? At the age of 10, after watching *Man of a Thousand Faces* on television, I was dismayed to find no books devoted to Lon Chaney, the actor or the man. As a teenager I, along with many others who admired this actor, tried in vain to emulate his great make-ups. Reading that he supposedly used celluloid discs (which he never did) to raise and extend his cheekbones in *Phantom of the Opera*, I was disappointed to see that my make-up did not resemble Chaney's Phantom, but rather a bad case of the mumps. I later found out that many who tried to look like the Phantom or sign their names with their feet as he reportedly did in *The Unknown* or drag themselves around like our hero in *West of Zanzibar*, had little accurate material to go by. My interest in collecting information on this actor grew into a hobby that has resulted in this book.

Over the years a lot of fiction has been printed about the life and career of Lon Chaney. This writing was no doubt the result of the authors' not spending the time to do the proper research or carefully checking the facts. This book is the result of six years of exhaustive research, and is as truthful and factual a presentation as is possible at this time. It is the intention of this book to clear up the fiction and errors others have reported, and attempt to set the record straight. I have preferred to let the facts speak and tell the story for themselves, avoiding the pitfalls of trying to put any words, other than his own, into the mouth of the subject.

This book is merely a piece of the puzzle. To appreciate Lon Chaney fully, the man and the actor, one must not only read about him, but should see as many of his movies as are available. The reviews and comments herein are of those who saw the films originally, and of those who either knew or worked with the man behind the thousand faces. I hope that if you aren't already a fan, you may become one, or at least an admirer of his work. Perhaps someday you may even want to see that old "boring medieval picture," *The Hunchback of Notre Dame*.

Michael F. Blake

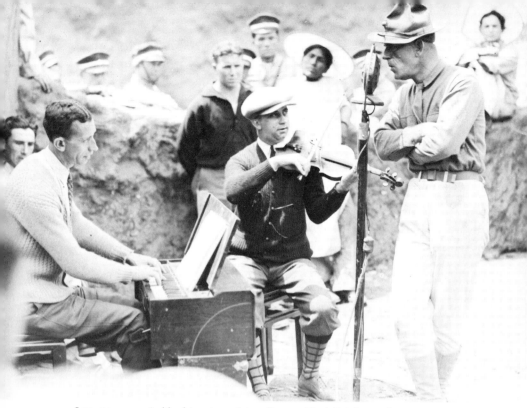

Lon, accompanied by his set musicians Sam and Jack Feinberg, sings a song during location shooting at Iverson's Ranch in Chatsworth, California. (*Tell It To The Marines*, 1927)

Victor Seastrom and Lon filming in the Hollywood Hills for *Tower Of Lies*.

Acknowledgements

While only one name may appear as author of this book, the author is only as good as his supporting cast. Thus, I would like to extend my gratitude to the following individuals and organizations for all their help on this project.

Robert G. Anderson
Bob Birchard
Mr. & Mrs. M. A. Bishop,
    Glacier Pack Train,
    Bishop, California
Larry J. Blake
Teresa A. Blake
Priscilla Bonner
1st Lt. J. D. Brader, USMC
Lawson Brainard
Bill Brent
Thomas Butler
James Cagney
Sterling Campbell
Gary Chaney
George Chaney
Keith Chaney
Lon Ralph Chaney
Rita Chaney
Ron Chaney, Jr.
Colorado School for the
    Deaf and Blind,
    Colorado Springs, Colorado
James Curtis
Crit Davis
Dick Dawson
Priscilla Dean
Oliver Dernberger
Beverly Diehl

Ray Downing
Thelma M. Dunphy
William N. Dunphy
Harry Earles
Larry Edmunds Bookshop
Betty Felch-Griffin
Tony Fiyalko
Dick Foster
Barry L. Friedman
Stella George
Sam Gill
Loren Harbert
Mike Hawks
Margaret Herrick Library,
    Academy of Motion Picture
    Arts and Sciences,
    Los Angeles, California
John Hill
Janet Hoffman
James Wong Howe
Adela Rogers St. Johns
Joyce Johns
Tom Kuhn
Henry Kurth
Burt Lancaster
Andrew Lee,
    Director of Research
    at Universal Studios

Los Angeles Public Library,
   Los Angeles, California
Col. Carl K. Mahakian,
   USMC (Ret.)
Make-up Artists and Hairstylists
   Union, Local 706, IATSE
Randal Malone
Leonard Maltin
Leonard McSherry
Patsy Ruth Miller
Laura A. Moore
Jack Mulhall
Bill Nelson
Jim Nicholas
Carroll Nye
Oklahoma Historical Society,
   Oklahoma City, Oklahoma
Anita Page
Cheryl Pappas
Kenneth Partridge
Penrose Public Library and the
   staff of local history division,
   Colorado Springs, Colorado
Harvey Perry
Joseph Pevney
Fred Phillips, S.M.A.
Pike's Peak Historical Society,
   Colorado Springs, Colorado
Pioneer's Museum,
   Colorado Springs, Colorado

Eddie Quillan
Mike Ragan
Esther Ralston
Philip J. Riley
Dr. James J. Roach, Jr., MD
Lillane Ross
Celeste Rush
Mary Jane Rust
San Francisco Performing Arts
   Library and Museum,
   San Francisco, California
San Francisco Public Library,
   San Francisco, California
Bob Scherl
Douglas J. Schiffer
William Self
Lamar D. Tabb
Steve Tanner
Takashi Teshigawara
U.S. Forest Service,
   Bishop, California
Charles Van Enger
Herbert Voight
George Wagner
Robert L. White
Patrick Wood
Ann Wright

I would also like to thank my wife, Linda, for all of her hard work, criticism and suggestions which helped me to see this labor of love come to life.

Beginnings of An Actor

"As a comedian he is irresistible and it would be hard to find his equal in dancing among many first class vaudeville performers."
—Review of Lon Chaney's theatrical debut in "The Little Tycoon." — 1902

Frank and Emma Chaney (Courtesy of the Chaney Family Collection)

The home on West Bijou Street where the Chaneys lived in 1894. It still stands today. (Photo courtesy of Patrick Wood)

In the early 1920's, a man about to step on a spider might well be cautioned by a friend, "Don't step on that spider! It might be Lon Chaney!" This good-natured line, which was in wide-spread use for nearly a decade, is symbolic of the fascination the movie-going public held for a chameleon-like actor who became one of the world's top motion picture attractions. Yet there was probably less known about Lon Chaney than any other star in Hollywood.

While the Hollywood publicity machine ground out countless stories on almost every aspect of a performer's private and public life, Lon Chaney created much of his own mystique by simply providing as little information about himself as possible. Chaney once said he'd get more publicity by remaining a mystery to the public than if he were more accessible.[1] More half-truths and outright fiction have been printed about Chaney than any other star from his period. Chaney was one of the biggest contributors to this fiction by rarely granting interviews, and then when he did, he was not always completely open and honest. In a few instances Chaney did become remarkably candid with a particular reporter, and in these interviews he gave the public a glimpse of a man who was often amused when mistaken for a studio grip instead of a movie star. He was once quoted as saying, "Between pictures there is no Lon Chaney. There is only the character I am creating."[2] While this certainly reflects his almost total immersion in each role, that statement is not entirely true. There *was* a Lon Chaney between pictures, as fascinating and as interesting as any character he portrayed on the screen. Despite his fame, Chaney remained a simple, sentimental fellow who never forgot a favor nor a bad turn.

Because of his propensity to remain a mystery, Lon Chaney was considered by many to be gruff and insensitive. However, actress Peggy Woods saw a different side of Chaney one day on the studio lot. Lon was on his way back to his dressing room when a commotion on the lawn caught his attention. Several baby birds, together with their nest, had fallen out of a nearby tree. Lon gently picked up the nest and, with his one free hand, climbed the tree and restored the nest and its frazzled tenants to a safe branch. When he climbed down and noticed the actress watching, he asked her not to tell anyone. "Everyone thinks I'm so hard-boiled that I'll never hear the end of it!"[3]

Writer Jim Tully was a close friend of Chaney's and in a *Vanity Fair* article, he observed the following about Lon:

> His sense of humor is bitingly keen. When the
> bones, often twisted to make a moron holiday, ache
> more than usual, his temper is uneven. It is said that
> one can tell how the great contortionist is feeling
> by the remarks he makes . . . But withal, his heart is
> warm.[4]

In one of Lon Chaney's more engaging interviews, Lewis L. Nichols of the *New York Times* wrote that Chaney

> is an interesting talker, emphasizing many of his
> points with gestures, and when he tries to make
> anything particularly plain, tossing in just a little
> characterization. His voice carries a curious spell

with it. As in his actions, his word pictures seem to stand out a bit from the background.[5]

William N. Dunphy, whose grandparents William and Mabel were close friends of Lon's, said his mother Thelma remembered Lon as "an outgoing person amongst his friends who was prone to teasing and practical joking. He was very good-natured and was a nice dancer."[6] In fact, an extra who worked with Lon on *The Big City* said years later that Lon's dancing was as graceful as, and in some ways better than, Fred Astaire's.[7]

Lon Chaney was the rare star who shunned the glamour of Hollywood and often took satisfaction in the fact that he could walk down the street and rarely be recognized. When M-G-M made an offer to give him a valet, Lon politely refused. He dressed conservatively, usually in a blue suit, red tie and his traditional cap, and was often described by writers as dressing more like a successful businessman than a movie star. He was considered to be shrewd, especially when it came to his career. When the studios started to make talking pictures, Lon held out, later stating, "I refused to talk because I am a businessman and I did not care to be a pioneer. The thing was imperfect at the time. It was experimental. Why should I, with my box office as it is, risk all of that for something that might have died stillborn?"[8]

Once when Lon was taking some visitors around the studio lot, they wanted to visit the set where John Gilbert and Jeanne Eagles were working. Gilbert, without explanation, refused to allow them on the set. The actress was very drunk and Gilbert thought it unwise to let outsiders see her in that condition. At a later date Gilbert tried to explain this to Lon, but Chaney never missed an opportunity to show his contempt. A personality problem between the two men went back to their acting together in *While Paris Sleeps*. Gilbert couldn't understand Chaney's single-minded dedication to his craft and Lon didn't care for Gilbert's playboy pose. According to his daughter Leatrice Gilbert Fountain, Gilbert once confided to a friend about Chaney, "I never have anything to say to that man. He looks right through me."[9] In a 1928 *Vanity Fair* article about Gilbert, Chaney told writer Jim Tully, "He is a good actor and thinks he is much better. . . . He loves to impress folks with his greatness by being unpleasant to them."[10]

Lon was once asked what he thought about other actors in general, and his reply was terse: "I'd rather not say."[11] Yet he did admire many in his profession, among them Emil Jannings, Gloria Swanson, Wallace Beery and character actors like Raymond Hatton and Tully Marshall.

While these anecdotes give a glimpse of Chaney the man, Chaney the actor was another story. Though he had no formal training, he was able to bring to his roles tremendous depth, power and sensitivity in an era where over-acting was common. Chaney approached his roles with complete concentration, carefully analyzing how a certain type of character should look or walk and what type of gestures he would use. He once said an actress who plays the part of a married woman must act, talk, and dress like a married woman. "It would never do to see her pick up a baby, when she is playing the part of a mother, and not know how to hold it."[12]

The seeds of this approach to acting took root in his hometown of Colorado Springs, Colorado. Lon Chaney was born there on April 1, 1883, just twelve years after its founding by railroad entrepreneur William Jackson Palmer. Palmer and his associates envisioned a city equal to gracious and fashionable eastern resort towns such as Newport or Saratoga Springs. One slight problem facing Palmer and his developers was an almost complete lack of water in the city; only two small creeks trickled through an eastern section of town. To justify the town's name, Palmer found springs six miles away in present-day Manitou. The springs were blessed with the foul-smelling odor of sulfur that would later, along with the dry climate, prove to be helpful to those suffering from tuberculosis.

At its founding on July 31, 1871, Colorado Springs was far from the peaceful resort Palmer envisioned. The treeless desert of yuccas and buffalo grass was populated by rattlesnakes; a harsh wind blew with such force it knocked over several locomotives and their cars. But people were attracted to the clean air, scenery, and the lure of gold and silver in the nearby mining town of Cripple Creek. By 1872, the dirt streets were graded and the Colorado Springs Hotel opened to accommodate the growing number of visitors, many of whom decided to call the town home. In 1881, the city built its first Opera House on Tejon Street, and in 1883 the Antlers Hotel, one of the grandest hotels west of the Mississippi, opened its doors.

Frank Chaney arrived in this growing town in mid-1877. At the age of 25, he was a professional barber, and whatever his impressions of Colorado Springs were, he could only express them with his hands — for Frank Chaney was deaf.

Frank Chaney was born on April 3, 1852, in Carroll, Ohio, of English and French descent. His father James farmed land he rented from his father, John Chaney, who had served in both the Ohio State Legislature and in the United States Congress in the 1830's and 40's. John Chaney was also selected to represent the state of Ohio when it nominated Andrew Jackson for president.

Frank had not been born deaf; his disability resulted from a case of typhoid fever contracted at the age of four. He attended a school for the deaf in Fulton, Missouri, where, during his teenage years, he had a sweetheart named Cora. After he left the school and went west to seek his fortune, opposition by Cora's parents (due to the sweethearts' five-year age difference) thwarted their plans to marry.

Frank Chaney settled in Colorado Springs, working in various barber shops until 1882, when he obtained a permanent position in Phil Strubel's barber shop and soon became shop foreman. For over

30 years Frank worked the head chair, even after the shop was sold in 1904 and the name changed to Cambells. He had gained the affectionate nickname "Dummy the Barber" from his patrons.

Frank Chaney was also nicknamed the "Millionaire's Barber" because he had many wealthy customers. Often Frank was given a five-, ten- and even twenty-dollar gold piece as a tip for his services. Winfield Scott Stratton was a well-known mining millionaire and one of Frank's regular customers. Frank went to Stratton's home to tend to his tonsorial needs. On the night of January 24, 1900, Mr. Stratton was particularly generous, giving Frank a $500 tip. On his way home that night, Frank was assaulted by two thugs who attempted to rob him. Frank, however, put up a good fight and managed to escape his attackers with only a few scratches and his wallet completely intact. His assailants were never caught. When Stratton heard about the incident, he told Frank that had he lost the money, he would have given him another $500.[13]

No doubt one of the reasons Frank Chaney chose to work in Colorado Springs was the Colorado School for the Deaf was located there. Not only did this school teach young children and adults who were born deaf, it also served as a magnet for social activities for all of the city's deaf community. It was here that Frank first met his future wife, Emma Kennedy.

Emma's parents, John and Mary Kennedy, were of Irish descent and born in Ohio; in 1855 they settled in Lawrence, Kansas, where Emma was born on October 13 of that year. It soon became apparent that their beloved daughter was deaf. No doubt spurred on by his daughter's disability, John Kennedy established the Mute Asylum in Baldwin City, Kansas, in 1864, and served as the steward of the Olastic Deaf and Dumb Asylum from 1866 to 1870. From there, the Kennedy family moved to Denver, where John Kennedy met with the governor and members of the state legislature in an attempt to establish a school for the deaf. The Colorado State Legislature voted to establish the school in Colorado Springs. The Colorado School for the Deaf opened in a frame building on April 8, 1874, on ten acres of land donated by Palmer's Colorado Springs Company at Cucharras and Tejon Streets, where it remained for two years. Kennedy was elected superintendent and his wife was matron. The school moved to the corner of Pike's Peak Avenue and Institute Street on January 6, 1876, where it still stands today.

By this time the Kennedys had two other children, a daughter Mattie and a son Orange, both of whom were also deaf. In 1879 Mattie Kennedy married Hugh Harbert, who for years edited *The Colorado Deaf and Blind Index*.

On December 5, 1877, Frank and Emma exchanged marriage vows in her parents' home. Frank and Emma Chaney's first child, Jonathan Orange Chaney, was born in Colorado Springs on August 5, 1879. After Lon's birth on April 1st, 1883, a third child, Earl, was born on May 14, 1887. He died on July 7, 1887, of pulmonary consumption. Their only daughter, Caroline (called Carrie for short), was born December 20, 1888. The following announcement appeared on June 11, 1893 in the Colorado Springs Gazette; "The household of Mr. Frank Chaney, popular deaf barber at Phil Strubel's tonsorial shop, was brightened yesterday by the arrival of a son." This was George, their last child.

For years, writers have thought Chaney's first name was Alonzo, but according to his brother George, his name at birth was Leonidas (Pronounced Lee-o-nah-dis).[14] Research on Frank Chaney's family tree shows that one of his older brothers was named Leonidas. In those days as now, children were often named after family members, and the Chaney family exhibits a propensity for naming children after relatives. Unfortunately there is no birth certificate for Lon in the few records on file from the 1880's in Colorado Springs; however, a city directory from 1908 and an article in a 1920 *Picture Play* magazine list his name as Leonidas.[15] In most of the city directories of

Colorado Springs from 1900 to 1908, as well as the U. S. Census of 1900, his name is listed as Leonard, an anglicized version of Leonidas. The first time he was listed publicly as "Lon" was in the 1902 review of *The Little Tycoon.* It seems that Lon was a nickname that stuck, and he used it for the rest of his personal and professional life.

Despite his parent's affliction, Lon steadfastly maintained that he had a reasonably happy childhood. His brother George once said that Lon felt no childhood was really unhappy, because youth had the opportunity to achieve happiness under any kind of circumstances. Lon claimed to be a pretty good football player and played a fair game of baseball; his childhood seems to have been filled with friendships, many of which endured until Lon's death. Dr. Lloyd Shaw, a Colorado Springs contemporary of Lon's, recalled that his brother Ray and Lon had jobs at the Opera House as stage hands, and when the occasion arouse, appeared in a "super" part.[16] (A "super" is short for supernumerary and refers to one who is used as an extra to fill up the stage.) Lon and Ray remained friends until Lon's death. Two other long-time friends were Lon's first cousin Hugh Harbert (the son of Mattie Kennedy and Hugh Harbert) and Harry Hughes, whom Lon often visited when in town during the 1920's.

Noble Johnson and his two brothers, Virgil and George, were boyhood friends of Lon who made their mark in Hollywood. The Johnsons were a well-known black family in the city and their father was an expert horse trainer. The three Johnson brothers started an all-black film company in the mid-teens that made and distributed films exclusively for blacks. Noble left the company to his brothers and went off on his own to become an actor. He worked at Universal in the late 'teens playing villains and eventually worked in such films as the original *The Ten Commandments* (1923), *The Mummy*

(1932), as the native chief in *King Kong* (1933) and as Red Shirt in *She Wore a Yellow Ribbon* (1949).

George Johnson recalled meeting Lon at M-G-M on the set of *West of Zanzibar* in 1928. George was at the studio visiting an advertising manager when Lon's name came up in the conversation. George mentioned that he knew Lon and learned that Chaney was working at the studio that day. George went over to the backlot and spotted Lon relaxing between scenes. He went up to Lon and nudged him. George said Lon mistook him for his older brother Virgil and, when he told him who he was, Lon excitedly replied "Oh! I know you too!" The two men shook hands and talked of their childhood memories of Colorado Springs.[17]

E. F. McKay, a one-time Colorado Springs resident, recalled to the *Oklahoma City Times* that he often saw Lon as a boy at Phil Stubel's Barber Shop, "He used to play around in the shop and in the street in front of it. Any old-timer in Colorado Springs knew 'Dummy' well, but none ever saw anything notable in the often dirty-faced boy who was to achieve fame."[18]

However, when Lon was in fourth grade, an event occurred which would have a profound effect upon his future. Shortly after giving birth to her son George, Emma Chaney was stricken with inflammatory rheumatism which rendered her bed-ridden for several years. Lon was forced to drop out of school to care for her as well as for Carrie and George. While Frank and John worked, Lon took charge of the household chores as well as seeing to his mother's comfort. It was here that Lon began to develop the talent that later won him praise as one of the great mimes of the silent screen. For three years, Lon took care of his mother in the silence of her bedroom, relaying the events of the day to her. To communicate with a deaf person, one uses not only finger spelling and hand gestures, but also facial and body expressions, interwoven into the language. Using every dramatic technique he could invent, Lon mimicked his friends and neighbors at play and work, and even performed an occasional skit. Through this daily ritual Chaney's talent of pantomime, with his graceful movements and his expressive hand gestures, began to grow and take shape.

When he was about 14, Lon's talent for expressing himself found an occupational outlet; he got a job as a tour guide during the summer months at Pike's Peak, taking visitors up by burro and pointing out the various sites of interest. For all his life, the mountains were Lon's Shangri-la. In later years, he spent most of his free time in the Eastern Sierra Nevada mountains of California fishing and camping.

During this time, Lon's older brother John had started working at the local Opera House as a stage hand, and occasionally as an assistant stage manager. Through his brother, Lon was introduced to what eventually became his livelihood. He got his start, humbly, as a prop boy for the sum of twenty-five cents a night.

While making *The Unholy Three* in 1925, Lon was introduced to Frederick Warde, a famous stage star visiting the M-G-M lot. "I don't expect you to remember me, Mr. Warde," Lon said, when the two were introduced. Warde paid Chaney a compliment on his work, but could not place him from an earlier meeting. "Do you remember once when you played Colorado Springs, you were taking an extra curtain call and a prop boy came out onto the stage to move a vase? Well, I was that prop boy!"[19]

Lon's stage experience grew from humble beginnings, and he remained a staunch supporter of working men and their unions throughout his life. A clear demonstration of this is in a story told about Chaney when he was a major star at M-G-M. He always finished work at 5 p.m. unless night scenes were called for. One day, filming was progressing slowly and it became obvious that they wouldn't finish the scenes with the extras by Lon's usual quitting time. If Lon left at 5 p.m., all the extras would have to be recalled for another day's work, and another day's pay, at their usual salary of $10 to $15. Irving Thalberg, M-G-M's production head, tried to persuade Lon to work longer so they could finish the scenes with the extras, thus avoiding the additional costs. Lon flatly refused, reminding Thalberg that he never held up production, even if it required him to arrive at the studio by 5 or 6 a.m. to apply his make-up so he could make his set call on time. "Besides," Lon told Thalberg, "these people need the extra day's salary."[20]

Anita Page, who co-starred with Lon in *While the City Sleeps,* confirmed hearing the stand Lon took:

> I loved it when I heard how Lon told Thalberg the
> extras would have to come back for an additional
> day's work because he wouldn't work late. That
> story was well known on the lot. He was the
> biggest male star on the lot and everyone respected
> him. You know Thalberg was Thalberg and when
> Lon stood up for the extras . . . what more could
> you say? Not only was he so brilliant [as an actor]
> but he stood up for his fellow man. He stood up for
> the crew on the set and was perfectly at ease with
> all of them. He was a very moral man. Nobody tried
> to take advantage of him.[21]

Until his death, Lon maintained his membership in the Stage Hands Union, later to become the International Alliance of Theatrical Stage Employees (IATSE). He was always proud of his affiliation with the union and almost every story or interview done in the 1920's mentions this fact.

While serving as a prop boy and later as a stage hand at the Opera House, he had his first exposure to the effects of theatrical make-up. Through cracks in dressing room doors, he watched various touring company stars change their appearances with the aid of grease paint, nose putty, and crepe hair.

However, at this early date, Lon did not seem to consider the theater a practical career choice. Although Frank Chaney continued to receive sizable tips, Emma's illness and four children at home must have rendered money very tight; from 1880 to 1914, the Chaneys resided at approximately 18 addresses in Colorado Springs. This, as well as his lean years as an actor, made an impression upon Lon that he never forgot. Tod Browning, who directed ten of his films, referred to Chaney as "the star who lived like a clerk."[22]

When Lon was 15, his father arranged for him to learn the trade of carpet laying and wallpaper hanging. In a 1927 *Photoplay* interview, Lon said he went to Denver to work at Cortdez and Feldhauser, the largest drapery house in the city.[23] He also stated that he stayed with the firm for three years, although no Denver city directories from this period list Chaney as residing or boarding there; however, in the Colorado Springs city directory of 1900, Chaney is listed as an employee of Brown's Wallpaper and Paint Company.

On October 1, 1898, the famous Antlers Hotel was destroyed by fire when burning embers from a nearby freight car fire were carried by the wind to the hotel. As soon as the ruins of the old hotel had been cleared, work was started on a new and even grander Antlers. During its construction in 1900, Chaney was one of the workers who helped install the carpets and hang the wallpaper. In the *Colorado Springs Evening Telegraph*, on the day of Chaney's death, the paper reported that "some of his work remains to be seen in the paper on the walls of the Antlers Hotel."[24]

By 1902, however, Lon had given in to his true calling, and was employed full-time as a stage hand at the Opera House. Shortly after his 19th birthday, Lon made his debut as an actor in an amateur play called *The Little Tycoon* presented at the Opera House on April 19,

1902. *The Colorado Springs Gazette* said the following of his performance:

> As the entertaining valet, Lon Chaney provoked laughter whenever he appeared on the stage and his dancing was received with loud acclamations of approval. As a comedian he is irresistible, and it would be hard to find his equal in dancing among many first class vaudeville performers . . . The Keyes boys also did excellent work, and one of the most finished bits of acting was contributed by John Chaney as the Lord. He did not have many lines, or much to do, but what did fall to his lot was given with a quiet skill which did very much to render the performance well-balanced and artistic.[25]

The Little Tycoon was a family affair, for not only did Lon and John appear in the play, but Benjamin, one of the Keyes boys, also performed. One year later, Benjamin married Lon's sister, Carrie.

Colorado Springs' Opera House where Lon got his start as a prop boy and later made his acting debut. (Courtesy of Pioneer's Museum)

The Colorado School for the Deaf and Blind as it stands today. This is the school Lon's maternal grandparents founded in 1874. (Photo courtesy of Patrick Wood)
Frank Chaney (second from right, arms folded) at Phil Strubel's barber shop in June, 1900. (Courtesy of Pioneer's Museum)

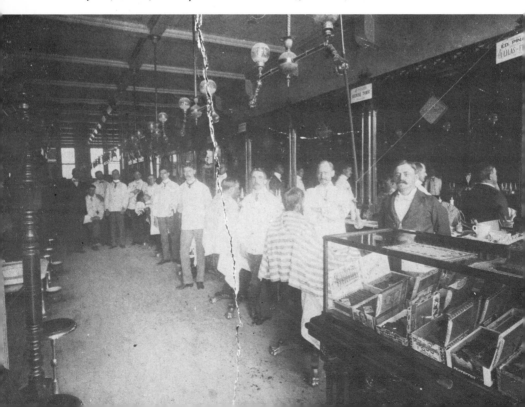

The Man of Musical Comedies
(1902-1912)

"I speak for more character parts for Lon Chaney, who as far as acting was concerned, was the unquestionable star of The Hen Pecks and certainly a man of unusual talent in character roles."
—In The Big Play World *column,* Los Angeles Times, *April 24, 1912*

(Left) Lon and Mlle. Vanity, the featured dancer of Fischer's Follies, April 1912.

Los Angeles Times, July 22, 1912

The acting bug had bitten Lon Chaney and his career as a carpet layer and wallpaper hanger was soon only a memory. But Lon maintained in a *Motion Picture Classic* magazine article of March, 1929, that it was a trade he could always fall back on if the "talkies" put him out of business.

In December of 1902, an article in the *Colorado Springs Gazette* stated that members of the local Stage Employees Union planned to present a series of comic operas at the Opera House. Both Lon and his brother John were mentioned as appearing in upcoming productions, including *Pirates of Penzance*.[26] Despite stories that have been published in the past, there is no evidence that Lon performed in *The Mikado* or *The Red Kimono* in Colorado Springs, although he may have been in these plays while he was touring with various companies.

Lon's next performance was in June of 1903, when he appeared with the Casino Opera Company at the Opera House in a production of *Said Pasha*. The June 9, 1903, *Colorado Springs Gazette* said, ". . . Lon Chaney, too, was good, and there were many others deserving of praise." The following month, the company became known as the Columbia Opera Company, and on July 13, 1903, opened a one-week stand at the Opera House with the comic opera *The Chimes of Normandy*. Chaney played the role of "The Assessor" in this production, and most of the same cast of *Said Pasha* also appeared.

Lon Chaney

In the 1904 city directory he was listed for the first time as "Lon F. Chaney, actor." Chaney must have been feeling confident of himself and his talents to list himself as an actor, having only performed in a few plays, but the listing also shows that he had made a conscious decision to make a career out of performing. That year, Lon and his first cousin Hugh Harbert went to San Francisco and Los Angeles to try their luck at getting into some stage shows. At that time, San Francisco and Los Angeles were usually the stopping points for most of the big touring companies. The tours started in Chicago, making one- or two-night stands through the midwest. Most shows played a week in St. Louis and Denver, then stopped off in Colorado Springs for one or two nights, followed by stops in Salt Lake City and Virginia City, Nevada, before arriving in San Francisco. According to Hugh Harbert's grandson, Loren, Lon's and Hugh's luck wasn't very good, and at one point they stood on street corners where Lon attracted a crowd with his eccentric dancing and his cousin Hugh played the violin and passed the hat.[27]   Shortly after this escapade, they returned to Colorado Springs. Lon rejoined the Columbia Opera Company which was preparing to tour the midwest with an assorted repertoire.

Over the next year and a half, Chaney toured Kansas, Missouri, Nebraska, North and South Dakota, Arkansas, Texas and what would soon become Oklahoma. During this period, Chaney's talents as a performer were really put to the test. Most of these shows had little to offer in terms of sets, props, orchestration and costumes. It then became the performers' responsibility to take what little they had and make a good show out of it, so the audience would return to see their other productions.

Chaney recounted those days of one-night stands during a three-part 1927-28 *Photoplay* profile, one of the few articles in which he discussed his early days and rise to stardom. He said that the company felt they were in the lap of luxury when they got to play in a theatre that had dressing rooms. In most theatres, a sheet was hung up on a rope in an area backstage, and women changed on one side of the sheet, men on the other. When the company played theaters with no dressing rooms, the actors had to store their trunks in the orchestra pit and go out in front of the audience, pick out their changes from the trunks and hurry backstage to dress. When they played small towns that had no theaters, a meeting hall or a store-front served as a stage; for footlights, the company had to make do with coal-oil lamps, which had a nasty habit of blowing out during the performance. It was then up to the performers to walk downstage and re-light the lamps while still delivering their lines. Lucky for the company that their audiences were starved for entertainment![28]

The troupe generally traveled from town to town in a freight train caboose because it was cheaper than a regular passenger train. These trains traveled so slowly that often Lon and several other members of the group occasionally hopped off the train and ventured out into the country to do some quail hunting, catching up to the train at a walk.[29] Aside from performing with the Columbia Opera Company, Lon also helped stage the musical numbers, arrange for transportation, and oversee the wardrobe — all for a weekly salary of $14. But this experience would prove to be invaluable to Chaney years later in motion pictures.

In the spring of 1905, the company arrived in Oklahoma City where auditions were held at Delmar Gardens for some local chorus girls. One of the locals to audition was a 16-year-old girl with a particularly beautiful singing voice; her name was Cleva Creighton.

Most stories relating to Lon and Cleva's romance and subsequent marriage give the date of their wedding as May 31, 1905; however, according to city records, Lon and Cleva were married on May 31, 1906 by Thomas H. Harper, pastor of the People's Temple Church. It seems unlikely that Lon and Cleva would have waited three months after the birth of their child to marry, since bearing a child out of wedlock was considered unthinkable at that time. Possibly the city records are incorrect, or the Chaneys were married while on tour and had a more formal ceremony the next year when they returned to Cleva's home town. However, another item supporting the city records appeared in the *Daily Oklahoman* on June 1, 1906: "A marriage permit was issued from the probate court yesterday to Lon Chaney and Miss Cleva Creighton, both residents of Oklahoma City."

Regardless of the actual marriage date, they left the touring company in December of 1905 and returned to Oklahoma City to prepare for the birth of their child. The 1905-06 city directory did not list Lon, but Cleva was listed as "Creighton, Frances C. Miss, actress - H. [home] 318 W. Potawatomie Ave."

To prepare financially for fatherhood, Lon got a job at Street and Harper Furniture Store on Main Street, recently purchased by a man named Francis M. Tull. Tull renamed the store "Tull's Grand Rapids Furniture Company." Lon remained with the new owner, taking charge of the rug department. Interviewed by the *Oklahoma City Times* at the time of Chaney's death, Tull described Lon as "an ordinary nice looking chap that worked hard," but added that the footlights were too tantalizing for Chaney and he couldn't stick to nailing rugs.[30]

On February 10, 1906, Lon's only child, Creighton Tull Chaney, was born. The boy's first name came from Cleva's maiden name, and the name Tull was taken from Lon's generous employer at the furniture store. Many years after Lon's death, a story surfaced that Creighton was born a bluish baby and did not cry out immediately, causing Lon to plunge him into the icy waters outside of their cabin to revive him. According to Lon's grandson, Lon Ralph Chaney, as well as Cleva's daughter by her second marriage, Stella George, the story is complete fiction.[31]

In May of 1906, Lon gave up his job at the furniture store to rejoin the Columbia Comic Opera Company which was about to begin its engagement at Oklahoma City's Delmar Gardens with a variety of musical comedies including *Said Pasha*, *Pinafore*, and *La Mascotte*. After playing this engagement, Lon played with various local companies and appeared in another local production of *La Mascotte* on April 25 and 26, 1907. A clipping in a 1907 edition of the *Oklahoma City Time Journal* said the following about his performance:

> Lon Chaney as the Prince Lorenzo was a decided hit. Mr. Chaney is a professional formerly with the Columbia Opera Company, and made a host of friends last year at Delmar Garden. His work was of the highest order and the comedy scenes between him and Charles Pryor were great. While it was known their work would be good, it was a delightful surprise to find the comedy so amusing.[32]

Even without much experience or training, Chaney's theatrical talents were earning positive notices. Yet the daily grind of putting a show together and performing had taught him much, and along with his youthful enthusiasm and God-given talent he was making headway to becoming a first-class performer.

Exact details of the next few years of Chaney's life are somewhat sketchy. The Oklahoma City 1907 city directory lists the couple as "Chaney, Lawn (wf [wife] Clevie) vaudeville, rms [rooms] 312 W. Washington." By 1908, they were back in Colorado Springs, living with Lon's parents and his brother George. That city's directory listed them as "Chaney, Leonidas F, carpet lyr [layer], bds [boards] 220 E. Vermijo Ave. (Mrs. Cleve)."

Lon Chaney

By April 1909, Lon and Cleva had left his home town and were in Chicago performing with the Cowpuncher Company. By October, Lon was performing in *The Royal Chef* at the Tabor Grand Opera House in Denver. The October 25, 1909, edition of the *Denver Post* said the following of its production:

> *The Royal Chef* one of those annual occurrences at the Tabor Grand which seem to retain their popularity with the patrons, inexplicably while other productions come for a year or two and are then heard of no more, packed two houses at the Tabor yesterday . . . . Walter A. Bohme as the Royal Chef and Lon Chaney as Lord Mito, furnished the amusement for the audiences. They were both very popular and received applause constantly.

The show played Denver for a week, then moved to Colorado Springs for a one-night stand at the Opera House on November 1. Cleva played "Trico," one of the Court Beauties in the production.

In 1910, Lon and Cleva were working in Los Angeles at a theatre called the Olympic on Main Street for a salary of $35 weekly. The Olympic was a "tabloid" musical comedy house which presented condensed versions of popular shows three to five times a day, seven days a week. After about six months, Lon and Cleva joined the Ferris Hartman Company at the Grand Opera House which was also located on Main Street. Other members of the company included Roscoe "Fatty" Arbuckle, who later started his motion picture career with Mack Sennett Studios; Robert Z. Leonard, who would direct his wife, Mae Murray, and Lon in a 1918 film for Universal, *Danger-Go Slow*; Frances White, who went on to become a headliner in vaudeville and musical comedies in New York; and a chorus girl named Hazel Hastings. The company toured the state, playing for a few months in

San Francisco and Oakland. Between tours, Lon also worked for other theatre companies, at one time serving as an understudy to the well-known musical comedy star Fred Stone. No doubt this was an invaluable training ground for Lon as Stone was considered to be one of the top performers of his time.

The Los Angeles City Directory of 1911 lists Lon and Cleva as living at 826 East 7th Avenue, but by August of that year, Lon was appearing with Max Dill and his company in *The Rich Mr. Hoggenheimer* at the Savoy Theatre in San Francisco. Max Dill was part of the famous Dutch comedy team of Kolb and Dill until June 1910, when the two performers parted ways and were not reunited until 1912. Dill's company left San Francisco by the end of August for a tour of the state. Coincidentally, as Chaney was rehearsing with Dill's company before their August opening, the Fred Karno Troupe was finishing an engagement at the Empress Theatre in the same city. Two performers in this troupe were Charles Chaplin and Stan Laurel.

By February of 1912, Chaney had signed up with Fischer's Follies. E. A. "Pop" Fischer was a well-known producer in the Los Angeles area. Prior to settling in Los Angeles in 1906, he had made his mark in San Francisco with musical comedies, employing the then unknown team of Kolb and Dill. With Harry James, Fischer's musical director in San Francisco, directing the current company, they planned to present only New York and Chicago hits during their musical comedy season. Arrangements had been made with entertainment greats like George M. Cohan, Weber and Fields, and the La Salle Theatre in Chicago to present top theatre hits, and Fischer considered taking some shows to Chicago or New York.

Fischer's Follies opened on March 17, 1912, at the Lyceum Theatre with productions of *The Neverhomes* and *The Song Birds.* The company changed shows every two weeks (with the exception of *Tillie's Nightmare* which ran four weeks to handle the crowds), doing one nightly performance and three matinees a week. The company also did productions of *When Johnny Comes Marching Home*, *Little Johnny Jones* (George M. Cohan's famous musical that introduced the two hit songs "Yankee Doodle Dandy" and "Give My Regards to Broadway"), *The Man Who Owns Broadway*, *The Chaperons*, *The Yankee Prince*, and *An American Idea*.

Lon appeared in all of these productions, served as stage manager, and choreographed the musical numbers while Cleva usually appeared in the chorus. Other members of the company included May Boley, Texas Guinan, Laura Oakley, Bob Lett, Herbert Cawthorne, and Mlle. Vanity, the featured dancer. But Lon's ability to "double in brass" — perform a variety of theatrical tasks — made him truly invaluable to a producer like E. A. Fischer or Kolb and Dill, who were known to be tight with a buck. Lon also found an admirer of his work in theatre critic Julian Johnson of the *Los Angeles Daily Times*. The following are excerpts from reviews by Johnson, as well as from his theatre columns *From the Mason to the Majestic* and *In the Big Play World* that appeared in the *Los Angeles Daily Times*.

The Hen Pecks (April 8, 1912):

> Lon Chaney, as Ravioli, the barber, gives a real
> character study. It is the best thing I have ever seen
> Chaney do, and marks him as one to watch for
> future work. As a dancer and as a player he is out of
> the ordinary.

From the Mason to the Majestic column (April 11, 1912):

> Lon Chaney, whose extremely clever and intelligent
> Italian character study is one of the features of *The
> Hen Pecks*, is the dancing master of the institution,

and the designer and engineer of all the choral steps. In the next show, *When Johnny Comes Marching Home*, Chaney will play a Kentucky colonel.

From the Mason to the Majestic column (April 17, 1912):

Lon Chaney next week will cease being a 'Guiney' and will be a southern gentleman. As the original slinger of dialect, Lon is the only bug under the Pop Fischer chip.

In the Big Play World column (April 24, 1912):

I speak for more character parts for Lon Chaney, who as far as acting was concerned, was the unquestionable star of *The Hen Pecks* and certainly a man of unusual talent in character roles.

Tillie's Nightmare (May 6, 1912):

Really the best single minute of Tillie's long vision was a fast and furious Russian dance by an apparition of Mlle. Vanity and Lon Chaney.

From the Mason to the Majestic column (May 9, 1912):

Poor Texas Guinan, the orchid-eyed prima donna of the Fischer Company, has been completely floored by her rebellious vocal cords. Last night she tearfully

resigned her part in Tillie to Mrs. Lon Chaney, the
pretty young wife of James' stage manager.

Man Who Owns Broadway (June 17, 1912):

Laura Oakley and Lon Chaney, both character
people, appear to do good on stage. Considering
the brief time in which he was required to get up
the chorus numbers, the dances speak loudly for
Lon Chaney's talent.

From the Mason to the Majestic column (June 20, 1912):

It is no disparagement to the others in the cast of
The Man Who Owns Broadway at Fischer's
Lyceum, to chronicle the belief that the best bit of
character work in the performance, excepting Bob
Lett's is contributed by Lon Chaney as the theatrical
man who is 'All O.K. with K and E.' In the original
Raymond Hitchcock production, this part was
played by Mark Sullivan, and if you don't consider
the clever imitations of well-known actors Sullivan
gave between the verses of the song, Chaney's
performance is just as good as his New York
predecessor.

The Chaperons (June 24, 1912):

It seems to me, that Lon Chaney, always notable for
his small parts, has another hit as Schnitzel, a bill
poster, which is really more nearly perfect than

anything else in the show. If I were getting together the biggest sort of troupe, wherewith to lay siege to Broadway, I should want this fellow Chaney for tiny things.

The Yankee Prince (July 1, 1912):

It seems to me, that Lon Chaney, playing the Irishman and Herbert Cawthorne, as Fielding, should have been reversed in the casting. Chaney would have made a better padre than Celt and Cawthorne might have had a good repetition of his Irish success of last week in *The Chaperons*. However, neither is bad although it seems to me that they might have been better the other way around.

An American Idea (July 22, 1912):

Lon Chaney, as the bogus Count, does an adroit piece of work — rapid, sketchy and varied. Considering the enormous amount of toll Chaney has in getting out the choral numbers in these weekly pieces, the fact that he found time to get up such a bright, clean-studied characterization of his own speaks loudly for his superior talent. DeSouchet is not as thorough-going as Chaney would have had him, doubtless with more time, but it is so good that I repeat what I said awhile ago —that Lon Chaney as a character actor of original sort is something worth a large managerial grab — and a quick one.

Lon Chaney

Fischer's Follies closed its final week on August 3 with a repeat performance of *Tillie's Nightmare*. The following night, the company began their summer shows with *I.O.U.*, with Lon and the chorus members remaining while Mlle. Vanity went to New York to perform in the Zeigfeld Follies. Fischer's summer shows had a daily matinee and two evening shows, with seats going for 10¢, 20¢ and 30¢.

Summer Flirts (August 12, 1912):

> The real hit of the show this week is Lon Chaney, who, as Bubbles a nigger with talking ways, has a part that suits him immensely. Lon does a dance that is quite the banner bit of the show.

Adolph and Oscar (August 18, 1912):

> Al Franks, Reese Gardner, and Lon Chaney all assume roles quite to their liking. The song numbers are unusually humorous in this lightsome show, and the dances equally so . . . . In these, Chaney, Gardner, and all three girl principals are to be seen at their best.

On August 31, 1912, the Fischer Comedy Company closed its summer season with the final performance of *The Kissing Bugs*, and once again Lon was out of work. Cleva, on the other hand, was becoming popular as a cabaret singer at the age of 23. The August 28, 1912 edition of the *Los Angeles Times* reported:

> A new ragtime singer to make her debut at Brink's is Cleva Creighton. She leaped into popularity with a late New York song hit which she has brought with her, *The Subway Glide*.

By the close of Fischer's Follies, Lon Chaney had not made the successful mark in theatre he had hoped for. However, he had honed his craft to such a degree that he was being noticed for his outstanding ability at dancing and his unique character work. Lon had no way of knowing that within 10 years his hard work and apprenticeship in the theatre, which improved his skills as a performer, would make him one of the foremost actors in motion pictures. While working with Fischer's Follies Lon's promising career as an actor became apparent. Here he had played a variety of small but notable character parts, establishing a "shorthand" for communicating the essence of the character to the audience in the limited amount of time allowed on stage. These small roles helped him to become adept at putting his character across — be it an Irishman, Frenchman, Italian or Southerner — and to very quickly get the audience to respond to his part. His superior dancing ability now became part of his characters, even if he never danced a step. Lon was agile and able to move gracefully on stage, making his characters more believable.

In playing these roles, Chaney also learned to understand the value of a good make-up and how it helped the audience to understand his character. In his early days of touring with various companies, Lon was taught how to use make-up for character roles by Edward S. Felch, a well-known stage actor in musical comedies.[33] During this period make-up had become part of Chaney's repertoire and he was becoming adept at using it. All these talents would later serve Lon Chaney well in his motion picture career.

Lon Chaney

Lon Chaney around the age of 22, when he started touring with musical comedy troupes. (Courtesy of the Chaney Family Collection)
Cleva Creighton, circa 1910. (Courtesy of the Chaney Family Collection)

Love and Heartbreak
(1912-1913)

"I hereby give and bequeath to Cleva Creighton Bush the sum of $1.00 and no more."
—*Last Will and Testament of Lon Chaney*

Savoy Theatre

Charles H. Muehlman, Lessee and Manager.

Commencing Sunday, January 26th, 1913
Regular Matinees Saturday and Sunday

KOLB and DILL
PRESENT
"ALGERIA"

Music by Victor Herbert.

Book by Roland Oliver. Lyrics by Glen MacDonough.

Produced under the Personal Direction of KOLB and DILL.

CAST OF CHARACTERS.

Louis Ostrander, a Chicago real estate magnate	C. WILLIAM KOLB
Michael Hoffmeier, his companion and foster brother	MAX M. DILL
Achu Hamid, Shiek of the Oasis of Ibid	Winfield Blake
Ishi, his first lieutenant	Percy Bronson
Abdul, Ishi's servant	Lon Chaney
Adlibb, generally useful	Silvion de Jardins
The Princess Isis, a noble seeress	Maude Amber
Osri, her maid of honor	Maxie Mitchell
Fatima, an Egyptian dancer	May Edythe Taylor
Lotus, the Shiek's first wife	Ella Crane
Deis, the Shiek's second wife	Rita Abbott
Iris, the Shiek's third wife	Becky Reuck
Ptolomie, the Shiek's fourth wife	Doris Vernon
Alexanderia, the Shiek's fifth wife	Irene Shay
Ibis, the Shiek's sixth wife	Rose Ford

Ladies of the Court of Isis, Moorish maids, water carriers, soldiers of the Shiek, palace guards, etc.

SYNOPSIS OF SCENES.

ACT I—Inside the Walls of the Oasis of Ibid.

ACT II—Scene 1—Throne Room of the Shiek's Palace.

Scene 2—Same as Act I.

MUSICAL NUMBERS.

Augmented Orchestra, Directed by Mr. Harry James. Staged by Mr. Lon Chaney.

Ida Wyatt, Ballet Mistress.

ACT I.

Overture.
1. Opening Chorus, "The Princess Sleeps."
2. "The Boule' Miche'" .... Percy Bronson
3. "Rose of the World" .... Maude Amber
4. "Ask Her While the Band is Playing"....Messrs. Kolb and Dill and Maxie Mitchell
5. "Twilight in Barakeesh" .... Winfield Blake
6. Sextette, "I Am Mrs. Achu"..The Misses Crane, Abbott, Reuck, Vernon, Shay, Ford
7. Finale.

ACT II.

1. Opening Chorus and Ballet.
2. "I've Been Decorated" .... Messrs. Kolb, Bronson and Chorus
3. "Love Is Like a Cigarette" .... Percy Bronson and Male Chorus
4. "Bohemit, Good-bye" .... Maude Amber and Chorus
5. "Little Bird of Paradise" .... Maude Amber and Chorus
6. Finale.

Ad for Kolb and Dill's *Algeria* at the Savoy Theatre in San Francisco. Not only did Lon play parts in this company, he also served as stage manager and choreographer.

Despite good reviews with the Fischer Company, Lon Chaney's years of struggling had not brought him any closer to success. He might do a show that would run five months, then be out of work for weeks or even months. During this time, Cleva worked steadily as a singer in cabarets, where she was expected to play up to the customers and share a drink or two at the table. Cleva's daughter, Stella George, said that her mother was the type of woman who never should have touched liquor.[34] Cleva's bouts with alcohol and Lon's frustration at her quick success and his lack of it must have caused tension in an already unstable marriage. Meanwhile, Lon, working or not, took care of Creighton and began to recognize the steady disintegration of his relationship with Cleva.

During this period, motion pictures were slowly moving from storefront nickelodeons to theaters specifically built for this new medium. To avoid the film patent wars in New York City, many film companies moved west, settling in Hollywood and its environs. Theatre was still the major entertainment source, and big stars such as John Barrymore, Sarah Bernhardt, Lewis Stone, May Robson and Marjorie Rambeau often played in various Los Angeles theaters. Most distinguished actors felt it was beneath their dignity to appear in films and frowned upon those who did. Some actors performed in motion pictures (then referred to as "flickers" or "movies") during the summer months of Broadway's off-season, and usually under an assumed name.

With the close of Fischer's Follies, Lon went back to San Francisco to work with Kolb and Dill, serving as stage manager, choreographer, and as an actor with the company. Harry James, who had been the musical director for Fischer's Follies, was now filling that capacity with Kolb and Dill. Lon started working with Kolb and Dill in their production of *Peck O' Pickles*. The company presented a total of five productions, including *In Dutch*, *The Motor Girl*, *Algeria*, and *Hoity-Toity*.

The *San Francisco Examiner* of February 2, 1913, said the following in its review of Kolb and Dill's *Algeria*:

> Percy Bronson and Lon Chaney as a couple of
> conspiring Ibidians bob in and out with cheerful
> regularity during the performance.

Journalist Clarence Locan, who later became one of Lon's closest friends, first met Lon during the production of *Hoity-Toity*. In a *Photoplay* article written shortly after Lon's death, Locan recalled noticing the chorus girls being lined up by an agile stage manager who minutes later was shifting scenery with the stage hands. The two men met briefly, shook hands, and Lon was off to do some more work.[35] Not only did Lon wear an astonishing number of hats during his association with Kolb and Dill, he often picked up outside jobs as well. During this same period, Lon was also employed by the producers of the play *The Talk of New York*, a George M. Cohan musical at the Alcazar Theatre, to stage their musical numbers.

Hoity-Toity closed its San Francisco run on March 16, 1913, and the Kolb and Dill company prepared for a road tour. The company arrived in Los Angeles in late April for their stand at the Majestic Theatre, where Kolb and Dill had played before in 1912. *In Dutch* was scheduled to start its Los Angeles run on April 27. Cleva, who had also been working in San Francisco, was scheduled to be the featured act at Brink's Cafe at the end of the month. On April 29, 1913, a photo of Cleva appeared with the following story in the *Los Angeles Herald:*

> The return engagement of Cleva Creighton, dainty singing soubrette who played at the cabaret show six months ago, is the feature at Brink's cafe this week.
>
> She has returned from San Francisco where she has been the furor of the cabaret shows and only comes to Los Angeles because of the fact that her husband, Lon Chaney, comedian, is here with Kolb and Dill for a short engagement.
>
> She brings with her the latest song hits and sings them in the same distinctive manner which won her popularity at the Brink's cafe during her former engagement here.

Events of the following evening, April 30, greatly changed the personal and professional lives of both Lon and Cleva. After finishing her early evening dinner show at Brink's Cafe on Spring Street, Cleva walked over to the Majestic Theatre on Broadway, where Lon was working. While exact details are unclear, Cleva allegedly had argued with Lon backstage during the show's performance. Standing in the wings of the theatre, she dramatically swallowed a vial of bichloride of mercury. *The Los Angeles Daily Times* reported the following story on May 1:

Dutch comedians were cavorting on the stage of the
Majestic Theatre to the merriment of the audience
last night, when Cleva Creighton, a cabaret singer,
behind the scenes, swallowed the contents of a vial
of bichloride of mercury after a misunderstanding
with her husband, L. F. Chaney, stage manager for
the theatre. She was taken to the Receiving Hospital,
where heroic treatment saved her life.

Miss Creighton, who is 23 years old and who resides
with her husband at the Percival Apartments, No.
845 South Hill Street, is employed in one of the
downtown cafes as an entertainer. She went to the
Majestic Theatre last night to talk to her husband.
The two had disputed about Chaney's joining the
Kolb and Dill forces and touring with them as stage
director. She objected to the change.

According to her story, she had walked on the stage
behind the scenes while Kolb and Dill were
hilariously performing in front. Chaney, she said,
ordered her off the stage. She rushed to a dressing
room. The crowd in front was roaring with
laughter, she said, when she lifted the vial of
bichloride of mercury, and drained the contents
with suicidal intent.[36]

The *Los Angeles Herald* gave their own version the same day:

Repentant after an alleged attempt to end her life
with poison and suffering physically and mentally,

> Cleva Creighton, noted cabaret singer, today admits
> life is not devoid of charm. Prompt treatment at the
> receiving hospital saved her life.
>
> The singer is the wife of Lon Chaney, stage manager
> of the Majestic company. Disagreements resulted
> from Chaney's determination to go on the road with
> the company when it leaves Los Angeles.
>
> At their apartments, 845 South Hill Street, Chaney
> today said the near tragedy was a terrible mistake.
> 'It is true we quarreled,' he said, 'but my wife had
> no intention of attempting suicide. She believed she
> was swallowing medicine. Our differences are all
> straightened out now.'

While Cleva recovered, Lon realized that their marriage could not continue, and on May 26, 1913, they separated. At first, Cleva kept Creighton with her. She tried to resume her career, but her suicide attempt had damaged her vocal cords and she could no longer sing. Lon took custody of the boy, who remained with him until Creighton's marriage in 1926.

On December 19, 1913, represented by William T. Blakely, Lon filed a complaint for divorce from Cleva. In the complaint, Chaney alleges

> . . . that at various times, and upon numerous
> occasions, between the 26th day of May, 1913, and
> the 19th day of December, 1913, in the City of Los
> Angeles, in the City of Ontario, in the City of San
> Bernardino, in the City of Bakersfield, all in

> California and at various other places, said defendant
> has committed adultery with one Charles Osmand, a
> bartender, and that for the greater part of said time,
> said defendant and said Charles Osmand have been
> living together as husband and wife. . . . Acts of
> adultery were committed without the consent,
> connivance, procurement, or previous knowledge of
> plaintiff, and plaintiff has not lived with said
> defendant since said time.

Chaney also claimed Cleva was unfit to have care and custody of the child and requested that he be given that privilege. The second cause of action stated that for more than a year prior to the divorce action, Cleva was guilty of "habitual intemperance from the use of intoxicating drinks" and that Cleva "inflicted great mental anguish" on her husband.

One of the most damaging complaints filed against Cleva was in the third cause of action. It stated that during the month of May, 1913, Cleva wrote the following letter to a D. A. Traeger, who at the time resided in Porterville, California:

> My dearest boy:
>
> Received your letters and will take a few lines
> before I go to breakfast. Creighton is in the bath tub
> and I am in my night gown. I sent you a letter about
> three days ago and gave it to a girl to mail. Did you
> get it? I told you that I was working at Clunes, 5th
> and Main. Gee, honey, you don't know how sick I
> am of work. I don't know what is the matter with
> me. The Doctor says I have lost control of my
> nerves. I am taking medicine all the time. Say dearie

I hope you can come here within two weeks as it
will be much easier for me to see you while I am at
Clunes. Well Don I must close and wash the baby.

Yours all the time with love,

Cleva

When Lon found the letter, he showed it to Cleva who admitted
that she had been in frequent correspondence with Traeger. She also
said she loved him, that he was going to send her money and that she
had no further use for Chaney.[37]

The complaint for divorce listed Lon and Cleva as being married
on May 31, 1905, not 1906. It also stated that Creighton was born in
1907, not the correct year of 1906. One can only assume that Lon,
possibly on the advice of his attorney, adjusted the dates to remove
any possible suggestion that Creighton was born out of wedlock,
which might have damaged his chances of obtaining custody.

An Order to Enter Default against Cleva was filed on January 27,
1914, by Chaney's attorney. Cleva, who at this time was living at
1615 South Los Angeles Street, did not show up for the trial held on
April 1, 1914, Lon's 31st birthday. The following day, the judge on
the case issued his decision: at the expiration of one year, the final
judgement and decree of the bands of matrimony between Lon and
Cleva be dissolved. The judge also wrote, "It is further ordered,
adjudged and decreed that plaintiff herein have the care, custody and
control of Creighton Chaney, the minor child of the parties hereto;
but that defendant be permitted to see said child at all reasonable
times, provided that defendant be not under the influence of liquor,
and that she conduct herself in a proper manner."

Not only did Lon have to endure the strain of the divorce trial,
but on April 8, his mother died at the age of 58 of a heart attack in

Colorado Springs. Emma was buried at Evergreen Cemetery in the same plot with her child Earl who had died in 1887. On June 9, 1914, Frank moved to Berkeley, California to live with Carrie and her family.[38]

When Lon took custody of Creighton after the separation from Cleva, he placed his son in a private home for children of divorce and disaster, and visited him every Sunday.[39] Creighton certainly had not had the most ideal upbringing in his first seven years, and he had never received any formal education until he was placed in this facility.[40] Creighton recalled the story told to him that when he was a baby, either his mother or father would rush backstage and heat a bottle of milk for him on a gas burner during performances. He said his father had constructed a hammock for him to sleep in backstage, woven out of string.[41] When he was about five years old, Lon would take him into a bar, where for 5¢ you could have a glass of beer and a free sandwich or a pretzel. Lon would place Creighton next to the sandwiches on the counter and then go over to the piano player and have him play a dance tune. While Lon kept everyone's attention with his dancing, Creighton stuffed his pockets with sandwiches and pretzels to eat later.[42]

Lon adored his son, but raised him sternly. From the time he was 14, Creighton spent his summer months doing odd jobs to earn spending money. "He's no rich man's son. He'll earn what he gets, the same as I did," Chaney told Adela Rogers St. Johns.[43] When Creighton was a student at Hollywood High, Lon refused to buy him a car, feeling kids had no business with cars and Creighton never drove one until he was 20.[44] After Creighton's death in 1973, a story came out that Creighton claimed he was physically abused by his father on several occasions for no reason. According to Lon's grandson, this story is "complete fiction."[45] Creighton was never allowed to get a summer job at the studio; Lon was dead set against it. He told writer Ruth Waterbury that he felt Creighton, at 6'2" was too tall to be an actor. At that height, he said, he'd have to have parts built around him and he could never build himself for a part.[46]

This in part was true, but the main reason Lon never wanted his son in the business was because he had seen what happens to actors. He knew how hard it was to make it in the business and was afraid Creighton couldn't survive the ups and downs. He once told M-G-M production executive M. E. Greenwood he'd rather his son be a good plumber than a movie star.[47] William N. Dunphy said his mother recalled that Lon had an on-going dispute with Creighton over his son's wanting to enter films using the name Lon Chaney, Jr.[48]

A touching portrait in the collection of the Chaney family is a photo of a young Creighton Chaney at about the age of six. It is inscribed by him to Frank and Emma. It reads:

> To Grandma and Grandpa,
>
> I wish you could speak to me,
>
> Love,
> Creighton

When Lon finally obtained his divorce from Cleva, he never mentioned her again until he made out his last will and testament. In all the magazine articles of the period, there was no mention of his marriage or divorce from Cleva. His second wife, Hazel, was credited as being Creighton's mother, and the boy, until his father's death, never knew Cleva was still alive, because Cleva was a subject that Lon steadfastly refused to discuss.

Lon about 1916.

This document was filed when Cleva failed to show up at the divorce hearings, January 17, 1914.

IN THE SUPERIOR COURT OF THE STATE OF CALIFORNIA
IN AND FOR THE COUNTY OF LOS ANGELES

Lon F. Chaney,
                    Plaintiff

            vs.

Cleva Chaney,
                    Defendant.

Order to Enter Default

The Defendant........Cleva Chaney..

....

having failed to appear and answer the Plaintiff's Complaint herein, and the time for answering having expired, you will therefore enter the default of said Defendant..

....

herein according to law.

    To the Clerk of said Court,

....

....

                                                    _____
                                                    Attorney for Plaintiff.

44

Apprenticeship
in the Movies
(1913-1918)

He was the hardest working person in the studio. There wasn't a thing he wouldn't turn a hand to. He'd help move props, lights or even make-up the extras. It was the trouper's spirit of him.

—Tod Browning

Lon gets the drop on William S. Hart in *Riddle Gwane* (1918).

At the time of Cleva's attempted suicide in April of 1913, motion pictures were making their presence felt as entertainment. Hollywood and the Los Angeles area were quickly becoming the center of motion picture production. Fortunately for Chaney he was in Los Angeles at the time his marriage dissolved; with his background in theatre, the motion picture industry gave Lon another opportunity to earn a living as an actor.

He started work at Universal Studios, which by 1912 had become one of the biggest and certainly busiest independent studios in Hollywood. Universal Studios was founded as the Universal Film Manufacturing Company in June 1912. The formation of this company grew out of problems stemming from what was known as "The Patents War."

The Motion Picture Patents Company — known in the industry as "The Trust" — was formed by Thomas A. Edison. The Trust, whose members included the film companies of Vitagraph, Essanay, Kalem and Lubin, was formed solely to eliminate not only independent film producers, but also the several thousands of independent theatre exchanges and exhibitors. Edison and his group wanted complete control of the growing industry, and insisted all licensed producers and theatre exhibitors and their exchanges pay him a licensing fee for using his camera and projection equipment. When lawsuits failed to stop the independents, the Trust resorted to hiring thugs to break cameras, steal film and generally harass producers. Many directors took to wearing guns on the set, and some of them hired cowboys to take care of any of the Trust thugs who might show up. This was one reason many film companies came to Hollywood. Along with the near perfect climate and varied scenery, they were far away from the New York offices of the Trust. And, if Trust thugs tried any strong-arm tactics, a film company could make a quick dash to the nearby Mexican border where they could continue to make pictures.

The Universal Film Manufacturing Co. consisted of a number of independent film companies such as Independent Motion Picture (also known as IMP), New York Motion Picture, Powers, Nestor, Rex, Champion, Eclair, Yankee, and the 101-Bison Company. With a large majority of the independent producers under one company, they prepared to file a single lawsuit against Edison and his group. Another independent film producer, William Fox, instituted a lawsuit under the Sherman Anti-trust act which helped to bring an end to the Trust and their monopoly.

Republican President Taft took no action against the Trust until Democratic Presidential candidate Woodrow Wilson, who favored stopping the Trust, began to gain public support. Nineteen-twelve was an election year and President Taft decided it would be in his best political interests to look into the matter.

The government did not challenge Edison's patents, but they did charge the Motion Picture Patents Co. and their own exchange company with using the Edison patents to create a monopoly. Because Trust lawyers used delaying tactics in the court system, the final ruling to break up the Trust was not effective until 1915. However, having to deal with the government left the Trust little time to harass the independents, who continued to make pictures. Various companies under the Universal banner continued to produce films under their own names, and Universal continued to release them until the early 1920's. From that point on, the companies were absorbed by Universal.

The early years of Chaney's film career are not well documented for several reasons. The films he made for Universal in the beginning of his career did not give credit for bit players, nor did the trade journals give any mention to anyone except the principal players. The exact date he began to work in motion pictures is still unclear today.

In a *Theatre Magazine* article of 1928, Lon stated that a stage show he was in got stranded in Santa Ana, California (about 50 miles south of Hollywood), so he headed out to Universal Studios and got work as an extra. Based on facts available, this is an inaccurate account of his entrance into pictures, and a typical example of how Chaney invented portions of his life story. What appears to be more likely is that he may have done some extra work as early as 1912, but did not fully make the commitment to motion pictures until after the repercussions of Cleva's attempt on her life. With all the bad press connected with that tragic event, Lon lost his job with Kolb and Dill and apparently felt his chances of obtaining work in the Los Angeles theatre district were greatly reduced. This probably channeled Lon into the motion picture industry, starting out at Universal, which was then located at the corner of Sunset Boulevard and Gower Street in Hollywood. This intersection became nicknamed "Gower Gulch" because so many extras loitered there, dressed as cowboys in hope of finding work in the westerns being made by small production companies with offices in that area.

The film historian attempting to compile a complete list of Chaney's early films faces an uphill battle. Many library holdings of period trade journals are incomplete. Also, only 40 of his over 150 credited screen appearances survive in one form or another because they were shot on unstable nitrate film stock. Nitrate stock was highly flammable (fires in theatre projection booths were not uncommon in the early years) and gradually decomposed and destroyed the print. (By the 1950's, a safety film stock was introduced to solve these problems.) In addition, most studios did not have the vision to even try to preserve their products for the future. Several studios scrapped their silent film prints for what silver they could obtain from the film stock, feeling sure there was no longer any profit in silent films, particularly after the birth of talkies.

Only fifteen of the films Chaney was known to have made at Universal exist in complete or partial form today. In contrast, of the twenty films from his career at M-G-M (including two early Goldwyn releases *The Penalty* and *Ace of Hearts,* obtained in the 1924 M-G-M merger), only four films are missing, and two of the sixteen remaining films are missing one or two reels. Nine films made at other studios during the period of 1919 to 1922 still exist.

Amazingly, several of Chaney's films, once thought lost, have turned up in the last 20 years. About 1972 a print of *Oliver Twist* was found in Yugoslavia without any titles. Blackhawk Films, with the aid of Jackie Coogan and producer Sol Lesser, made up a set of new titles and released the film to collectors. It was shown in 1975 at Filmex, the film exposition in Los Angeles, where Coogan and Lesser described the challenge of creating new titles for a film some 50 years after its original release.[49] In another instance, the owners of a home in Georgia replaced their old porch in 1983 and found several metal film cans. One of the cans contained a complete print of *The Oubliette,* a 1914 3-reeler with Chaney playing a villain.[50] A third film came to light when a group of film preservationists located a man in France thought to have prints of silent films previously considered lost. When the preservationists contacted him, they asked if he had a copy of Chaney's *The Unknown* and he showed them where he kept all his films. Unfortunately, if the film had no opening title and was not easily identifiable, the man simply marked the film can

"Unknown"! But the searchers' persistence paid off and a print of the film was found there in the early 1970's.[51]

In the book *Big U,* which describes Universal during the silent era, author I. G. Edmonds mentions that Chaney appears unbilled in *Suspense,* directed by Lois Weber and Phillips Smalley and released in July, 1913.[52] This was one month before Chaney's first known billing in a one-reel IMP comedy called *Poor Jake's Demise,* released on August 16, 1913. Allan Dwan, a director at Universal in Hollywood's early days, told Peter Bogdanovich that Chaney was working on his crew as a prop man and would wear false teeth and weird make-up. Dwan asked Chaney if he wanted to act and Lon replied that he did. Chaney went on to tell him he had worked once in a stock company and liked it but was working as a prop man to earn a living. Dwan said he put him to work and thereby "discovered" Lon Chaney. While it is an interesting story, Allan Dwan did not discover Chaney nor did he give Lon his break in pictures.[53] Chaney had appeared in four films before his first known screen credit in an Allan Dwan film.

Lon continued to work steadily at Universal without benefit of a contract from 1913 until he left after a salary dispute in mid-1918. Most of his early films were one- to three-reelers that took only a few days to make, and even though he did not have the lead role, he was generally given a featured part. In many of his films he was cast in character parts and was allowed to experiment with various types of make-up and characterizations.

The film-making husband-and-wife team of director Joseph De Grasse and screenwriter Ida May Park saw something unique in Chaney. They encouraged him in his character roles, and Lon made sixty-four films for them between 1914 and 1918. Lon even took up the megaphone himself when he directed six films for the Victor Company at Universal in 1915 (*The Stool Pigeon, For Cash, The Oyster Dredger, The Violin Maker, The Trust,* and *The Chimney's Secret*). Of these, he wrote the scenario for one (*The Oyster Dredger*) and appeared in three (*The Violin Maker, The Trust* and *The Chimney's Secret*). Lon also wrote the scenario for two films in 1914 — *Her Escape* and *The Menace To Carlotta*. Sadly, none of these films exist today.

In a *Movie Magazine* article entitled "My Own Story By Lon Chaney," Lon said he was offered the chance to direct by studio officials because of his background as a stage manager. He said he wasn't given the chance to carry out his own ideas and do things his own way, so after six films, he went back to acting.[54]

Carl Laemmle, president of Universal, was a man with his own ideas, too. He dreamed of building a studio with dressing rooms, a prop warehouse, commissary, hospital, film labs, blacksmith shop, stables, and even police and fire departments — in other words, a real "city" built entirely for the making of motion pictures. Laemmle wanted it to be bigger than Thomas Ince's Inceville which was mainly an outdoor studio. In 1912, when he came out to Los Angeles to look at sites for the building of his studio, Laemmle settled on a 250-acre chicken ranch in the city of Lankershim (now known as North Hollywood), three miles north of Hollywood through the Cahuenga Pass. From the onset, his staff objected that the property had too many trees and hills to be suitable for a studio, but Laemmle ignored them and pressed on.

The following year, construction began on Laemmle's dream project. Universal City Studios, like Inceville, began as rows of outside stages and sets, constructed to take advantage of the natural sunlight. Muslin cloth was placed above the sets and then pulled over to diffuse the glare. Later, glass enclosed stages were built, and by the early 1920's, cement enclosed stages began to be used. With the arrival of sound, the inside walls of these stages were padded to reduce outside noise, coining the term "sound stages."

From the Cahunega Pass to the studio a paved roadway was laid, eliminating the dusty road which became a virtually impassable swamp when it rained. The road, however helpful, did not eliminate the site's major drawback: the stream running alongside the property regularly overflowed its banks, occasionally even flooding out the sets. Once when this happened, the studio simply took advantage of the mishap by writing a movie about a flood.

On March 15, 1915, Universal City Studios was dedicated as the first real city built entirely for the making of motion pictures. Opening ceremonies for the brand new studio began with the presentation of a gold key to Carl Laemmle from actress Laura Oakley (a colleague of Lon's from the Fischer's Follies days), and then continued with everyone on the studio payroll acting as guides, ushers, stuntmen and performers for the public as well as for invited guests, because Laemmle wanted to show everyone how movies were made. The response was so great that Universal began a tradition of studio tours for an admission fee of 25¢. In the early 1920's the tours were discontinued because constant interruptions by tourists proved to be too costly to productions. But in 1964, Universal decided to bring back the traditional tours, and it has proven to be a financial bonanza to the company ever since.

Long-time Colorado Springs resident Earl Cox visited the new studios at Universal City shortly after their opening and described it to the *Colorado Springs Gazette* as a "marvel in design." He also said he ran into Lon while he was directing one of his films. The paper reported,

> One of the principal directors is Lon Chaney, a son
> of 'Dummy' Chaney, who was a veteran barber of
> this city. The young man got his first schooling at
> stage work in the Grand Opera house here, under
> the late S. N. Nye, and developed a special aptitude
> for it. Mr. Cox watched him direct several scenes.[55]

During this time, a major turning point in Lon's personal life took place with his marriage to Hazel Hastings; five years younger than Lon, she had been one of the chorus dancers with the Ferris Hartman Troupe when Lon and Cleva worked there. During the old Ferris Hartman days, Hazel was married to a legless man who ran a cigar counter in her hometown of San Francisco. Although it is unclear exactly how she and Lon became reacquainted, writer Adela Rogers St. Johns said the reunion occurred when Hazel was performing at Jahnke's Tavern on Spring Street in downtown Los Angeles.[56] This version of their meeting seems possible, since Lon was living in an apartment at 123 North Grand Avenue at the time, just a few blocks from the tavern.

On November 26, 1915, in the Santa Ana, California, courthouse, Lon married the woman he often referred to as "my beloved wife." Creighton Chaney came home from his boarding school to live with his father and step-mother at 1607 Edgemont Avenue, just south of Hollywood Boulevard and across the street from the famous estate of Aline Barnsdale in the East Hollywood area.

By 1915, Lon was earning $45 per week at Universal, without a signed contract. On two different occasions in 1916, he was featured in articles in Universal's trade magazine *Motion Picture Weekly*. "Lon Chaney, A Master Of Make-Up" appeared on September 16, and displayed seven photos of Lon made up in some of his character roles. "Making Up With Brains" in the December 2 issue featured two pictures of Lon; one as himself, and the other as Pancho Villa. The November 17 *Photoplay Journal* featured a full-page article on Lon with three photos of him in various roles, entitled "Rich Man, Poor Man, Beggarman, Thief — Lon Chaney."

As his film career blossomed, Lon received generally good notices for his work, despite being assigned featured or supporting roles. By the end of 1916 Lon had appeared in 79 films portraying a wide variety of roles that allowed him to portray vivid characters, much like he did on stage (e.g., a hunchbacked fisherman, moonshiner, cowboy, Spaniard, a crippled half-breed, an old doctor, and several villains). In addition, he wrote and directed several films, including *The Oyster Dredger* and *The Chimney's Secret*. This sampling of reviews from various industry trade journals illustrates that his work was not going unnoticed:

Tragedy of Whispering Creek

And then there is Mr. Chaney in the role of the Greaser. Mr. Chaney has used his own ideas in working out the character, a pervert, in this play and what he has given us is startling to an unusual degree. True, he paints a horrible picture for us — one that is apt to cause a feeling of revulsion. But, that is as it should be. In fact, Mr. Chaney has created a new character — one that will live long — that will be copied as a newer standard for others.
— *Universal Weekly*

Place Beyond The Winds

Lon Chaney portrays well the part of the half breed." — *Moving Picture World*

The Gilded Spider

There was not a member of the cast that seemed distinctive with the possible exception of Lon Chaney, who did fairly well as the Italian. His work was not big, although it showed up to decided advantage when considered with the other members of the particular cast. — *Wid's Film Daily*

Lon Chaney's Giovanni is a strong piece of character portrayal. — *Motion Picture News*

The Desert Breed

With the desert so convenient, what more natural impulse than that Director De Grasse should take his Pauline Bush - Lon Chaney - William Dowlan combination to the places where the sands run white and men and women grow less amenable as their distance from the center of civilization increases. At least, that is what happens when a good cast like this takes to the desert, for it is truly a notable trio, notable for this particular picture as well as for past reputations. — *New York Dramatic Mirror*

The Oyster Dredger

This two-part drama featuring Warren Kerrigan and Vera Sisson is a good, interesting picture, well acted and ably directed. — *New York Dramatic Mirror*

The Chimney's Secret

This story of the young bank cashier who masquerades as a miserly peddler is not entirely

new, but will offer a surprise to many observers.
It is quite dramatic in its way and well constructed.
Lon Chaney and Gretchen Lederer play the leads. —
Motion Picture World

A Doll's House

Lon Chaney, as the forger friend of the husband
who is redeemed by the love of the woman he had
failed to get early in his life, had poise and authority
and made his part register in every scene. — *Wid's
Film Daily*

Fires of Rebellion

Lon Chaney, who did the city tempter part, was a bit
too 'wicked,' in his characterization, there being a
tendency on his part to keep a leer on his face at all
times. — *Wid's Film Daily*

The Price of Silence

Lon Chaney supplies an excellent heavy
characterization. — *New York Dramatic Mirror*

The Flashlight

Lon Chaney, as the hermit, had a rather bum beard,
but was very satisfactory. — *Wid's Film Daily*

Lon Chaney

Girl in the Checkered Coat

Lon Chaney, as a 'willam,' had poise and authority.
— *Wid's Film Daily*

Life at the Universal Studios lot was much like a small town where everyone knew each other, even if they never worked together in a film. And like any good citizen in any small town, Lon made many friends. During this period, Jean Hersholt and Lon were reported to have shared a dressing room at Universal for a time. Years after Lon's death, when Herscholt was under contract to M-G-M, Hersholt took up residence in Lon's old M-G-M dressing room and prominently displayed an autographed picture Lon had given him.

Adela Rogers St. Johns recalled that once when she was on the Universal lot to interview Priscilla Dean, Lon called her over to his dressing room. He showed her his first make-up case, a small black box in which he had assorted shades of greasepaint, tubes of putty, crepe hair for beards and moustaches, as well as a few false teeth. She recalled his eagerness to show her how the materials worked, much like a child on Christmas morning.[57]

Jack Mulhall, who was a star in the 'teens and 1920's, worked with Lon on several Universal films: *The Price of Silence, Place Beyond the Winds, The Grand Passion, Danger — Go Slow*, and later in the 1922 feature *Flesh and Blood*. He said Lon kiddingly gave him the nickname "Gashouse," because of Jack's upbringing in New York during the gaslight era. Once, while they were on location for the day in the local mountains, Chaney began to sketch the scenery on a paper bag after finishing his lunch. Lon was about to throw his well-done sketch away until Mulhall asked if he could have it. He kept it for several years.[58]

And as any small-town resident will attest, life behind the scenes at Universal City often proved to be more dramatic than the movies themselves. Film historian Bob Birchard recalled how Lon Chaney once saved the life of an actress off-screen. This woman had an affair with one of the studio's prominent directors and became pregnant, a serious taboo not only in Hollywood at that time but also to society in general. The actress, in the privacy of her dressing room, tried to self-induce an abortion, causing herself much pain and putting her life in jeopardy. Lon happened to be walking past her dressing room when he heard her cries of anguish. Rushing into the room, he picked her up and took her to the studio hospital where she received emergency medical attention.[59]

But Lon's primary function at Universal was to make movies — and make movies he did. *Hell Morgan's Girl* was released in March of 1917 and gave Lon some of his best notices yet. ("Dorothy Phillips, William Stowell and Lon Chaney have given us some big scenes and a lot of truly worthwhile little touches." — *Wid's Film Daily*). The film took place on San Francisco's Barbary Coast in 1906. Chaney played the gang leader Sleter Noble, who had an eye for the daughter of Hell Morgan, the saloon/gambling-hall owner. When she falls in love with Roger Curwell, a down-on-his-luck socialite, Sleter plots his revenge, only to be killed in the dramatic climax which takes place during the San Francisco earthquake.

As Lon's popularity with the American movie-going public grew, he was also acquiring an international reputation; Japanese film historian Takashi Teshigawara said that the release of the Universal/Bluebird features during the period of 1919 to 1921 made Chaney one of the most popular American actors in Japan.[60] (Most of the Bluebird features with Chaney were released in the United States during 1916 to 1918, playing in Japan up to two years later.)

Lon's father, Frank, moved to Los Angeles in 1916 from Berkeley where he had been living with Lon's sister Carrie and her family. Since the death of Lon's mother, Frank suffered greatly from loneliness and upon arriving in Los Angeles, went to several social functions given by the Los Angeles School for the Deaf. At one party he was introduced to a widow named Cora Marker. It was not until their second encounter that they discovered, much to their delight, that they were in fact the long ago sweethearts from the deaf school in Fulton, Missouri. On February 6, 1917, Frank and Cora were married, fulfilling a promise they had made to each other some 42 years earlier.[61]

By 1918, Lon had been working at Universal for five years at $75 a week without a contract, while other, less-talented actors were earning more. At his wife's urging, he went to see studio manager William Sistrom. He asked for $125 a week and a five-year contract. Sistrom refused his request and added that Chaney would never be worth $100 a week.[62] (Interestingly enough, this is the same man who was reported to have said Clark Gable had "big ears and no star potential.") Because of Sistrom's remarks, Chaney left his "home" lot, determined to prove the studio manager wrong. At that point, the reality of the business hit Lon square in the face. For all of the years he spent at Universal working steadily, he was virtually unknown anywhere else. At first, Lon didn't worry, as he had saved his money and felt confident of finding work elsewhere. But weeks grew into months and he still had nothing to show for his decision except a smaller bank account. By his own admission, he began to believe that maybe Sistrom wasn't such an idiot, and was considering returning to Universal to take what salary he could get.[63]

Happily, Chaney's luck changed. William S. Hart was then the leading box-office star of westerns and had his own production company. There are conflicting stories concerning the way Lon got the role of Hame Bozzam in Hart's next picture, *Riddle Gwane,* but in his autobiography Hart mentions seeing Lon as the heavy in *Hell Morgan's Girl* and felt he would be good as the villain in his upcoming film. Hart goes on to say both E. H. Allen, Hart's studio manager, and his director Lambert Hillyer interviewed Lon but felt despite Lon's strong face, he was too short to play opposite Hart. Hart overrode their judgment and supposedly told Chaney, "Inches never made an actor. You're an actor, you've got the part."

In a 1988 interview, however, film historian Bob Birchard tells a different version of this story. He claims that in a letter Lambert Hillyer wrote to author George Mitchell, Hillyer says his mother had seen Lon in *Hell Morgan's Girl* and called his performance to Hillyer's attention. It was Hart who had to be sold on Chaney because of his height, not the other way around. Regardless of which story was correct, Lon had the job, and he was paid $125 a week for his performance.[64]

Motion Picture News, in reviewing the film, noted,"Lon Chaney has a prominent character role, and plays it up to the minute."

For four weeks, Hart's company went on location in the northern area of the San Fernando Valley known as Chatsworth. One tradition on all of Hart's locations was a nighttime kangaroo court. The "crimes" were usually nothing more serious than someone helping to do someone else's job. The "punishment" would be a whipping on the rear end with a pair of chaps. Of course, all this was done good-naturedly and taken in stride (unless, of course, you were on the receiving end). Lon found out the hard way when he was found guilty of chopping wood for the cook. According to Hart, he noticed Chaney did a lot of standing and walking but very little sitting during the next few days. Hart's crime of loaning leading lady, Katherine MacDonald five dollars to beat the cowboys at craps caught up with him. The judge appointed Chaney to swing the chaps on the producer/actor. No one had apparently realized how strong Chaney was, and it was Hart who did very little sitting for some time to come.[65]

After working with William S. Hart, Chaney returned to Universal at his now-standard weekly salary of $125. He appeared in several pictures, including *Danger — Go Slow!*, directed by Robert

Lon Chaney

Z. Leonard (a former member of the old Ferris Hartman Troupe with whom Lon performed) and starring Leonard's then wife, Mae Murray.

Lon Chaney had come a long way in the growing motion picture business in just five short years. His training on the stage and his varied work at Universal taught him a great deal about creating a character. He was yet to experience the luxury he would have later in his career when he would have weeks, sometimes even months to work out ideas for a character. Lon once said he would never play an old man with the stereotypical make-up or performance. Both in the physical and mental make-up of his characters Lon Chaney did something to make them unique. For each new role, he painstakingly analyzed the way a character acted, looked and moved. "Think your character out," he often told young actors — a piece of advice he never neglected to follow himself.[66]

William C. Dowlan and Lon in *Tragedy of Whispering Creek* (1914).

Arthur Shirley, Cleo Madison, and Lon (right) in *The Fascination of the Fleur de Lis* (1915).
Jay Belasco and Lon in *The Grip of Jealousy* (1916).

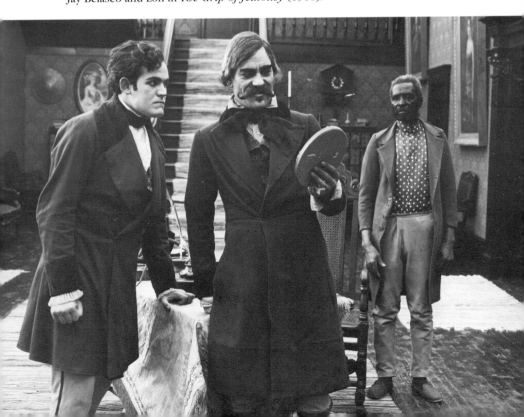

(Right) Lon, Dorothy Phillips, and William Stowell in *Hell Morgan's Girl* (1917).

Lon (standing left) with the cast of *Father and the Boys* (1915). Director Joseph De Grasse (with cap and black scarf tie) is to Lon's right. Veteran stage actor Digby Bell is seated in the front row, second from left.

A Bogus Cripple
Gets Noticed
(1919-1920)

---

*"God," Tucker said. I wanted to say that
too, but not for the same reason.*
— *Lon's description of his screen test for*
The Miracle Man

As the bogus cripple in *The Miracle Man* (1919). This role brought Chaney to the attention of Hollywood.

T**he Wicked Darling**, a 1919 melodrama for Universal, marked the beginning of a Chaney's ten-year association with director Tod Browning. In the film, Lon played the lead villain, and *Variety* noted, "Particularly commendable is the work of Lon Chaney as 'Stoop,' a crook." The teaming of Lon and Browning was to become one of the most important aspects of Chaney's film career. On the surface the two men really don't seem to have a lot in common, yet a closer inspection of Browning's early career shows parallels to Chaney's. They were a year apart in age (Browning was born in 1882) and had played a wide variety of parts on the stage, including roles in musical comedies; they started in pictures at roughly the same time and both had directed films.

Tod Browning had aspirations of becoming a jockey in his native town of Louisville, Kentucky, but his height put an end to that dream. At the age of 16, he ran away from home to join a traveling sideshow, becoming the "barker" for "The Wild Man of Borneo" (actually a black man from Mississippi in make-up). He toured one season with Ringling Bros. as a clown before abandoning the circus for vaudeville. Browning eventually appeared with the Willard and King Company and toured the United States and Europe. When that ended, he went to work for the Whallen and Martel Burlesque Company in Chicago, playing a variety of parts including a blackface routine with comedian Charlie Murray. The company was known as "The Whirl of Mirth," and Browning stayed with them for several seasons. In 1913 he got his start in pictures playing comedic roles for D. W. Griffith at Biograph. When Griffith moved to the Mutual Film Company, Browning followed and in 1914 was given his first opportunity to direct a comedy entitled *The Lucky Transfer*. He made an appearance in 1916 as racing car owner in the modern story segment of Griffith's *Intolerance*. He continued to direct at Mutual before moving to Metro pictures for a year and then on to Universal in 1918. Most of his films at Universal had an underworld theme and usually starred Priscilla Dean, Universal's leading female star from 1919 to the early 1920's.

After *The Wicked Darling*, Priscilla Dean and Lon worked together on a feature for Universal called *Paid In Advance*, set in the Klondike Gold Rush period. In an interview with the author, Ms. Dean told about a scene in the film where she and Lon were supposed to be arguing. As the conflict warmed up, she began to beat him. When Lon pushed her away, she grabbed for his hair, which was a long, straggly wig. Lon was a perfectionist when it came to make-up and had glued the wig down so well that it felt exactly like his own hair. As Ms. Dean pulled on the hair, something had to give, and it certainly wasn't Lon's wig. Her fingernails pulled completely out of her fingers! She said Lon was terribly distressed by it all and, on her way to the hospital, she made a promise to herself that she'd be more of an actress and less of a realist in the future.[67]

On August 31, 1919, *The Miracle Man* was released by Paramount Pictures. Originally a novel by Frank Packard, it was adapted for Broadway by George M. Cohan. The film version was written and directed by George Loane Tucker who entered films in 1910 with Laemmle's old Independent Moving Pictures (IMP) company. In 1913, Tucker had made Universal's first real hit, *Traffic in Souls*, a five-reel picture based on a true story of white slavery in New York City.

The Miracle Man tells the story of four crooks who try to take financial advantage of miracles performed by a blind faith healer known as the Patriarch. One of the crooks, "Frog" (played by Chaney), is able to contort his body to appear crippled. The plan is to have Frog crawl up to the Miracle Man and pretend to be healed in front of a large group of spectators. The crooks could then steal the donation money Frog's performance was sure to inspire. However, the plan is dashed when a young boy who is truly crippled, throws down his crutches, and runs up to the Miracle Man, thus providing a true faith healing. The virtue of the faith healer and their witness to a true miracle reforms the crooks and they give up their life of crime.

Tucker had planned to cast a real contortionist in the role of "Frog," but none of the men he interviewed could act. When Tucker and Chaney met, the director said that if Chaney could do an effective "unwinding" scene before his crook pals, the part was Chaney's. Chaney was neither double-jointed nor a contortionist as many have thought. He said he got the idea of the twisted legs from a habit he had since childhood; while sitting, he'd cross his legs, then double cross them, wrapping his left foot behind his right ankle.[68]

Chaney described his screen test to writer Ruth Waterbury in 1928:

> When I came to the studio on the test day, Tucker
> was already behind the camera. He gave me one
> glance and called 'Camera.' I flopped down,
> dragging myself forward along the floor, my eyes
> rolling, my face twitching, and my legs wrapping
> tighter and tighter around each other. Tucker didn't
> speak and sweat rolled off me. Finally I heard a
> single whispered word from him. 'God,' Tucker
> said. I wanted to say that too, but not for the same
> reason."[69]

Lon Chaney

The *New York Times* commented, "Unusually good work is done by Thomas Meighan, Betty Compson and Lon Chaney in a picture which will please all movie enthusiasts and convert a few more."

Julian Johnson of *Photoplay* said, "I do not recall that the silver sheet has ever offered anything any better than this, and few pieces as good. . . . Lon Chaney is so good as the Frog that I cannot think of anyone who could have played that grotesque monster as effectively." (This is the same critic who praised Lon's work in Fisher's Follies in his *Los Angeles Daily Times* column.)

Lon's role as the "Frog" involved more physical than facial make-up. Originally Lon had planned to have a hump on his back and a withered hand. When he learned that he would have to "unwind" before the camera twice, Lon discarded this idea. After many unsuccessful experiments, Lon came up with the idea of letting his beard grow out, wearing dirty clothes and rolling his eyes up into his head to appear blind when begging on the streets. Chaney is first seen this way on the screen leaving the audience revolted by his appearance. His brother George said Lon got inspiration for his character from a crippled beggar he had seen in Chicago during his musical comedy days.[70]

When the crooks put their plan into action and the "Frog" is healed by the faith healer, Chaney is clean-shaven and wearing a better suit of clothes, helping his character gain sympathy from the unsuspecting townspeople. As he is "healed," Chaney uses his entire body to give the effect of a terribly disfigured man who is now miraculously rejuvenated. He snaps his wrist from a coiled position and then moves it around to show the process of his character's "healing." The lifeless and twisted legs are slowly untangled and as he begins to stand, Chaney thrusts his body and spine into place as if he were being manipulated by a chiropractor. As he rises, Chaney's bent right leg snaps into position. He stands before the faith healer and assembled townspeople proclaiming his "miracle." For the benefit of the townspeople, Lon's character has an expression of amazement and hope all through his transformation. The impact of the healing sequence is further enhanced by the reaction shots of the townspeople at this event. When Chaney's character is rejuvenated by the goodness of the faith healer, he (along with the other crooks) changes from a scheming, manipulative criminal to a warmer, benevolent man.

This was actually his first role playing a cripple.[71] The movie was one of 1919's major hits both with box office and critics. His salary was $125 a week. Lon Chaney's performance brought him to the prominent attention not only of Hollywood but also the film-going public. In 1932, Paramount made a sound version of the film with John Wray in Chaney's role. Today, all that exists of the silent version is the healing scene and another brief clip.

By now Lon was becoming known as both a prominent character actor and master of make-up. Jane Daley, who later played Lon's wife in *West of Zanzibar*, worked in 1919 as an extra on *False Faces*, in which Lon played the villain. She appeared with two other extras as a haunting vision to a German U-Boat captain. She said she was paid $5 for the day and that Lon applied her make-up to give her the appearance of a sea corpse.[72]

In *Victory*, a later 1919 release based on the novel by Joseph Conrad, Lon played the villainous Ricardo for director Maurice Tourneur. The *New York Times* reported,

> No screen actor whose name comes to mind can
> equal Mr. Chaney in the impersonation of intense,
> strongly marked types. He does with consummate
> skill and fine finish the kind of acting that many
> attempt with lumbering ponderousity and maladroit
> exaggeration.

Lon Chaney

In playing Ricardo, Lon followed Conrad's description which painted the character as "a muscular, short man with eyes that gleamed and blinked, a harsh voice, and a round toneless, pock-marked face ornamented by a thin, disheveled moustache sticking out quaintly under the tip of a rigid nose." Lon used rigid collodion to create the pock-marks on his face. Rigid collodion, also known as common or nonflexible collodion, is a viscous liquid consisting of an alcohol and ether solution in which guncotton or pyroxylin is dissolved; the resulting adhesive film will draw the skin together. When rigid collodion is applied with a soft brush or Q-tip and allowed to dry, it gives the effect of a scar or, in this case, pock marks. Additional coats give a deeper look and can be peeled off or dissolved with acetone.

Chaney also wore a drooping, thin black moustache. The hair to make moustaches or beards came from crepe-wool hair, a form of cotton-wool which is still sold in assorted shades, plaited into a braid. When unraveled, soaked in water, and allowed to dry, the hair straightens and stretches out. It can then be applied with spirit gum (an adhesive), trimmed to the desired length, and given shape with the aid of a heated curling iron. To hold the shape and style in place, a hairstyling material called Bandoline was either combed into the piece or applied with the fingers. By the mid-20's, moustaches, beards, and sideburns were sometimes made out of real hair and actually sewn, or ventilated, into a fine piece of lace. This allowed the piece to be used over and over by simply applying spirit gum to the desired area and placing the lace piece (which had already been trimmed and styled) to the face. Both methods are still used today in make-up for motion pictures, but Chaney generally preferred to lay the hair on the face daily instead of using lace pieces.

Chaney was often quoted as saying that he watched people in all walks of life, collecting ideas on how a character should look. Generally he was able to walk around unrecognized by wearing his traditional cap and heavy-rimmed glasses. Not only did he observe features, but he also studied mannerisms and gestures. Chaney always felt that make-up was merely the prologue to the total picture of the character. Most film scripts did not give much of a description, and Lon's conception of the character came after reading the script or possibly from discussions with the director. However, when a film was based on a novel, like *Victory* or *Treasure Island*, he consulted the original source material.

Chaney worked with Maurice Tourneur again on *Treasure Island*, released by Paramount in 1920. In this version, Lon played a dual role as the blind pirate Pew and the surly pirate Merry. In playing Pew, Lon wore a pair of false teeth, a scraggly wig, heavy eyebrows and, to simulate blindness, he rolled his eyes back up into his head for the length of the scene. He did not use the thin, opaque white skin from the inside of an egg shell over his eyeball as has often been reported. As Merry, he wore the same wig, a scar on his right cheek, an enlarged nose made from nose putty, and a moustache to complete the look of the character.

The film was generally well received, and again, Chaney received good notices. "The most vivid acting is done by the dependable Lon Chaney in two roles," the *New York Times* reported.

Later that year, Chaney made his third and final film with Tourneur. In this story, Chaney played a wax sculptor who plots to steal the girl from co-star John Gilbert. The picture was made under the working title *The Glory of Love*. Due to unknown production problems (possibly legal or distribution), it was not released until 1923 under the title of *While Paris Sleeps*. The three-year gap was noted by *Variety*: "Lon Chaney plays the heavy and, from the role, it is quite evident it must have been shot long before the day he started starring."

In *The Gift Supreme*, he was the villain in a social drama ("Of the character actors, Chaney takes all the honors" — *New York Times*) and in *Nomads of the North* he was the leading man in a James Oliver Curwood story set in the Canadian north woods. ("In this particular picture, Lon Chaney was less successful than usual. . . What he lacked was the romantic bearing to capture the heart of a girl like Nanette."—*Variety*).

In the seven years since his first-known screen credit, Lon Chaney had carved a niche for himself in motion pictures, appearing in featured but prominent roles and gathering favorable reviews. His abilities with make-up were fast making him one of the most popular character actors in Hollywood. At 5 feet 10 inches and 155 pounds, his average stature allowed him to build himself up for a wide variety of parts with the use of make-up, padding and altered body posture. But his physical strength, in addition to his other attributes, would soon be called upon in his upcoming performance in *The Penalty*.

Lon and Seena Owen in Maurice Tourneur's *Victory* (1919).

In dual role of the blind pirate Pew and the surly Merry in Paramount's *Treasure Island* (1920).

Lon and Hazel on one of their many camping trips in the early 1920's.
(Courtesy of the Chaney Family Collection)

Don't Step
On That Spider!
It Might Be Lon Chaney!
(1920-1923)

---

*"He was a real loner on the set. He
made Howard Hughes look like Pia Zadora."*
—*Jackie Coogan*

LON CHANEY

T*he Penalty* was a major career boost for Chaney. Goldwyn Pictures bought the rights to the 1913 novel by Governeur Morris, which told the story of a young boy injured in a tragic accident. The boy had his legs needlessly amputated above the knees by an inexperienced doctor. Years later this boy is known as "Blizzard," ruler of the San Francisco underworld. He swears revenge upon the doctor who maimed him and plans to hold his daughter hostage. In return for her release, the doctor must graft new legs from his daughter's fiance onto his stumps. Instead, the doctor corrects a brain lesion that had controlled his evil motives. In the book, Blizzard goes on to become a philanthropic force in the community, but in the film, he is killed by one of his former henchmen, paying the penalty for his life of crime.

Chaney was signed to star in the film by studio manager Abe Lehr at a salary of $500 a week. It was from Lehr that Chaney learned just how much his appearance in a film was really worth. He overheard Lehr talking with the studio casting director, Clifford Robertson (father of actor Cliff Robertson), saying that he could not believe they had gotten him for only $500 a week when they were prepared to pay $1500.[73]

To give his character the effect of walking on stumps, Lon devised quite an intricate device. First, leather belts were used to hold his legs strapped up behind him. The pants of his costume were

As the ape-man in *A Blind Bargain* (1922).

oversized which easily allowed him to get his doubled up legs into them. He then placed his strapped legs into leather stumps, which had straps running length-wise up the pant legs, attaching to a belt Lon wore around his waist. He wore a padded chest piece under his shirt and vest. This gave Lon a fuller look to his upper torso. The jacket, which was oversized in length, helped to hide his strapped-up legs. Wearing the harness and oversized clothing, Chaney walked on his knees with the aid of weighted crutches, and all of his scenes were shot without the use of trick angles or photography. His great-grandson, Ron Chaney, Jr., remembers hearing that for several weeks prior to filming, Lon put the harness on at home and practiced walking around.[74] Nonetheless, he suffered severe lower back strain due to the harness, and was only be able to wear it for short periods of time before having to unstrap it and have his legs massaged.

Fortunately, according to his grandson Lon Ralph Chaney, Lon was a very strong man, being able to grab hold of a ceiling beam and do several one-arm pull-ups.[75] He became a member of the famous Hollywood Athletic Club in September of 1922, and he worked out there regularly until his death. Lon's physical strength and stamina, due in part to years of dancing and scene shifting, helped him in this role as well as in many others.

Although *The Penalty* gathered mixed reviews, Lon received positive notices for his performance. "It is needless to say that the picture is Chaney more than anyone else," *Variety* wrote, while the *New York Times* observed, "In the midst of a purely mechanistic arrangement of incidents, and surrounded by puppets, Chaney creates a character. . . [Chaney] has another vivid impersonation."

Chaney's character of Blizzard, like the "Frog" in *The Miracle Man*, involved more physical than facial make-up, or as Lon would refer to it, "an attitude of body." Blizzard is charming and cunningly manipulative when dealing with the doctor's daughter. Yet when it comes to his henchmen, he rules them with an iron hand, putting complete fear into them so they'll follow his orders.

The sheer physical aspect of the role could have overshadowed the performance but Chaney etched out a strong portrayal. One has to wonder if the intensity Lon brought to this role might have been due in part to the pain produced by his harness. In one sequence of the film Chaney has gained the trust of the doctor's daughter, for whom he is modeling for a bust entitled "Satan: After The Fall." As he recognizes his growing influence over the girl, he becomes over-zealous in professing his feelings.

In this scene Chaney is sitting on a modeling platform, and with intense passion, begins to express his feelings to the young woman, not only facially, but with his hands. As he pleads for her not to forget him, his intensity builds and the young woman nervously laughs out of fear of his passion. Her laughter enrages Blizzard and his exploding anger is shown in a tight close-up. As she backs away from his grasp, Chaney falls off the platform, his emotions devouring his whole body. Standing on his stumps without the aid of his crutches, he makes an attempt to walk over and grab her. The visual impact of his efforts along with the anger on his face presents to the audience the terrifying image of a man gone mad. When Lon realizes his error he suddenly stops cold. Quickly switching gears, he deliberately exaggerates, wholly within his character, the anguish of losing his temper. Chaney attempts to regain her confidence by holding his head down as he speaks to her, much like a child would to its mother after being scolded. He slyly glances up at the young woman to see if his strategy is working. This glance conveys how devious Blizzard really is. His feigned sincerity solicits sympathy from the young woman. Yet one can see Blizzard's shrewd manipulation as he tries to right his mistake. Chaney does all of this mainly through facial expression since most of the scene is shot in medium close-ups, demonstrating again Chaney's unique ability to convey emotions to the audience, usually without committing the sin of overacting.

Lon was given second billing behind Priscilla Dean in Universal's *Outside the Law*, his first film of 1921, and his second film under the direction of Tod Browning. Leo McCarey worked as an assistant director on this picture. A few years later McCarey worked at Hal Roach Studios, directing some of the best short subjects in which Laurel and Hardy appeared, and later such well-known films as *Duck Soup* and *Going My Way*.

In *Outside the Law*, a crime melodrama set in San Francisco, Chaney played a dual role of the vile "Black Mike" Silva and an Oriental, Ah Wing. In an interesting plot twist at the climax, Chaney (Ah Wing) murders Chaney (Black Mike) in a clever double exposure. "Silky Moll" and her gangster father "Silent" Madden have become faithful followers of Chang Low, a Chinese shop owner who has introduced them to the works of Confucius. He hopes to help them shed their criminal past, but these hopes are dashed when Silent Madden is framed by Black Mike Silva for a policeman's death. Black Mike and "Dapper" Bill convince the disillusioned Silky Moll to join them in a jewelry heist. Before the robbery, Bill confesses to her that the plan is all a double-cross by Black Mike. They turn the tables on him, stealing the jewels and hiding out until he eventually finds them. The couple manages to escape to Chang Low's where Black Mike and his gang follow them and a bloody shoot-out erupts. After the battle, Silky Moll's father is released and she and Bill profess their love to each other and go straight.

Again Chaney gathered good notices for his part. "Chaney . . . makes his 'Blackie' sneaky role so vicious he throws the house [audience] right into the young couple's laps," *Variety* commented.

One can tell by the way Tod Browning uses Lon in this film that the director had an appreciation for the actor's talents. Although the film starred Priscilla Dean, Browning gave special attention to Lon.

For example, the part of Ah Wing is an insignificant role having no major scenes to propel the story forward. Yet with Chaney playing him, the character gains a realistic Oriental substance and personality as compared to the characterization of Chang Low. (In the 1930 remake, Browning did not include the character of Ah Wing.) This film demonstrates Browning's recognition that Chaney could play a variety of parts (even dual roles) — a harbinger of things to come for the two men when they worked together later at M-G-M.

To effect the Oriental make-up, Chaney used two strips of fishskin, a thin, transparent, tough skin used for medical purposes. These two strips were cut three inches long and five-eighths of an inch wide. On one end, each piece was cut to a rounded, pointed "V." Slightly behind the outside corners of the eyes, spirit gum was applied about an inch and a half back. When the adhesive was tacky, the strips of fishskin were placed over the spirit gum and pressed onto the face. Two strips of adhesive tape, each 3/4" wide, were cut long enough to reach around the head, from one piece of fishskin to the other. Taking one strip of the tape, keeping the adhesive side away from the hair, Lon fastened one piece of the fishskin by pressing it onto the adhesive tape. Gently pulling on this side of the tape would slant the eye. Carrying the tape around the head, the other piece of fishskin was pulled to slant the other eye and affixed to the other end of the tape. Taking the second strip of adhesive tape and placing the adhesive side in, Lon placed it over the first piece of tape, sticking them together. This gave the fishskin a double hold and prevented it from coming loose during the day's filming. A black wig covered up the tape. After applying the make-up base color, a light black line was drawn down from the inner corner of each eye. Chaney also shadowed under the cheekbones and wore a set of false teeth. The rest of the effect of appearing to be an Oriental was accomplished through acting skill. Chaney adapted a specific body posture for the role of Ah Wing; he hunched his back slightly, pulled his arms back, and took short steps, thus changing the appearance of the size of his body with minimal adjustments.

As good as his ability at make-up was, the acting was what finally made his performance believable. One scene in the film has Black Mike (Lon) and his two henchmen plotting a crime while eating at a restaurant. As they get up to leave, the henchmen leave a tip, which Black Mike pockets. Little bits of business like this gave Chaney's characters life.

In 1920, enjoying the fruits of Lon's success, he and Hazel bought a little bungalow at 1549 Edgemont Avenue, just down the street from the house where they had lived since 1915. They sold the house in 1922 and moved to 7152 Sunset Blvd. That building, which is still standing, is a two-story structure with two apartments on each floor. At that time the now-legendary street consisted mostly of single-dwelling homes instead of the shopping malls and high-rises that proliferate today.

For Those We Love, Lon's next film, was a Goldwyn Pictures release produced by and starring Betty Compson, who hired Chaney as her co-star. Lon played Trix Ulner, a gambler who befriends the heroine and helps her to clear her brother who was framed for a robbery. ("Miss Compson has a corking company supporting her, which includes Lon Chaney and others of equal note, but even they cannot pull the picture through." —*Variety.*) Lon then began work on a four-episode feature called *Bits of Life,* directed by Marshall Neilan. Lon again played an Oriental in the segment called "Hop" which also featured Anna May Wong. It told the story of Chin Gow, who was raised to believe that girl infants were undesirable. When his wife gives birth to a baby girl, he beats the wife and threatens to slay the child. A friend of Chin Gow's wife gives her a crucifix and while nailing it to the wall, the nail penetrates Chin Gow's skull as he lies on a bunk on the other side of the wall, killing him. ("Lon Chaney as the Chinese of the third story gives a striking performance." — *New York Times*.)

About this time, the joke "Don't Step On That Spider! It Might Be Lon Chaney!" became well-known. It is attributed to director Marshall Neilan, who was at a party when he observed another guest about to crush a spider.[76] Lon's incredible ability with make-up intrigued the public to such a degree that he became the subject of many jokes. Later in his career, he was mentioned in several comic strips, including the famous "Mutt and Jeff."

Lon's last film of 1921 was a Goldwyn picture based on Governeur Morris' novel *Ace of Hearts*. Leatrice Joy and John Bowers played opposite Lon in a story about a death club whose zealots meet regularly, and whoever draws the ace of hearts is pledged to rid the world of "one who has lived too long." ("The picture is done in splendid, dignified style and has as its featured actor, Lon Chaney, whose work ever since his playing of 'The Frog' in *The Miracle Man* has added to his reputation as an actor of utmost sincerity and skill." —*Variety*.

In December of 1921, Lon and his wife went to New York City where he played in Hope Hampton's production of *The Light in the Dark*, in which he played a kind-hearted crook who steals the Holy Grail to help cure the heroine. The film was not released until September of 1922, and received weak reviews. ("Lon Chaney is a somewhat more kindly crook than is his wont." —*Variety*.)

After completing the film, the Chaneys stopped off in Colorado Springs and stayed with his old boyhood friend Harry Hughes. While he was in town, Lon appeared at the deaf school his maternal grandparents had founded and gave a talk to the students in sign language.[77] During his stay, Lon gave an interview to writer C. S. Dudley. In the interview, which appeared on January 1, 1922, in the *Colorado Springs Gazette*, Lon discussed the upcoming role of

Lon Chaney

Quasimodo in *The Hunchback of Notre Dame* as well as the movie business in general:

> "A German company offered me practically
> anything to go to Germany and make the picture,"
> [Chaney] said yesterday. "I turned the offer down.
> They were planning to make the picture in three
> months. It can't be done. It would take three hours
> a day to make up for the part alone.
>
> "Now I am in correspondence with other
> companies, and the picture may actually be started
> before very long.
>
> "Do you know I have been dreaming of playing that
> part for three years? I have even gone so far as to
> plan the make-up, and I have a device by means of
> which I could strip to the waist and still appear to
> be the hunchback. I could be lashed with the whip
> and the blood would apparently come on my
> body."

It is doubtful any company other than Universal was considering *The Hunchback of Notre Dame*. As to the reference of a German company wanting to make the film, nothing has ever come to light regarding Lon's assertion.

Chaney went back to Universal for a starring role in *The Trap*, originally titled *The Heart of a Wolf* prior to its release in May of 1922. The story has Chaney playing a good-hearted trapper in the Canadian Northwest who is betrayed by his friend and plots revenge. Virgil Miller was the cameraman and this was one of the earliest films to employ the use of panchromatic film stock. It was also the first time the title "Man of a Thousand Faces" was used to promote publicly Chaney's unique and increasingly famous gift for elaborate character make-ups.

Despite lovely location footage shot in Yosemite, California, *The Trap* received weak reviews, such as *Variety's*, "Too much star in closeups every few feet makes this feature a very draggy affair . . . The picture gives Chaney a chance to hog footage right along in close-ups. This becomes rather tiresome, as all the emoting he does does not carry the story forward at all."

At least one other person in the motion picture industry found Lon's emoting tiresome as well. In 1921, Rudolph Valentino approached Rex Ingram, who was directing him in *The Conquering Power*, and told him he felt he was being repressed in his performance. Valentino said he had spoken to Lon Chaney who urged him to take more freedom in his roles and be less limited. Ingram told Valentino that he felt Chaney was a contortionist actor who played his roles a bit too vividly for his liking, and preferred his actors to be restrained.[78]

Fortunately, however, most people did not share Ingram's opinion, and Lon's popularity continued to climb. His next starring role was in an independent film produced by Irving Cummings entitled *Flesh And Blood*, which cast him as an escaped convict who disguises himself as a cripple to elude the police so he can see his daughter. (". . . Chaney's plastic face is crossed by all the emotional expressions" —*Motion Picture*.) According to an article in the *Exhibitors Trade Review,* one scene in the picture was shot with color film using Chinese actors.[79] Unfortunately this sequence does not exist in any known print. In *Voices of the City*, originally released under the title *The Night Rose*, Lon played O'Rourke, a dapper gangster pretending to aid a young couple who witnessed his gang kill a policeman. O'Rourke secretly plans to kill the young man when the D.A. links the couple to his activities and the shooting. O'Rourke's mistress kills him before he can harm the couple.

The film, produced by Goldwyn pictures and Lon's third film directed by Wallace Worsley, gave Chaney positive notices for his work. *Variety* observed, "Lon Chaney, as always, gets the utmost out of the role of a powerful leader of lawbreakers. He has a gift for quiet emphasis in pantomime which fits nicely into this lurid tale."

Apparently the tale was a little *too* lurid, for according to the August 19, 1922, *Exhibitors Trade Review*, the film came under the ban of the New York censors. After certain scenes were removed, it was approved for exhibition in the state of New York. Until the formation of the Motion Picture Producers Association (MPPA), every state had their own Board of Censors and could deem any film unsuitable for showing if it offended local sensibilities. After the MPPA was formed, a set of rules was drawn up for the producers to follow.

Lon was next signed by producer B. P. Schulberg to star in the lead role of a film based on Wilbur Daniel Steele's novel *Ching, Ching, Chinaman*. Chaney played the role of Yen Sin, a Chinese man washed ashore in a storm and confronted by racial and religious prejudice of local New Englanders. Eventually, Yen Sin exposes their hypocrisy and paves the way to happiness for a pair of the young lovers. Exterior scenes were filmed in Balboa, California, and the Louis B. Mayer Studios were leased for interior scenes.

In the 1920's, Orientals were nearly always played as cold-hearted villains, and exhibitors felt the film-going public would not accept them in heroic roles. As a result, no major theatre chain would touch the film, even with the title changed to *Shadows*. It was finally distributed to the smaller independent theatre houses without advance payment in exchange for a share of the profits.[80] The National Board of Review praised the film and Robert E. Sherwood included *Shadows* on his Best Moving Pictures of 1922-23 list, giving the film some much-needed prestige and publicity. *Variety* commented, "Lon Chaney as the Chinaman gave a corking performance and successfully withstood the strain of dying through about 2,000 feet of film."

Priscilla Bonner co-starred in the film and in a 1992 interview, she remembered what it was like working with Chaney:

> There was a deep sadness about his face. There was a haunting quality that stayed with you. It was something that you couldn't put your hand on. You couldn't quite identify what it was — it was strange. I think that it came from the parents, the deaf mutes. How would you feel if your parents were deaf mutes? It's a sadness that can't be thrown off. It would affect your personality and I think it affected him. I think perhaps, it helped to make him a magnificent pantomime artist.
>
> [Working with Lon as an actor was]. . . Wonderful! That is where the kindness came in. I was a struggling actress, he was so kind to me. He was so helpful to me. . . . Marvelous. He was a top actor, a magnificent actor. . . . I saw every picture he ever made because I admired him enormously. It was just a joy to be able to work with him and see how he handled himself, he was so easy. [Lon was] a superb human being, warm, soft spoken. He had a very warm personality.
>
> In this film he played a Chinese. He was not heavily made up. He did have his eyes taped a little, but the

rest of it was in his mind. He thought Chinese. Even
his gestures and everything, he became the
character of a Chinese. He was Chinese and I felt he
was Chinese. Now you may think that I'm a little
crazy, but that is the truth. It was in his mind. He
thought he was Chinese. He became Chinese in his
mind and he reflected it. He would even speak in an
accent and use his voice.

I never saw him touch up his make-up. Didn't seem
to me he even had powder. I think when he
portrayed any nationality, he went among them and
listened and watched and learned. Then I think he
would copy it and give his interpretation. I don't
think he ever broke character between scenes that I
recall. He took direction from a person he trusted
and respected. He wasn't eccentric. Lon had a good
rapport with everyone on the crew. They all seemed
to love him, everybody did. One time during filming
he came over and sat beside me on the set and we
just talked. I don't remember anything exactly —
nothing very profound.

Once Marion Blackton was with us and we were
talking about Lon. She agreed [with what I said
about him] and she knew him for a longer period
than I did. She said, "I would say he was somewhat a
man of mystery."[81]

While on location in Balboa, Lon's appearance caused a lot of
attention, according to the *Santa Ana Register's* September 5, 1922
edition:

"Swathed in greens and decorated with asters of
varying hues, a small river boat, borne along by a
rattan sail, presented a new phase of 'the dead
steered by the dumb' as it plied its course in and
about the harbor while Chaney, in gorgeous oriental
robes, was 'shot' from all angles."

Oliver Twist was released in November of 1922 by Associated
First National and marked the fourth time since 1909 that the
Dickens classic was filmed. Lon was cast in the role of Fagin and
child star Jackie Coogan was cast as Oliver. According to Coogan,
Chaney was the only actor considered for the Fagin role. During a
tribute to Chaney at the Academy of Motion Picture Arts and Sciences
in 1983, Coogan recalled working with Chaney on the film:

I was introduced by our director Frank Lloyd to this
man who was nothing remarkable, short, very tan,
he was bowlegged, very charming, and we talked
about four or five minutes and found out he danced
on the stage. We did a few breaks (dance steps) and
after he left I forgot him.

We had been filming four to five weeks before Lon
came to work. On the way to work that Monday
morning, I remember my dad saying to me, "Jack,
you're going to meet the fella who's gonna play
Fagin in the picture, and it's the fella you met, Mr.
Lon Chaney." I remarked that I remembered him as
the fella who dances and my dad said, "He won't be
dancing in this picture, and . . . get set because he
does his own make-up and he is gonna be pretty
grotesque."

Lon Chaney

Well, I was seven and a half and I thought I knew everything. We went on the set at 9 a.m. and Frank Lloyd introduced me to Chaney and this thing turned around. He scared the bejesus out of me! This man with a few strokes of grease paint and glue turned himself into something that was as evil as anything in the world. And at seven and a half, I was pretty impressionable. I was so frightened by this man; the only thing that got me out of it is when we started to do our scene and I got close to him, was the smell of spirit gum which he had used so cleverly. It brought me back to my senses and I was able to work with him. He was with us three weeks and I must say that I've worked with only two people in the years I was in the business, Mr. Chaplin and Mr. Chaney that . . . they were everything.

When we finished our first scene together (where Fagin teaches Oliver to pick pockets) I always looked at the assistant cameraman after a scene and he gave me a wink which meant it was okay. So the director said we'd print that and go in closer to cover the scene. I went back to a chess game I was having with my tutor and suddenly I could smell him coming closer to me, because of that spirit gum odor. He put his hand out and we shook hands and there was no longer that feeling of coldness and iciness and reptilian dislike that I felt before when he touched me. He was a warm man and he looked me right in the eye and said, "Jackie, you're all right."

Coogan also said that Lon was "a real loner on the set. He made Howard Hughes look like Pia Zadora." In an interview for *Motion Picture* magazine, Chaney explained his portrayal of Fagin: "I'm not playing him essentially as a Jew, but as a character of more universal appeal — a man of wits who has no particular racial limitations. This will, I think, be my best piece of work."[82] *The New York Times* commented on Chaney's role: "There's Fagin, too, vividly present in the person of Lon Chaney."

To play Fagin, Chaney used a long scraggly beard and a pair of bushy eyebrows made from crepe-wool hair. False teeth, fitted over his own, were made out of guttapercha, a hard dental rubber used by dentists to make temporary fillings. Chaney heated the guttapercha (which came in round sticks or flat strips) over an alcohol lamp or gas stove until it became pliable, then he placed it into his mouth and molded it into shape. While the guttapercha was still warm, he pressed individual false teeth into the rubber. This gave a far more realistic look than the other commonly used method, which was to carve the shape of the teeth out of the rubber and paint them with tooth enamel.

The long drooping nose was modeled out of nose putty. A combination of clay and resin, nose putty came in the form of stiff sticks which had to be softened by kneading between the fingers or by placing in a spoon and heating over a candle or alcohol lamp. Spirit gum was first painted onto the area of the nose to help the putty adhere better. The softened putty was then placed onto the nose and modeled to the desired shape. Since nose putty had such a flat color, red liner paint was painted over the putty before the grease paint foundation was applied, to prevent the nose putty from photographing darker than the grease paint.

Aside from nose putty, plasto wax, which was also known as mortician's wax, was sometimes used to create a false nose, cover the eyebrows, or build up the cheekbones. Both nose putty and plasto wax had a tendency to crack away from the skin where there was a lot of facial movement, but plasto wax had the additional drawback of being more susceptible to melting after several hours under hot lights. This made nose putty preferable in filming situations, and it was the medium Chaney generally used.

To further emphasize Fagin's age, Lon employed the use of highlights and shadows and finely painted lines applied with grease paint and eyebrow pencils. He also used the trick of cutting cotton-wool in a crescent moon shape to create realistic-looking eyebags. Spirit gum or flexible collodion was painted over the cotton-wool as a sealer, allowing the grease paint, mixed with a little olive oil, to be painted over it and used for additional days of filming.

All this cumbersome make-up made relaxing between sets difficult for Lon; however, Esther Ralston, who played Rose Maylie in *Oliver Twist*, recalled his amusing way of taking a nap under these most restrictive circumstances. She said Lon would slump in his director's chair, stretching his legs out in front of him and letting his arms hang off either side. He then placed a small dinner bell on his stomach and close his eyes. Within a few minutes, he was asleep and the bell would slowly slip off his stomach and fall to the floor. The noise would awaken him and this method helped to keep him refreshed through long days of filming.[83]

In March of 1922, *Photoplay* ran a one-page article called "Lon Chaney's Make-Up," which was the only time Chaney ever showed in a set of four pictures how he achieved some of his various make-up effects. It was also one of the few times he allowed his make-up case to be seen and used for publicity. This layout was taken during the production of *A Blind Bargain*, Lon's his fifth picture made for Goldwyn Studios and his fourth film directed by Wallace Worsley.

A Blind Bargain was one of the few true horror films Lon ever made, despite his reputation as a "horror" actor. Based on the novel *The Octave of Claudius* by Barry Pain, it tells the story of a prominent surgeon, Dr. Lamb, who is obsessed with prolonging human life. He carries out his experiments in the secret chambers of his mansion where one of his earlier efforts, a hunchback half-ape, half-man assists him in his work. Dr. Lamb befriends a young man, Robert, who has been left destitute after World War I. Robert offers his services to the surgeon if he will perform a needed operation on his mother. Before Dr. Lamb can begin to carry out his procedures on the young man, the ape-man tells Robert what is in store for him. Robert escapes with the aid of the ape-man, who then releases yet another of Dr. Lamb's failed experiments from his cage. Justice triumphs when this monster kills the surgeon.

Chaney played both roles of Dr. Lamb and the hunchback ape-man. The film employed double exposure, allowing the two characters played by Chaney to appear in the same scene. The make-up Lon devised for the ape-man became the model for similar make-ups of this type. He wore a closely cropped black wig with a low hairline, and extended his eyebrows across the bridge of the nose. He repeated the trick of cotton-wool under the eyes that he had used in *Oliver Twist*. To obtain the effect of a broad nose, the use of highlights and shadows as well as placing the ends of rubber cigar holders in the nostrils were used. These ends were cut about 3/8" off the cigar holders, allowing Chaney to get the desired look and still breathe freely. A set of false teeth gave a protruding look to his mouth. He also added a slight hump to his back and walked in a stooped manner to give a simian gait to the character.

A Blind Bargain received favorable reviews. *Photoplay* said, "Lon Chaney's fine acting in two widely divergent roles is the outstanding feature of this picture." *Variety* was even more positive:

> . . . beyond the work of the star himself, there is
> nothing to raise this film above the average feature. .
> . . Chaney, doubling as the doctor and the

hunchback, gives a credible performance and allows
for some double photography that is by no means
unworthy of mention. Always at his best in a
grotesque make-up, Chaney predominates in the
character of the man-ape, using the ungainly lope of
the supposed animal as a means of locomotion
throughout the interpretation of the character."

Lon next appeared as the crooked lawyer in Metro Pictures *Quincy Adams Sawyer*, a rural comic melodrama based on Charles Felton Pidgin's novel. ("Lon Chaney and Elmo Lincoln do good work as the villains," *Variety* reported.) He also appeared as one of the brothers in the 1923 release of Metro's *All The Brothers Were Valiant*, from the sea novel by Ben Ames Williams. ("Chaney appeared straight for once, minus character make-up, and did well with a hybrid sympathetic and negative role." — *Variety*) Lon then returned to Universal to star in their 1923 programmer release, *The Shock*, portraying Wilse Dilling, a crippled gangster of the San Francisco underworld. The climax of the film features the 1906 earthquake and is one of the few films where he ends up with the leading lady. ("Another hideously clever characterization by Lon Chaney as a cripple of the underworld." — *Photoplay*)

In the five years since Chaney had left Universal, he certainly proved the studio manager's statement wrong. Nevertheless, despite leading roles in some features, he had yet to graduate to the ranks of world-wide stardom. When a film historian looks at the career of an actor, several roles inevitably stand out as career milestones. For Chaney, *Hell Morgan's Girl, Riddle Gwane, The Miracle Man* and *The Penalty* were certainly significant in advancing his career. But the role of Quasimodo in Victor Hugo's *The Hunchback of Notre Dame* was the film that would boost Lon Chaney to international acclaim.

As Fagin in *Oliver Twist* (1922).

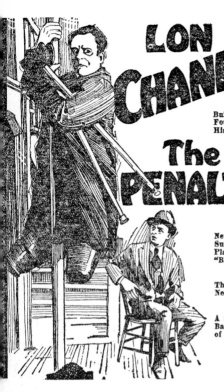

LON CHANEY

Built the
Foundation of
His Career in

The PENALTY

Never Has He
Surpassed His
Playing of
"Blizzard."

The 1926
New Edition

A Story of the
Barbary Coast
of Olden Days

Metro-
Goldwyn-
Mayer
Picture

The Penalty (1920)

In the dual role of the gangster "Black Mike" Silva and the Chinese shop keeper Ah Wing in Tod Browning's *Outside the Law* (1921).

Filming *Ace of Hearts* (1921) for Goldwyn Pictures. Director Wallace
Worsley (right, bending down) stands on the cat walk next to camera. Lon is
seated at the table (left) next to Leatrice Joy.

Preparing to leave for location shooting from Yosemite Lodge for *The Trap*
(1922). Lon, in costume, points out something to director Richard Thornby.

Lon (in his Chinese make-up) with director Tom Forman and Producer B. P.
Schulberg on the set of *Shadows* (1922)
Lon and Wallace Beery clown around during production of *A Blind Bargain*.

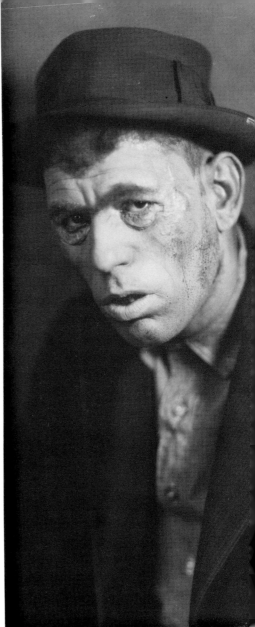

(Left) As the mad doctor in *A Blind Bargain* (1922).
(Right) The original make-up for the ape-man in the same film. The final
transformation appears on page 78.

The Bell Ringer of Notre Dame

(1923)

———————————

"Remember, my dear, you are an actress. You don't have to live the part, just act it. The point is not for you to cry, make your audience cry. You have to be in control of yourself."

—*Lon Chaney's advice on acting*
to Patsy Ruth Miller

In 1918 Irving G. Thalberg accepted the position of secretary to the general manager at the New York office of Universal Studios. His proficiency and skill soon caught the eye of company president Carl Laemmle, who appropriated Thalberg to work for him exclusively. Laemmle was so impressed with his new secretary he even sought his opinions on the films being made and released by the company.

In 1920, Thalberg was asked to accompany his boss on a trip to the studio in California. Along the way, Laemmle was working on plans to set up a new management team at the studio. It was common knowledge in the industry that Universal had a revolving door when it came a studio manager's longevity. Laemmle was expected to stay for only a week, and summoned Thalberg to his office at the studio to notify him that a fourth member was being added to the team that would run and supervise production at the California studio — Irving Thalberg. (Tarkington Baker, Maurice Fleckles and Isadore Bernstein were the others.)

Laemmle left for New York, and the four-man team set about running the studio. However, the ideas and comments Thalberg proposed went largely ignored. Frustrated, Thalberg finally went to his boss and explained his stifling situation. Laemmle backed his former secretary's ideas, which led to the other three team members being transferred to other studio departments. At the age of 20,

The Hunchback of Notre Dame (1923)

Irving Thalberg, the legendary "Boy Wonder," became the sole head of production at Universal Studios.

Thalberg's rapid ascent in Hollywood history is all the more remarkable considering that he had a rheumatic heart, and doctors held little hope that the boy would live past the age of 30. But despite spending much of his childhood bedridden, he graduated from high school with the rest of his class and took courses in shorthand and speed typing which landed him a secretarial position with an import trading firm at 18. He left there and joined Universal at the invitation of Mrs. Carl Laemmle, who had been a childhood friend of Thalberg's mother in their native Germany.

During Thalberg's boyhood, he had enjoyed reading the classics. One of his favorites was Victor Hugo's *Notre Dame de Paris,* known to English readers as *The Hunchback of Notre Dame.* In 1922, he persuaded Carl Laemmle to approve production of an elaborate film version of the novel at the then-unheard-of budget of $1,250,000. Not unexpectedly, Laemmle was quite hesitant to do such a costly feature, for at that time Universal was mainly producing westerns, melodramas, comedies and weekly serials. The company, unlike other studios, had produced very few prestige pictures with the exception of Eric Von Stroheim's *Foolish Wives.* Thalberg felt that it was time for Universal to take this important step. Interestingly, Chaney mentioned his desire to play the role over a year and a half prior to actual production, so Thalberg may possibly have discussed the project with him while Lon was working on *Outside the Law* or *The Trap.*

The Hunchback of Notre Dame was one of the first spectacle pictures ever produced. Patsy Ruth Miller, who played Esmeralda in the film, said "Back then a film with such a budget was a big thing. It was unheard of to make a movie for so much, but now — millions here, millions there."[84] The sets covered 19 acres on the studio backlot, and over 750 crew members — carpenters, masons, property men and costumers — were hired. A special building was constructed just to house and distribute the costumes for the extras, who often numbered in the thousands. Every arc light in the studio, and most of the available lights in other Hollywood studios were put to use by 105 electricians for the nearly two months of night filming required by the picture.

Wallace Worsley was assigned to direct the film, with the aid of 10 assistant directors. One of these assistants was William Wyler who later directed such Hollywood classics as *Dead End, Wuthering Heights, Best Years of Our Lives,* and the remake of *Ben-Hur.* The Western Electric Public Address Apparatus, used for the first time in motion pictures on the set of *The Hunchback of Notre Dame,* allowed Worsley or his assistants to give directions to cast and crew throughout the enormous set, a definite advantage over the megaphones normally used at the time.

The largest part of the set was a stunning recreation of the Notre Dame cathedral. The set of the cathedral ended just above the doors, and for wider shots of the building, the upper portion was constructed as a large scale hanging miniature which was mounted between the camera and the building, and lined up to blend in perfectly with the full-scale set. Other sections of the cathedral were built on a hill for low-angle shots, as well as for safety so if someone fell they would not be seriously injured.[85] The cathedral set remained on the Universal lot until it was destroyed by a fire in 1967.

By this time in his career, Chaney's reputation for unusual make-up and bizarre characterizations made him the obvious choice for the role of Quasimodo. He received $2,500 per week for the role. There is an interesting yet unsubstantiated story regarding how Chaney negotiated his weekly salary. Supposedly Universal refused Lon's initial salary request of $1,500 a week. When they could find no other actor suitable for the role, the studio again contacted Chaney, who now asked for $2,000 a week. Universal again went looking for someone else. Unable to sign anyone, Universal contacted Lon once more. He advised the studio that his salary was now $2,500 a week and he would raise it an additional $500 every time they called.[86] The picture began filming on December 16, 1922, and was completed on June 3, 1923, with Patsy Ruth Miller, Norman Kerry, Ernest Torrance, Raymond Hatton, Brandon Hurst, and Nigel de Brulier playing the other leading roles.

Chaney's make-up faithfully re-created Victor Hugo's description of the character of Quasimodo. The author had described the hunchback as having "a tetrahedron nose . . . horse-shoe mouth, of that little left eye stubbled up with an eyebrow of carroty bristles, while the right was completely overwhelmed and buried by an enormous wen; of those irregular teeth, jagged here and there like the battlements of a fortress; of that horny lip, over which one of those teeth protruded, like the tusk of an elephant . . . his prodigious head was covered with red bristles; between his shoulders rose an enormous hump, which was counter-balanced by a protuberance in front; his thighs and legs were so strangely put together that they touched at no one point but the knees, and seen in front, resembled two sickles joined at the handles."

A great deal of fiction published over the years has led to misconceptions about how Chaney achieved his make-up masterpiece. The hump he wore to give the appearance of a hunchback did not weigh 70 pounds as has so often been reported, nor was it made of rubber. According to Patsy Ruth Miller, the hump was made of plaster and weighed no more than 20 pounds.[87] To hold the plaster hump on his back, Chaney designed a leather harness which also prevented him from standing. This harness fitted around his waist like a belt, with straps over his shoulders which attached to the front part of the belt, thus keeping him in a stooped position. During filming he had a special stool with arms on it that would allow him to rest between scenes.[88]

It took Lon three hours a day to apply all the make-up necessary to become Quasimodo. To distort his cheekbones, Lon did not use nose putty or plasto wax, but built-up cotton and flexible collodion. Spirit gum was first applied to the cheek area. Before the spirit gum dried, cotton was pressed onto the gum, and then a coat of flexible collodion or spirit gum brushed over the cotton. Another piece of cotton was placed onto the area and covered with another coat of collodion. This procedure continued until the desired effect had been achieved. A final coat of collodion applied over the entire piece blended the edges into the skin, and a topcoat of greasepaint completed the effect. This method of layering cotton and collodion allowed Lon to use these pieces for several days with a minimum of maintenance and repair. Flexible collodion had a composition similar to "New Skin" and, used as a sealer, should not be confused with nonflexible collodion, which is used to make scars.

For the wart on the eye, Lon covered his right eye with adhesive tape and applied nose putty. (This, incidentally, strained his eyesight to such a degree that he had to wear glasses off-camera for the rest of his life.)[89] Crepe-wool hair was used for bushy eyebrows, and nose putty changed the shape of the tip of his nose. The nose was further accentuated by the use of cigar-holder ends placed in the nostrils. The effect of jagged teeth was made with the use of guttapercha, and an additional piece of this material was placed in the lower jaw to create a protruding effect. Understandably, this made talking very difficult, and Lon rarely engaged in conversation on the set while made-up. In the scene where Quasimodo is placed on the whipping wheel, Chaney wore a rubber shirt, allowing him to appear bare-chested; the front seam and collar were covered with crepe-wool hair applied directly to the rubber. A light brown, matted wig completed Lon's transformation. In some early scenes crepe-wool hair was placed on the back of his hands to give them a hairy, animal-like appearance. However, this particular effect was soon discarded, with no loss to the effectiveness of Lon's characterization; in his autobiography, director Tay Garnett recalls visiting the set one chilly night and observed that even the most jaded extras avoided looking at Lon in his make-up.[90]

In an interview for the April 21, 1923, issue of *Movie Weekly*, Lon told Grace Kingsley how he felt make-up helped him in playing his parts:

> In one way make-up helps you in putting a characterization over. It aids you in getting into the spirit of the part while you are looking into the mirror, and when you see the interest in the faces of your co-workers. But in another way it hinders.
>
> When a make-up is as painful as that which I wore as Blizzard in *The Penalty*, when I had my legs strapped up and couldn't bear it that way more than twenty minutes at a time — when I have to be a cripple, as in *The Miracle Man*, or have to keep a certain attitude of body as I did in playing Yen Sin in *Shadows*, it sometimes takes a good deal of imagination to forget your physical sufferings. Yet at that, the subconscious mind has a marvelous way of making you keep the right attitudes and make the right gestures when you are actually acting.

Patsy Ruth Miller, who played the role of Esmeralda, recalled her memories of Lon Chaney and the making of this epic film:

> Lon was very serious when working, but he had a fey sense of humor. Unlike many of the stars I

worked with in that day, he was extremely kind, thoughtful and protective towards me. He once reprimanded me for smoking, saying "Just because I do it doesn't mean you should." He wasn't a very socially [out-]going man, on or off the set. He had his own friends, who rarely visited the set, except his son who was there quite a few times. Because of his make-up and harness, he didn't mingle much with the cast or crew, and unless he had a suggestion or advice to give me, we rarely spoke to each other while he was in make-up.

Lon directed as much as Mr. Worsley did in the scenes we did together. Mr. Worsley was a nice man, but I didn't care for him much as a director. As far as reports of Lon fainting from exhaustion, I never witnessed it nor heard of it. I think it was more of the writers' imagination than truth. But I know Lon was very tired, and as a matter of fact, we all were. When we did the night scenes, we'd film from 5 p.m. until dawn and the rest of the time we'd start at 9 a.m. and go until 6 or 7 p.m. Occasionally we'd shoot longer and this was my routine for 6 months on this picture!

Lon was a perfectionist. If he felt the scene didn't play right, he'd insist on doing it over, but he was never excessive in doing scenes over and over. He had a way of getting his point across without quarreling. The thing I remember most about Lon was his kindness and his sense of humor. When I was doing the scene in the tavern where Norman

Kerry is trying to seduce me, and I'm looking at him
calf-eyed, I heard Lon's voice from off-camera say,
"Oh, Mr. Kerry, are my eyes too big for pictures?"

Lon did warn me once not to be such a pushover for
a hard luck story. He had seen me giving money to
an extra who looked like a pathetic old woman. Lon
said she was not old, not pathetic, and not poor, and
I was being played for a sucker. He said generosity
was okay but never be played for a sucker.

By the end of filming, we had all become a family
and saying good-bye was pretty emotional. Lon, who
was not a demonstrative man, actually gave me a
good-bye kiss!

In one of my big emotional scenes, I was overdoing
it a bit in rehearsal and Lon came up to me very
quietly and said, "Remember, my dear, you are an
actress. You don't have to live the part, just act it.
The point is not for you to cry, make your audience
cry. You have to be in control of yourself."[91]

Despite the fact that Patsy Ruth Miller didn't "care for [Wallace
Worsley] much as a director," Chaney must have, as he was
supposedly instrumental in having Worsley hired for the film. No
doubt the two men had a good working relationship (since they had
made four other films together) and Worsley probably let him play
the scene the way Lon envisioned it. Chaney once said he never
worried about who the studios handed him as a director. With the

exception of Rupert Julian, with whom he later worked on *Phantom of the Opera*, it doesn't appear he had any problems with any of the directors he was assigned.

During the production of *Hunchback*, Lon was doubled by Joe Bonomo, who had worked with him on *The Light in the Dark* doing stunts and playing small parts. Bonomo was used in the scene were Quasimodo slides down a rope in front of the church to rescue Esmeralda from the King's guards. The first man to try the stunt was sent to the hospital after he received severe rope burns on his hands and the insides of his legs. Bonomo had aluminum foil sewn into both his pants legs and his thick leather gloves and was able to do the slide in one continuous movement without any trouble.[92] Harvey Perry was also hired to double Lon in some scenes and was given a make-up job by Lon himself, just in case the camera caught a glimpse of his face.[93] Audiences of 1923 had no idea that Chaney, or any other star for that matter, was ever doubled by stuntmen. They assumed that stars did all their own acts of daring — a myth propagated by the studios; the program book for *The Hunchback of Notre Dame* states that Chaney did all his own stunts.

The night work on the backlot at Universal in the winter was described by Earl Miller, the chief electrical engineer on the film, as "rain, fog, wind and mud — days, weeks, months of it . . . those foggy cold nights and the miles we walked, night after night, up and down that cobblestone street and out in that mud, I wonder how the picture was ever completed."[94]

In his autobiography, Tay Garnett described the numerous delays that took place in shooting the sequence on the night he visited the *Hunchback* set. First there were problems with the camera, then a light went out. Each time a new setback occurred, the extras doused their torches and sat down, complaining about the long hours. When things were finally ready, the assistant director would yell to the extras, "Light your torches and pull up your tights!"[95]

Lon Chaney

One of the most interesting items this author discovered while researching this book was a letter Lon wrote during the production of the film to his cousin Hugh Harbert, who was then living in Seattle:

Dear Old "Dutch,"

I received your letter and it was sure a surprise. I know old "kid" I owe you a letter, but if you knew how tired I have been on account of this picture I am doing now, you would excuse one this once anyway. Well Hugh, I am sure glad to hear you have found something that will make a little business of your own. While there are thousands of hair tonics on the market, no doubt there is room for one more. After all, it isn't how many are on the market, but how good are they? Now enclosed find a check for one hundred ($100.00) dollars as per your letter and you can consider me a partner more or less. But however you can use your own judgement about that. It is a good thing by the way you did not need any more as I have invested almost all my ready cash in real estate and I am just beginning to build my own home and as a result I am just a little bit low on the ready cash. I hope and trust old boy that this proposition is a great success as I know of no one I would rather see get along than yourself. Let me tell you something Hugh, while I have been very fortunate and have gotten to the top of my profession, I am still the same guy you knew back in the old days. I will admit I have a great many more responsibilities and am older, the thought and principle is still there, thank God. I sure would like to see you bud, and who knows that in the near future I may. I have been working awfully hard on this picture and it is coming to a close now, and naturally everybody is more or less anxious to get through. As a result, we are working night and day. We expect to finish about the 10th of next month. I am then going to take my wife and hop on a train and go to Glenwood Springs, Colo. and take the first real rest I've had in over 20 years. Think of that. I hope to be able to stay 3 weeks. It all depends on how soon we finish this picture as I start another one July 2nd or 3rd. So that's how it goes. I sure am sorry to hear about your Dad, but I try to convince myself that it is all for the best. Dad has not been at all well himself. He had a touch of Bright's Disease [kidney disease], but fortunately I caught it in time, sent him to the hospital, and at the end of two weeks he was out of danger. But he must adhere strictly to a diet prescribed by the doctor. Should he fail to do so, he will not live any time at all. Still, he looks very well and is in good spirits. All the rest of the folks are in first class health. I see John once and awhile, and he looks good. Belle of course is just going through the change and does not feel extra well, but as good as could be expected. Their two boys Keith and Frank are sure two mighty fine young men. They are both in the movie business. Keith is a cameraman and Frank is an electrician. Frank is about to get married I believe. My boy, you know is a whale of a kid now. He is 5 ft. 10$^3/_4$ inches and is 16 years old. Not a bad looking guy

either. Well bud, I guess I will close for this time and
I want you to keep me posted from time to time as
to how this new venture of yours comes out. With
all the good luck in the world to you and yours, I am
always your cousin

> Lon
> 7152 Sunset Blvd.
> Hollywood, Calif.[96]

On June 19, 1923, Lon and Hazel arrived in Colorado Springs by
train. The following day, the *Colorado Springs Gazette* reported on
the arrival of the home-town celebrity:

CHANEY COMES TO COLORADO SPRINGS
TO RESTORE BROKEN HEALTH

Strenuous Work in Recent Motion Picture Success Has Played
Havoc with Nerves of Colorado Springs Star of the Silver Screen;
Visits Harry Hughes

Lon Chaney, one of the greatest character portrayers
in motion pictures, is in Colorado Springs, his
boyhood home, for a few days. Mr. Chaney arrived
here yesterday and is visiting his old friend, Harry
Hughes, 2122 North Tejon Street. Mr. Chaney will
remain here until Thursday or Friday, when he will
go on to Glenwood Springs to rest his nerves,
broken by his strenuous work in *The Hunchback of
Notre Dame.*

Known as "the Man with a Thousand Faces," Mr.
Chaney has played several big roles in motion
pictures of the last few years. . . . One of the
requirements of his role in *The Hunchback of Notre
Dame* is that of distorting his body and remaining in
a cramped position for hours at a time. The pain he
has undergone in some of his late pictures has been
very severe. He left Los Angeles a short time ago
with the intention of taking a six weeks rest and
when he gets to Glenwood Springs he will hike for
the mountains and shut himself out from civilization.
He is accompanied by Mrs. Chaney.

Although Chaney's portrayal of Quasimodo in *The Hunchback of
Notre Dame* aggravated a back condition which had developed
during his work on *The Penalty*, the pain Lon suffered from the
making of these films has been greatly exaggerated by over-
imaginative writers. While the rigs required by his grotesque
characterizations were not particularly comfortable, they were not as
excruciating as some writers made out. Rumors to the contrary,
however, were very prevalent at the time of Lon's death, when it was
commonly believed that his life and career were cut short by his
physically demanding roles. The fact that Lon was a heavy smoker
and actually died of cancer may not have been sensational enough for
a celebrity who seemed so much larger than life.

Before Thalberg departed Universal in February 1923, he decided
The Hunchback of Notre Dame should be sold as a special attraction
instead of a typical Universal programmer. The New York office of
the studio wanted the film right away to fulfill their need for
theatrical releases, but Thalberg took a gamble. He ordered Worsley
to shoot additional crowd scenes which pushed the budget up an

extra $150,000. The higher cost and the additional footage insured the film's release as a special attraction.[97] An exclusive campaign was mounted for the film with an original score compiled by the well-known composer Dr. Hugo Riesenfeld, the leading movie theatre musical director at that time. This score, consisting of classical music and original compositions, could be played by a symphonic orchestra, a small ensemble or a simple keyboard organ.[98]

On August 30, Lon and Hazel left Los Angeles to attend the film's New York benefit premiere for the American Legion at Carnegie Hall. *The Hunchback of Notre Dame* began its Broadway run on September 2 at the newly built Astor Theatre, and played there for 21 weeks before it started its regular ticket price release throughout the country. The film was released with several scenes tinted to intensify the picture's changing moods. The night scenes had a blue tint, candlelight sequences were amber, magenta was used for the flashback scenes about the kidnapping of Crazy Godule's child, and the torture chamber was a garish green.[99] When it started its general run, the film was trimmed down from 12,00 feet to 10,000 feet or about 12 reels to 10 reels.

While reviews of the film were mixed, Chaney's performance was praised by the critics and public alike. *Photoplay* commented,

> In spite of the liberties taken with the Victor Hugo
> novel, this picture is a superb and remarkably
> impressive spectacle . . . the picture is very much
> worthwhile because of the acting of Lon Chaney in
> the title role. His performance transcends anything
> he has ever done, both in his make-up and in his
> spiritual realization of the character.

In its year-end review of top films, the *New York Times* noted,

> *The Hunchback of Notre Dame* with Lon Chaney
> playing the ugly, repugnant, bent-backed bell-ringer
> is a film which people are going to talk about.
> Chaney wanted to make his work count, and he has
> gone to great pains and borne no end of discomfort
> to give a realistic and faithful performance of the
> Hunchback of his conception.

Time magazine felt it was

> A legitimate example of movie elephantiasis . . . All
> this would have been futile, as it so often is with
> spectacle productions, if the story had not furnished
> it with backbone and if Lon Chaney had not
> provided a singularly fine performance in the title
> role."

The industry trade paper *Variety* flatly called the film

> . . . a two-hour nightmare. It's murderous, hideous
> and repulsive. . . . Mr. Chaney's performance as a
> performance entitles him to starring honors — it
> makes him ever more on screen, but his make-up as
> the Hunchback is propaganda for the wets. His
> misshapened figure from the hump on his back to
> the deadeyed eye on his face can not stand off his
> acting nor his acrobatics, nor his general work of
> excellence throughout this film . . . Produced as it is,
> *The Hunchback of Notre Dame* may become a

detriment to the box office it plays for, other than
on main thorough-fares in the larger cities similar to
Broadway in the largest.

Regardless of *Variety*'s assessment, Chaney's Hunchback is generally accepted as one of film's greatest performances. In a particularly poignant scene, Quasimodo has been whipped for trying to abduct Esmeralda. While sitting in the sun on the pillory, Quasimodo cries out for water. Chaney shows the hunchback to be thoroughly drained of any strength; as he slowly sits up, he strains against his shackles and makes an attempt to free himself, much like a chained animal. His visible eye and mouth express his pain and thirst. Esmeralda comes to him with a jug of water and at first glance, Chaney only sees the jug and not who is holding it. When he recognizes the gypsy girl, he recoils from her like an animal afraid of humans. Able to use only his mouth and his one visible eye, Chaney shows his apprehension struggling with his need by looking from Esmeralda to the jug and back again, his tongue constantly licking his quivering, parched lips in an attempt to moisten them. However desperate Quasimodo's thirst may be, he is hesitant to accept it from someone who was so repulsed by his features. Yet when Esmeralda extends the jug closer to him showing she only means to help, Chaney lets Quasimodo give in. He eyes the jug once again and then with a smile, drinks heartily.

After consuming the water, Chaney pulls away from the jug with a huge sigh of relief. Esmeralda gently pulls his torn shirt up over his back. Chaney winces from the pain, then graces her with a slight smile, much like a young school boy holding hands with his first love. When the priest comes to free Quasimodo from his shackles, the gypsy girl leaves. Quasimodo never takes his gaze from her. When his left hand is free, Chaney extends it towards her and then gestures to the priest by pointing to his chest and lips that she gave him water. These gestures are a perfect example of Chaney's mastery of pantomime.

Burt Lancaster once said "Chaney could express with his whole body in a few gestures what pages of dialogue couldn't. When he first looks upon the gypsy girl with fascination and she snubs him because of his looks, Chaney's whole body caves in. What he was able to express with his one eye was amazing."[100]

The film enjoyed a successful run at the box-office, appearing on several Top 10 lists of 1923, and was Universal's biggest hit of that year. Lon Chaney had now become a world-wide household name and, during the run of the film, several theatres held contests for their patrons to see who could best resemble Chaney's Quasimodo.

Forty-nine years after its initial release, Orson Welles, who introduced the film on the PBS series "The Silent Years," said of Chaney's performance:

> In *The Hunchback of Notre Dame*, he was not merely horrific, he was exactly what the hunchback ought to be. Exactly what he was in the Victor Hugo novel, a sort of human gargoyle who looked as though he climbed down the front of the cathedral of Notre Dame. And with all that make-up glued onto him and limping under that hump, there's still a performance. It's simply not somebody running around in a disguise. It's a huge performance, entirely satisfactory in its own terms. And of course totally dims the rest of the picture which is full of second-rate Griffith or Cecil B. DeMille-anry, which dates rather quickly. But not this performance of Chaney's.

Theatre owners used a variety of stunts to promote *The Hunchback of Notre Dame*. Here Billy Bart walks the streets of Salt Lake City with a sign on his back to advertise the film.
(Left) The Rialto Theatre in Omaha, Nebraska.

(Right) Director Wallace Worsley, Patsy Ruth Miller, and Lon looking over the script between set-ups.

Seven Falls – Colo. Springs.

124

Lon playing with his dog Sandy in Garden of the Gods during his 1923
visit. (Courtesy of Loren Harbert)
Lon sits on the running board of a car while visiting Garden of the Gods
in Colorado Springs. (Courtesy of Loren Harbert)

Upon completion of the film, Lon and his family went to Colorado
Springs for a rest in June 1923. Here they visit Seven Falls. Left to right:
Creighton, Mrs. Harry Hughes, Lon, Hazel, Harry Hughes, and his son.
(Courtesy of the Chaney Family Collection)

Leaving for the New York premiere of *The Hunchback of Notre Dame*.
Left to right: actor Walter Long, Creighton, John Chaney (standing next
to Creighton), Lon, and Hazel.
Lon buys tickets from ten-year-old Muriel Lawler for the New York premiere
at the Astor Theatre.
(Below) This greeting card accompanied the gift certificates that Lon handed
out to studio employees at Christmas.

A Star in M-G-M's Heaven (1924-1927)

At Christmas time at the studio, he had a huge box he carried around and in it were gift certificates from a department store in Los Angeles. He'd hand them out to all the office workers and crew members and say, "Here's a Christmas card for you." Everyone on that lot really thought a lot about him.

—*Harry Earles*

Phantom of the Opera (1925)

Before Metro-Goldwyn-Mayer became one the largest and most powerful studios in Hollywood, the lot itself had a long history, beginning with its 1916 construction in Culver City as the site of the Triangle Film Company. At that time, Triangle was a combination of the production companies of Thomas H. Ince, Mack Sennett, and D. W. Griffith. When personal disagreements split up the triumvirate, their twelve-acre studio lot was leased to producer Samuel Goldwyn who eventually bought the property as well as an additional twenty-three acres. It was here that Chaney made *The Penalty*, *Ace of Hearts*, *Voices of the City*, and *A Blind Bargain* for Goldwyn, but the producer's tenure on the property was short-lived due to poor financial management.

In the meantime, the Hollywood-based Metro Studios was becoming too small for the volume of features its president, Marcus Loew, wanted to produce. Loew, also the president of Loew's theatre chain, wanted to supply his theatres with additional feature motion pictures. Therefore, Loew had his attorneys negotiate the purchase of the Goldwyn facility in Culver City while he looked for someone to run and oversee his growing studio. Loew was eventually introduced to independent film producer Louis B. Mayer, and was so impressed with him and his film operation that he agreed to buy Mayer's company, designating Mayer as first vice-president and general manager of his new operation. Irving Thalberg, who had joined Mayer's company in February 1923 after a falling out with Carl

Lon Chaney

Laemmle at Universal, was kept on as the second vice-president and became supervisor of production. Samuel Goldwyn was bought out and, although his name remained part of the new company, he never received any share in the studio's profits or glory.

Metro-Goldwyn-Mayer was officially dedicated on April 26, 1924. That Saturday was a pleasant, balmy day in Southern California and the studio that would become one of the most important in Hollywood had all the stops pulled out. A Navy band played on the studio lawn where Mayer, Thalberg, Harry Rapf and other M-G-M executives sat on a platform festooned with bunting. Next to the platform stood a large key bearing the word "success." Against this backdrop an estimated 600 people, many of them stars in their own right, listened to a program of speeches and telegrams of congratulations. With celebrities like Chaney, John Gilbert, Norma Shearer, Roman Novarro, Mae Murray, Marion Davies, and later Greta Garbo under contract, the studio could rightfully claim it had "More Stars than there are in Heaven."

He Who Gets Slapped was the first feature to be produced and released by the fledgling company. The play on which it was based, by Russian writer Leonid Andreyev, had a successful run on Broadway in the early 1920's. The film version, directed by Victor Seastrom, starred Chaney, John Gilbert, and Thalberg's future wife Norma Shearer, and marked the beginning of Lon's six-year association with M-G-M.

In the film, Chaney played a struggling scientist in Paris who is betrayed by both his wife and his benefactor, Baron Regnard. The Baron not only steals his scientific essay, taking the professional credit, but his wife as well. Disillusioned, the scientist runs away to become a clown in the circus, changing his name to "He Who Gets Slapped," because his role lets his fellow clowns slap him no matter what he does. HE becomes a huge success, and eventually falls in love with a young bareback rider, Consuelo. When HE professes his

130

love to her, she playfully slaps him, thinking he is clowning. Consuelo's father, a down-on-his-luck Count, has arranged for her to marry Baron Regnard, who by this time has left HE's wife. When HE learns of this, the clown plots his revenge against the Baron and Consuelo's father with the aid of a lion. During the conflict, however, HE is stabbed by Consuelo's father. HE dies dramatically in the circus ring before his audience, who believe it to be a new act, until he finally collapses in Consuelo's arms.

George Davis, a famous European clown, coached Chaney for his role as HE, for which Lon used a traditional whiteface clown make-up. In contrast, for his part as the struggling scientist, Lon wore a goatee to give himself an aristocratic look.

Mike Ragan, a well-known character actor in films in the 1950's, recalled his experiences working as a child extra on this picture:

> The set was this one-ring circus with bleachers surrounding it. I was sitting in the upper part of the bleachers next to where the circus performers made their entrances and exits. I was looking over the rail when I first saw Lon, standing in his clown make-up and costume. Two men stood in front of him holding stilts. He climbed onto them with such ease, just like he'd been doing it forever. I was in awe of him. When he got his balance on the stilts he told someone he was ready and he looked over at me. Because he was on the stilts we were then at the same level and made eye contact. Lon was no doubt aware of my staring at him, he smiled at me in his make-up and said "Hello, son." All I could do was nod at him, totally speechless with my mouth open! Here was one of my favorite actors who talked to me and all I could do was nod at him![101]

Shot in 37 days, *He Who Gets Slapped* was released in November of 1924. It was an instant critical and box-office success. *Photoplay* said, "Lon Chaney does the best work of his career. Here his performance has breadth, force and imagination." The *New York Times* claimed,

> Never in his efforts before the camera has Mr.
> Chaney delivered such a marvelous performance as
> he does as this character. He is restrained in his
> acting, never overdoing the sentimental situations,
> and is guarded in his make-up.

Variety felt that

> Lon Chaney as 'HE' stands out as possibly the
> greatest character actor of the screen. In this role,
> he displays an understanding of character beyond
> anything that he has done heretofore. Those who
> have seen him in *The Hunchback* will want to see
> him in this, and they are going to be agreeably
> surprised at his work.

Before the release of *He Who Gets Slapped*, Chaney appeared in a forgettable melodrama for Paramount entitled *The Next Corner* in which, *Variety* noted, "Lon Chaney has a weak part and gets into the fore only now and then in subordinate situations where he has little to build on." Obviously Lon was waiting for another challenge — and when opportunity knocked, he answered. On October 29, 1924, Chaney returned to Universal for the last time to begin filming his most famous and memorable role, *Phantom of the Opera*.

From the beginning of the project, Lon strove to come as close to the novel's description of the Phantom as possible. In the Gaston Leroux novel, the Phantom is described as looking "extraordinarily thin and his dress coat hangs on a skeleton frame. His eyes are so deep that you can hardly see the fixed pupils. You just see two big black holes, as in a dead man's skull. His skin, which is stretched across his bones like a drum head, is not white but a nasty yellow. His nose is so little worth talking about that you can't see it side-face; the absence of that nose is a horrible thing to look at."

Over the years, many writers have propagated myths about how Lon's Phantom make-up was actually accomplished. Stories range from Lon placing celluloid discs in his cheekbones (which is, of course, physically impossible), to placing wire pins in his nose to distend his nostrils. To achieve the Phantom's skull-like appearance, Lon employed the same cotton and collodion technique he used in *The Hunchback of Notre Dame* for the raised and extended cheekbones. The up-tilting of the nose was done by gluing a strip of fishskin onto the top of the nose with spirit gum, pulling it up until the desired look was achieved, and then gluing the rest of the strip of fishskin to the bridge of the nose and lower part of the forehead. Shading around the eyes with a dark liner gave the hollow-eyed look which was further emphasized with a thin line of highlight color under the lower eyelashes. The jagged teeth were made of guttapercha, accentuated by using a dark lining color on the lower lip. Lon used a skull cap with a wig sewn onto it and a fine piece of muslin on the edge of the cap. Gluing the muslin edge allowed it to blend easily into the forehead. His ears were glued back with spirit gum, completing the hideous look.

While the make-up for the Phantom is very effective, Chaney knew from his days on the stage how lighting could enhance or ruin a good make-up creation. Lon said in an interview that a lot of the success of the make-up was due to the placement of the right shades of greasepaint in the right places, some not on the most obvious areas of the face.

He was very exacting when it came to doing make-up tests, something that he learned back in his early days at Universal. He got a cameraman on the lot, Virgil Miller, to shoot a series of short make-up tests to see how various kinds of make-ups would come across on film.[102] A brief piece of a make-up test from *Road To Mandalay* still exists and gives an idea of what Chaney looked for in these tests. Lon is seen in extreme close-up looking into the camera; he turns right, left, moves away from the camera, and then finally swings back into the lens. During this procedure, his face is constantly changing expression to help him in determine how his make-up would register on the screen in a variety of situations.

To keep the public in suspense about the Phantom's appearance, Universal had Chaney's make-up "blanked out" in all the promotional photos, lobby cards and programs. This also helped to heighten the audiences' reaction when they finally did see his face. Despite the numerous remakes and Andrew Lloyd Weber's Broadway hit musical, Chaney's make-up has endured and is still considered by motion picture make-up artists as one of the truly classic make-up creations in film history.

As in the case of *The Hunchback of Notre Dame*, Universal spared no expense for the production of *Phantom of the Opera*. Over 250 dancers from the Chicago, Metropolitan, and other opera companies were brought to the studio for the dance numbers that were supervised by noted dance producer Ernest Belcher. The Masked Ball sequence and several ballet scenes were shot in the early two-color Technicolor process — a technique that was far from routine at that time.

The first steel and concrete stage ever built in Hollywood was also erected for this film. It housed the entire interior set of the Opera House as well as the backstage area and the grand staircase. The stage, which still stands today on the Universal Studios lot, is now known as Stage 28. It is the only remaining set in Hollywood from any Lon Chaney film, and, sadly, only the opera box seats stand untouched. Several other films over the years have been shot using this set including *One Hundred Men and a Girl*, the 1943 re-make of *Phantom of the Opera*, *Torn Curtain*, *The Sting* and even Chaney's film biography, *Man of a Thousand Faces*.

The cellars and subterranean lake, as well as some exterior streets of Paris, were built on other stages on the Universal lot.

A studio reader's memo dated May 8, 1924, offers an opinion on the potential for the film version of *Phantom of the Opera*:

> Properly developed, cast and directed, this story would make a magnificent and intensely interesting picture, in my opinion. It would have all the effectiveness of splendid sets, absorbing characters, and spectacular action. And at the same time, it would be an understandable, straight-away story with a strongly romantic and melodramatic flavor. Although it would be an expensive picture, it need not cost a fortune. Artistry in the sets and direction is more needed than money.
>
> It has three splendid characters—a perfect role for Lon Chaney, a part for some stunning young woman, and a role for a likeable, almost boyish young man, who will be an effective contrast with Chaney. If we do it, for God's sake let's not botch it.[103]

Unfortunately, the film was plagued with problems from the very start when it went into production on October 29, 1924. Rupert Julian was signed to direct, and early in the production, he and Chaney clashed over the portrayal of the Phantom. Julian wanted a much broader performance than what Chaney had envisioned, and relations between the two men were so strained that they rarely spoke to one another. Cameraman Charles Van Enger, who acted as the go-between, later said:

Julian would explain to me what he wanted Lon to do, and then I'd go over to Lon and tell him what Julian had said. Then Lon would say to tell him to "go to hell." You have to remember, Julian was a bigger star than Lon was when they worked at Universal in the teens, and after he replaced [Eric] von Stroheim on *Merry-Go-Round*, he thought he was as good, if not better, a director than von Stroheim. A lot of the friction was brought about by Julian himself, who could be a prima-donna. When we filmed the scene of the chandelier crashing, he wanted it to be filmed with almost no light, bordering on total darkness. I explained that it was not going to show up on the film if we did it that way, but he was insistent. So I went ahead and lit the set the way I felt it would show up best, and then, to pacify Julian, I inserted the darkest filter I had into my eyeglass [which was used by cameramen to view how the lighting would show up on film with the appropriate filter on the camera lens] and he thought it was great. Of course, if we had shot it Julian's way, the footage would have had to have been scrapped.[104]

After filming was completed, a work print was assembled and previewed in Los Angeles in January, 1925. Carl Laemmle was unhappy with the film's reception at the preview, and ordered additional shooting and re-editing. A major concern was the original ending of the film, which had the Phantom found by the mob, lying dead at the keyboard of his organ.

A studio report of the original ending dated March 9, 1925, discussed problems with that sequence:

The ending is not logical or convincing. A monster, such as the Phantom, the official torturer, etc. and

who delighted in crime could not have been
redeemed through a woman's kiss, nor could a girl
who had witnessed his diabolical acts, have been
moved to kiss him merely because he dropped his
head sadly. His death rang false moreover, better to
have kept him a devil to the end.[105]

Edward Sedgwick, known as a comedy director, was hired to direct a new climax in which the Phantom escapes the mob by stealing a carriage and, in a frenzied chase through the streets of Paris, careens past the Notre Dame cathedral (from Chaney's other Universal hit, *The Hunchback of Notre Dame*) to the banks of the Seine river, where the mob corners and kills him.

In April, 1925, the film, in its new form, was previewed at the Curran Theatre in San Francisco. However, all the recently added footage, except the chase scene, was deleted from the picture before this preview. After the disappointing San Francisco showing, new scenes with comedian Chester Conklin were added, as well as new title cards. After viewing this "final" version, Laemmle ordered the comedy scenes junked and still new title cards written to account for the many changes. Unfortunately, lost in all these many changes were some ballet scenes photographed in the two-color Technicolor process. The film finally premiered on September 6, 1925, at the Astor Theatre in New York, where it ran for 9 successful weeks, despite mixed reviews.

"Obviously the title role was one for Lon Chaney, and he gives a superb performance. Here was another chance to distinguish himself as an unrivaled artist in character make-up, and he has done just that," commented *Motion Picture World*. *Photoplay* said, "In spite of the horror of his role, Lon Chaney wins, at times, sympathy." The *New York Times* observed, "Lon Chaney impersonates the Phantom. It is a role suited to his liking, and one which he handles with a certain skill, a little exaggerated at times, but none the less compelling."

Variety, on the other hand, said

> Universal has turned out another horror. This newest of U specials is probably the greatest inducement to nightmare that has yet been screened. . . . Lon Chaney is again the 'goat' in the matter, no matter if it is another tribute to his character acting. . . . Following the 'Hunchback' thing, it becomes a moot question whether or not Chaney's name in connection with a picture is going to keep children away from a theatre . . . However, the kick of the picture is the unmasking of the Phantom by the girl. . . . The resultant 'shot' is from the front. Between Chaney's horrible facial make-up and the expression thereon, it's a wallop that can't miss its objective. . . . It's impossible to believe there are a majority of picture goers who prefer this revolting sort of tale on the screen.

Chaney's Phantom was a combination of terror, anger and pathos, instilling fear and horror in those around him throughout most of the film. Yet when he first comes in physical contact with the girl he worships, he is shy and hesitant in approaching her. Chaney conveys this by a simple gesture; he approaches Christine from the back, and as he is about to touch her shoulder with his hand, he hesitates, as if dreading her reaction to his masked face. When he does touch her it is done with extreme gentleness.

In contrast, there is nothing gentle about Chaney's famous un-masking scene. Christine, under the spell of his melodious music, is intrigued by her masked admirer. Chaney has worn the mask throughout the early part of the film and at one point he warns

Christine not to touch it. However, the prohibition only tantalizes Christine (to say nothing of the audience) and fuels her desire to see what he looks like underneath.

While wearing his mask, Chaney's Phantom is confident of himself and afraid of no one. When Christine rips off his mask, however, his confidence turns into rage as his hideous face is exposed by the one he loves. While Christine cowers on the floor at his feet, the Phantom looms over her jabbing an accusing finger into her face. Chaney then raises his hands above him, looking up to the heavens as if to call damnation upon the girl. His uplifted hands start to shake with fury and he bends down to Christine, grabbing her head and forcing her to look at his features. "Feast your eyes — glut your soul, on my accursed ugliness!" he cries, laughing maniacally. Then just as suddenly he stops. Pushing himself away from her, he realizes she has seen his dark side and his hopes of winning her love are destroyed. Chaney covers his face in his hands, his body slumping, the face that sparked fear now drawn into a the mask of tragedy. As Christine pleads for her freedom, the Phantom clasps a hand over his heart and slowly leans against a pillar, his head resting against his right arm, his hand curling into a fist. Here in this famous scene Chaney at first scares the hell out of the audience and then just as quickly is able to win their sympathy for his character.

There were many reports that people actually screamed or fainted when actress Mary Philbin unmasked the Phantom. While many reports may have been the result of Universal's publicity machine, the late well-known character actor, Eddie Quillan, verifies at least one of them. At this time, Eddie and his vaudevillian family were playing at a theatre in San Francisco. During a break between shows, Eddie and his family took a walk and noticed an ambulance in front of a movie theatre where *Phantom of the Opera* was playing. Eddie went over to find out what happened and was told a lady had fainted during the unmasking scene.[106] Lamar D. Tabb, a long-time fan of Lon Chaney, saw the film when he was 14 years old in his hometown of Dayton, Ohio. He recalled that when Chaney was unmasked, the entire audience uttered a synchronized and very audible gasp.[107] Author Robert Bloch (*Psycho*) said when he first saw Chaney un-masked for the first time, he "gazed upon the face of naked fear."[108]

Many writers have reported the story of how Thalberg loaned Lon to Universal to make *Phantom of the Opera* because he knew that such a prestigious picture would enhance the reputation of their new star, now under contract with M-G-M. In truth, the evidence available shows that Universal had Chaney in mind for the role by May 1924. When Lon started work on *He Who Gets Slapped* on June 17, 1924, he signed a contract for just the run of this picture and was paid $12,500 for the engagement (breaking down to $2,500 a week). On January 6, 1925, while still in production on *The Unholy Three*, Lon signed a one-year contract with M-G-M, at a weekly salary of $2,500 beginning on February 15, 1925. He also had two additional one-year options on his contract, with salary increases at $2,750 and $3,000 a week, respectively.[109] There was no mention in this contract that there had ever been a previous one, thus supporting the belief he was never loaned out to Universal, but was freelancing at the time he began work on *Phantom of the Opera*. Another item which supports this theory appeared in the *New York Morning Telegraph* on October 14, 1923. In the article, it says that Lon was considering two contracts, one from Universal and another to make pictures with the Anderson Company. This company, headed by Carl Anderson, was formed under the auspices of the Motion Picture Theatre Owners of America to produce pictures. At any rate, by the beginning of 1925, Lon was back at M-G-M.

Chaney's first release of 1925 was *The Monster*, with Lon playing the role of Dr. Ziska who, along with other patients, take over the asylum in which they are confined. The film, based on the play by Crane Wilbur, was a tongue-in-cheek melodrama with Lon playing the role more for laughs than chills. Despite the moody atmosphere created by director Roland West, the film received generally weak reviews. *Variety* felt "Lon Chaney does not make the crazed surgeon as terrifying a picture as he might have and, in that, the film lets down to a certain extent." The *New York Times* commented

> The ludicrous situations and comical antics of the players are all the more surprising, as one does not expect much fun in a film featuring Lon Chaney . . . Mr. Chaney does not have very much to do, but his various appearances are effective . . . Mr. Chaney looks as if he could have enjoyed a more serious portrayal of the theme.

The Monster was not produced by the studio, but by Roland West Productions and Tec-Art. In the February 14th, 1925, issue of *Moving Picture World*, M-G-M announced that it would distribute the film, and bought all the rights to the picture from Roland West in 1927.[110]

Chaney and Tod Browning then teamed up for what would become one of their most successful efforts. Browning had recently overcome a heavy drinking problem which had idled his career for two years, and had what he thought was a sure-fire project for his comeback. The film was *The Unholy Three*, and became one of the major hits of 1925.

It was based on a 1917 thriller novel by Clarence Aaron ("Tod") Robbins about a trio of sideshow performers — a ventriloquist, a midget and a strongman — who, when their sideshow is shut down, form an alliance to commit robberies. Using a bird store as their front, the ventriloquist masquerades as an old woman, Mrs. O'Grady, selling parrots to rich customers who later find themselves the trio's victims. They are successful in their crimes until the midget and strongman commit a murder during a heist. They plant the stolen jewels on their unsuspecting employee Hector, who is in love with Rosie, the ventriloquist's girlfriend. He is framed for the murder and faces conviction when Echo intervenes.

Browning had peddled the idea to every studio in town and was flatly turned down by everyone except Irving Thalberg. Industry consensus was that Thalberg had bought the rights to a gruesome thriller that was destined to be a flop. *The Unholy Three* was a major box-office success for the studio, appearing on a total of 60 Top Ten Film Lists for 1925.

The film was a perfect vehicle for Lon and its success was the foundation of a long collaboration for the actor and director. In the novel, it is the midget who is actually the brains of the group; Echo the ventriloquist (Chaney's role) is not really a hardened criminal, but a schizophrenic who talks only through his ventriloquist dummy. As Chaney plays him, however, Echo is assured of himself as a thief; yet when the murder is committed, he is the only one of the three conspirators who is fearful of the complications. His relationship with Rosie is a mitigating factor; he truly loves the girl, but his jealousy gets the better of him when she shows signs of affection to Hector, the innocent bird store employee.

Hector is arrested for the murder, and at Rosie's urging, Echo goes to the trial to see if he can save the young man. In this sequence, Chaney's performance is restrained, yet he is able to show Echo's anxiety and guilty conscience with only the most subtle of body gestures. While he watches Hector handle a letter he has written as Mrs. O'Grady and planted on the defense table, Chaney sits on the edge of his seat (along with the audience) urging him to read it. The note tells Hector to take the witness stand again and silently mouth the Lord's Prayer.

When Hector takes the stand, Chaney beams with confidence, sure that his plan will work. As the young man starts to mouth the prayer, Echo throws his voice, telling the story of the Unholy Three. In Chaney's close-ups we see his lips and throat muscles move, giving the impression of throwing his voice. The prosecuting attorney terminates Hector's testimony and Chaney's expression flashes through anger to despair; he slumps in his chair, his confidence shattered at the failure of his plan. While Chaney looks on helplessly, the judge begins to give instructions to the jury. He fights to maintain control as he asks the man sitting next to him if he thinks Hector is guilty. When the man responds affirmatively, Chaney's expression shows disbelief and he seems on the verge of tears. Just as the jury is about to head to the deliberating room, Echo recalls Rosie's promise to forget Hector if only Echo will save the young man. Chaney jumps to his feet, his arm outstretched, yelling for the jury to stop. Realizing that he cannot turn back, he seems dazed until he glances over at Hector. It is then that the ventriloquist knows why he is doing this and his confidence returns, allowing him to make a full confession.

Lon received praise from the critics for his performance, with the industry paper *Variety* summing it up best:

> And then there's another thing about this picture,
> and that is that Lon Chaney stands out like a million
> dollars. He's done that before, but always with a
> more or less grotesque make-up. No make-up this
> time. He isn't all hunched up, he isn't legless, he
> isn't this, that, or the other things in deformities.
> He's just Lon Chaney, and he's great. He must have
> had a hard time convincing 'em that as just plain Lon
> Chaney he could be as great as though he was this,
> that, or the other form of a cripple, but from now
> on it's going to be another story.

Lon Chaney

The *New York Times* wrote, "Not often does one see so powerful a photodrama as *The Unholy Three* . . . Mr. Chaney gives a brilliant, restrained and earnest performance."

Mae Busch was the girl pursued by both Chaney and Matt Moore, who played the unsuspecting bird store employee, Hector; Victor McLaglen and Harry Earles completed the trio of sideshow performers turned crooks. Earles, born in Germany, came to America with his sister Daisy in an act they had called "The Dancing Dolls." Five years later he revived his role as Tweedledee the midget in the talking version of the film. In 1932, along with his sister Daisy, he starred in Tod Browning's *Freaks,* and then left the picture business to tour with Ringling Bros.-Barnum & Baily Circus. In 1939, he and his three sisters appeared as Munchkins in *The Wizard of Oz,* with Harry playing one of the "Lollipop Boys." After 25 years with the circus, he retired to Sarasota, Florida, where he died in 1985. Shortly before his death, he talked about Lon:

> He was a very kind and considerate man. Being new to the picture business, he helped me a great deal in my acting and I learned a great deal from him. But he was that way to a lot of people. There was a former soldier [retired Marine Sgt. Frank McCloskey] whom Lon had been friends with. He ran a newsstand in Los Angeles and he needed to have some surgery performed but couldn't afford it. Somehow Lon heard about it and hired someone to run his newsstand while Lon personally drove him to the hospital and helped to pay for his surgery.

> Once I went into this novelty shop on Hollywood Blvd. and while I was looking around, I heard a voice that was very familiar, but the man's face was completely unknown to me at first. Then I suddenly

realized that it was Lon behind the glasses and the beard! No one else had any idea who he was, and I went up to him and pulled on his pants leg and asked him what was he doing there. He made a quick gesture to be quiet and asked me not to let on who he was.

At Christmas time at the studio, he had a huge box he carried around and in it were gift certificates from a department store in Los Angeles. He'd hand them out to all the office workers and the crew members and say, 'Here's a Christmas card for you.' Everyone on that lot really thought a lot about him. He was very well liked.[111]

The Unholy Three, as originally shot, contained one sequence that does not appear in any existing print. In this scene, Hercules and Tweedledee pull off a robbery on their own because they were impatient with Echo who wanted to stay behind to keep an eye on Rosie and Hector. During the burglary, which takes place on Christmas Eve, they awaken the little girl of the house. When she sees Hercules, she exclaims "Santa Claus!" much to the giant's surprise. She thinks Tweedledee is a gift for her in the guise of a little brother and she tries to hug him. The midget responds by choking the girl. She screams, awakening her father, who is shot to death by Hercules. This scene was cut from the final version of the film because it was considered too intense for audiences of 1925.

Tower of Lies, directed by Victor Seastrom, was Lon's next picture for M-G-M. Here Lon played the part of Jan, a simple, hardworking Scandinavian farmer. When his daughter Goldie is born, the drudgery in his life turns to happiness. He and his daughter play a favorite game in which he is the emperor of a fictional kingdom. Years later, Jan's landlord dies, and the landlord's son demands payment on all notes from farmers, including Jan. To prevent her parents' eviction, Goldie goes to the city, promising her father she will return in a few months. When she buys the farm for her parents but does not return as promised, Jan loses his sanity and reverts to dressing up as the fictional emperor, playing with the neighborhood children. Time passes and Goldie finally returns, dressed in fancy clothes, which leads the neighbors to suspect she has turned to prostitution. The rumors are too much for her to bear, and she returns to the city, unaware that her father is following her. At the boat dock, Jan stumbles and is drowned.

Variety commented:

> Notwithstanding that *Tower of Lies* is a sincerely made picture and excellent from artistic and literary viewpoints, it is too heavy for the picture audience . . . The thread of fantasy in the theme is well planted by the director, and the acting of Chaney goes a long way toward making it bearable, but the theme itself is ponderous and, in its scenario form, advanced largely by means of subtitles.

The *New York Times* concurred, saying,

> The necessity for strong dramatic action in the course of telling a grim story has been overlooked in translating to the screen... it seems to the viewer as if Mr. Chaney had had too much to say about his own performance, for he overacts and his make-up, consisting largely of a rich crop of iron gray hair and whiskers and beard, seem to fit well without looking as if they belonged to him. Mr. Chaney's exaggerated actions and expressions appear to have been contagious, for Mr. Seastrom himself betrays a weakness for overemphasizing a number of points.

The character of Jan required Lon to age from his late 30's in the beginning of the film to his 60's at the end. This transformation was done by the simple use of highlights and shadows as well as the emphasis of wrinkles, grey hair, beard and a wig with a receding hair line. *Tower of Lies* is one of the four M-G-M pictures which Chaney made that does not survive today.

In the wake of *Hunchback*, *Phantom*, and *The Unholy Three*, the number of projects with which Lon's name became associated attests to his box-office stature. A 1925 studio theatre exhibitors' herald mentioned that Lon was scheduled to appear in a film version of Sutton Vane's stage play *The Span of Life*, co-starring Pauline Starke and William Haines. Later, in 1927, *Hate*, *Ordeal*, *The Wandering Jew* and *Seven Seas* were all announced as upcoming Chaney vehicles, but for one reason or another, none of those projects ever materialized for Lon. *Hate* was to be an adaptation of Frank Packard's novel *The Four Stragglers* in which Lon would play the feared and brutal leader of a band of Apaches that dominate the underworld of Paris. *Ordeal* was a sea novel by Dale Collins, scheduled to start production right after *London After Midnight*. *The Wandering Jew*, an adaptation of a popular novel by Eugene Sue, was a project that M-G-M had in the planning stages for some time. *Seven Seas* was based on the character of Cheri-Bibi created by Gaston Leroux, author of *Phantom of the Opera*; a version of this novel, entitled *Cheri-Bibi*, was scheduled to be Lon's next picture at the time of his death. It was eventually brought to the screen under the title of *The Phantom of Paris*, starring John Gilbert in the title role.

In late August of 1925, Lon and Hazel drove up to Seattle, Washington, to visit with his cousin Hugh Harbert. According to Hugh's grandson, Loren Harbert, the visit by Chaney was big news in his neighborhood:

> My dad said that the neighbors were curious by the
> fairly new and fancy car that my grandfather's guests
> drove. And then when Lon filmed the family out on
> the front lawn with his new 16mm camera, that's
> when everyone got interested in who this person
> was. Nobody had anything like that and was quite a
> thing to see in those days, and to top it off, Lon
> Chaney was staying right in their neighborhood![112]

While driving through Northern California on their trip, the Chaneys spotted the names of Lyle and Emerson on a vaudeville bill at a theatre. Clinton Lyle was an old friend of Lon's from his musical comedy days and after their reunion Lon persuaded Clinton and his wife Florence Emerson to come to Hollywood and get into pictures.[113] He became one of Lon's closest friends, appearing with Lon in *The Big City* and *While The City Sleeps*.

M-G-M picked up the first option on Lon's contract in January of 1926 and then, in April of that year, Lon signed a new one-year contract for $3,000 a week. The contract had four renewable options for one year each, at weekly salaries of $3,250 for 1927, $3,500 for 1928, $3,750 for 1929, and $4,000 for 1930, with the same stipulation as his previous contract — that he not make more than four feature films during each contract year. Louis B. Mayer approved the new contract as well as picking up the first option (for 1927), and Lon was given a cash bonus of $2,125 for appreciation of the services rendered during his 1925 contract.[114] With wealth, however, came tax problems; the April 17, 1926, edition of the *New York Times* carried a story that the United States Revenue Department made Lon Chaney a defendant in a tax lien action alleging taxes in the amount of $1,600 were sought for his 1920 income. There is no record of any further court action, and it was probably settled out of court.

Lon was one of the few stars who invested his money heavily in Southern California real estate, mainly in the Hollywood area. By 1926 he owned four homes, all of moderate proportion compared to his peers in the film industry. He and Hazel lived in a modest two-bedroom Tudor-style house with a three-car garage located at 604 Linden Drive in Beverly Hills. Lon purchased this house in 1926 and sold it for a small profit in 1929. In contrast, the house was last sold in 1986 for the outlandish sum of $800,000. Unfortunately, the house was demolished to make way for a larger home and can no longer be viewed.

The other homes the Chaneys owned in the Hollywood area housed either Lon's relatives or his in-laws. His son Creighton lived in the home at 735 N. Laurel Avenue from 1926 to 1936. Lon's father and step-mother lived at 7764 Warring Avenue until 1934. 1151-53 N. Vista Street, which Lon and Hazel bought in 1924, is where Hazel's family lived. Later, after Hazel's death, they bought the building and lived there until 1938. Additionally, in 1925, the Chaneys acquired five lots in the Tahoe Cedars Additions in Placerville, California.[115]

At this time, Creighton Chaney was working as a salesman for General Water Heater Corporation, and on April 25, 1926, he married the boss's daughter, Dorothy Hinckley. Within two years, Creighton was promoted to secretary of his father-in-law's company, and Lon was pleased that his son had chosen "a sensible profession." Lon Ralph Chaney's birth in July of 1928 made Lon a proud grandfather. Lon delightfully spoiled the boy, as well as his second grandson Ronald Creighton, who was born in March of 1930.

After *The Unholy Three*, Lon teamed up with Tod Browning again to make *The Blackbird*. In this 1926 feature made under the title *The Mockingbird*, Chaney plays a Limehouse crook called the Blackbird. The Blackbird's ability to masquerade as his supposed twin brother the Bishop, a kindly cripple who runs a rescue mission, provides him with an alibi from the police. Both the Blackbird and another thief, West End Bertie, are in love with Fifi, a local music hall favorite. In order to win Fifi's affection, the Blackbird frames his rival for the murder of a Scotland Yard man. Fifi runs to the Bishop for advice and he uses the situation to undermine West End Bertie. He then changes out of his Bishop disguise in order to confront Fifi and plead his love. However, the Blackbird's ex-wife shows up one step ahead of the law and tells Fifi who really committed the murder. When the police arrive, the Blackbird slips into another room to switch back into his disguise as the Bishop. As he finishes his transformation, the police break down the door, knocking the Blackbird down and breaking his back. Dressed as the kindly Bishop, he dies without ever revealing his true identity to the police. This persona — a grotesque character who is eventually destroyed by love — was a typical theme in many of the films Browning made with Chaney.

The *New York Times* said,

> This stirring piece of work is heralded as *The Blackbird*, and in it the unfailing Lon Chaney is featured in a sort of dual role in which he has the opportunity of satisfying his penchant for portraying a twisted and crippled character. . . . Mr. Chaney's depiction of the two types of the crook is one of the finest exemplifications of screen artistry one would hope to behold.

Photoplay magazine selected the film as one of the month's best picks, and observed,

> Lon Chaney has placed himself in the foreground as one who can accurately analyze any human soul and any human emotion. This is one of the finest

characterizations to Chaney's credit. He doesn't
resort to heavy make-up to put over his character.
Even when he appears as the cripple, he shows how
he merely throws his shoulders and hips out of joint
and hobbles on crutches . . . Don't pass it up.

In playing the two characters, Lon employed stark differences in personality as well as in physical appearance and gestures. The Blackbird is harsh and gruff, with slicked-down hair and pinned-back ears. In contrast, the Bishop, who is paralyzed on one side and walks on crutches, is the perfect example of a gentle and caring man. Lon had to maintain the crippled posture of the Bishop throughout the film. The effect was aided by his costume, which had the paralyzed side tailored a bit longer. In one scene, Lon had to make a quick change in front of the camera from the Blackbird to the Bishop and appears to throw his shoulder and hip out of place to assume the posture. In reality, Lon never did throw his joints out of place and merely acted as if he was really contorting his limbs.

The Road To Mandalay was his next 1926 release under Tod Browning's direction. Lon played Singapore Joe, the one-eyed ruler of a Singapore dive, who makes frequent trips to Mandalay to do his shady business and visit his daughter. Raised by Joe's brother Father James since her mother's death at childbirth, she confides to her surrogate father that the one-eyed man gives her the chills, unaware that Joe is her real father. When she falls in love with one of Joe's partners, the Admiral, Joe shanghais her lover and heads back to his dive in Singapore. Joe's daughter follows them and is about to fall prey to English Charlie Wing, one of Joe's other cohorts, when her father intervenes. In an ensuing fight with the Admiral, Joe is stabbed by his daughter. With all the strength he can summon, Joe tells the Admiral to take his ship and save the girl while he holds off English Charlie Wing. Joe collapses when they have made good their escape, and his daughter finds happiness with the Admiral, never knowing about her father or his ultimate sacrifice.

In a 1953 article for *Films in Review*, writer George Mitchell claimed that Lon put collodion in his left eye to give the effect of a blind eye and, since then, the statement has been published repeatedly. This practice would be extremely dangerous as collodion contains a solvent that could permanently damage the eye, and it is definitely not the technique Chaney used. In reality, Lon had one of the leading opticians in Los Angeles, Dr. Hugo Keifer, make a white glass shield, similar to present-day contact lenses, to cover the eye and create the illusion of blindness. Chaney trimmed the hair of his left eyebrow and ran a collodion scar on his forehead down into the eyebrow and below the eye to further accentuate the dead eye. The close-cropped haircut, as well as finely-painted lines on his face (which was something he did in many of his make-ups) gave his face a textured look, helping to intensify the progress of his character's age. In scenes cut from the final release print of the film, he appears as a younger man with a full head of wavy hair, and minus the scar and dead eye. This transformation was accomplished with the use of a wig and "straight" make-up, consisting of applying base make-up, shading the upper eyelids, and penciling in the eyebrows which gave the face its softer look. The lenses on motion picture cameras in Chaney's time, as well as the film stock, were not as penetrating and sharp as they are today, and thus his make-ups do not show the detail that one can see in an original still photograph. Despite the deficiency of the camera lens, Chaney never appeared to take a short-cut in his application of make-up, although he undoubtedly knew what he could and could not get away with in front of the camera.

The Road To Mandalay must have set something of a record in its day as it went into production March 19, 1926. Filming was completed on April 19 (for the most part, Browning's films took an average of five weeks to make), and the film was playing at the Capitol Theatre in New York on June 27, 1926.

Variety said three days later:

> Chaney has another of these characteristic roles.
> This time his deformity is a sightless, white eye. It is
> remarkable how this particular detail contributes a
> sort of mood and tempo to the whole production.
> . . . The picture is Chaney, who unquestionably has
> a big following. At the Capitol Monday they had a
> good attendance at 2 o'clock and for the 4 o'clock
> show it was capacity downstairs. This, on a perfect
> June day, must have had some bearing on Chaney's
> draw.

Photoplay magazine quipped, "It's not the story but Lon Chaney's fine performance that puts the ginger in this cookie." *Variety*'s review points out that Chaney's popularity with the audience was the main drawing card of the film, as *The Road To Mandalay* was not as strong a picture as Browning's *The Unholy Three* or *The Blackbird*.

While Chaney was alive, he was often referred to as the greatest character actor on the screen. Since his death, he has been unfairly labeled as a "horror actor." This misconception is due partly to the easy television and video accessibility of Lon's more gruesome film roles in *The Hunchback of Notre Dame* and *Phantom of the Opera*. Film historians and writers tend to look only at these two films, which admittedly were important ones, ignoring his other films in which he played an equally demanding, though less grotesque, variety of characters. To say Lon Chaney was merely a horror actor is akin to saying Laurence Olivier was only a Shakespearean actor or Gary Cooper only played cowboys. Unfortunately a film star is sometimes remembered and judged by only a few outstanding pictures, and not by his overall film career.

The film that best illustrates Lon's ability to do "straight" work is *Tell It To The Marines,* which was Chaney's next picture for M-G-M.

Lon Chaney

The film remains one of his finest performances and demonstrates that he could be a serious actor without any make-up. Chaney was cast as Sgt. O'Hara, "a hard-boiled egg," who whips new recruits into shape. Claire Windsor and Charles Ray were originally announced to co-star in the film, but were replaced with Eleanor Boardman as the nurse and William Haines as the smart-mouthed recruit who eventually becomes a Marine under Chaney's guidance. Lon's long-time friend, Eddie Gribbon, played Cpl. Madden, and Warner Oland, who later gained fame for his portrayal of Charlie Chan, was the Chinese bandit leader who clashes with the Marines in the exciting climax of the picture. This film's scenario became the model for military-theme films from that point on, including such pictures as *To The Shores of Tripoli*, *Sands of Iwo Jima*, and *The D. I.*

"Skeet" Burns is a wise-cracking youth who enlists in the Marine Corps only to get to San Diego so he can go to Tiajuana and bet on the horses. He relates this plan to another train passenger who happens to be a Marine general traveling in civilian clothes. Upon arrival in San Diego, the general spots Sgt. O'Hara who is sending off a group of Marines on another train. The general tells the sergeant of the young man's plan and O'Hara goes after him. Skeet manages to give the sergeant the slip in city traffic and is off to the races. O'Hara smiles, knowing the young man will be back. Several days later Skeet shows up at the Marine base without a dime. After being sworn in, he soon learns that becoming a Marine is not as easy as he thinks. Training at the base does have one appealing aspect for the young man in the form of Navy nurse Norma Dale, also the object of Sgt. O'Hara's affection. After a rocky start to their romance, Skeet leaves on a tour of duty, promising to come back to Norma.

On Tondo Island, a native girl attempts to seduce Skeet, but when he refuses her advances, a fight ensues between Skeet and the natives, with O'Hara coming to the young man's rescue. When Skeet meets up with Norma in Shanghai, she tells him she wants nothing to do with him because of his conduct on the island. While discussing the situation with Sgt. O'Hara, Norma receives orders to go to Hangchow to help with an epidemic in an area overrun by Chinese bandits. Shortly after she arrives, the bandits capture the Americans and hold them hostage. The Marines, including O'Hara's squad, are sent to Hangchow to rescue them. When the Marines arrive, Skeet and Norma are briefly reunited before O'Hara's group is detailed to hold the bandits at the bridge at all costs while the Americans escape. It is here that Skeet proves himself worthy of being a Marine, even when the squad is overwhelmed by the bandits. After his enlistment is up, Skeet and Norma marry. He goes back to see O'Hara at the Marine base, where he offers the sergeant a partnership in a ranch he has bought. O'Hara declines, stating "I snort and beef a lot, but I think the world of each lousy rookie!" With that, O'Hara goes back to work making Marines out of young men.

With the help of General Smedly D. Butler, who in February, 1926 assumed command of the Marine base in San Diego, M-G-M was not only given technical assistance but the use of the Marine base itself. In return for their cooperation, the studio lent a steam shovel to the San Diego base to help landscape the complex. *Tell It To The Marines* was the first motion picture made with the full cooperation of the U.S. Marine Corps. The eight-and-a-half week shooting schedule, under George Hill's direction, was kicked off with one of the most impressive ceremonies ever to signal the start of a motion picture. Literally the entire studio, from stars to carpenters, assembled on the studio lawn to watch this impressive event.

As the USMC band played, Major J. P. Wilcox, USMC, on behalf of Major General John A. Lejeune, Commandant of the Corps, presented M-G-M with a new American flag, to be flown at the studio. Louis B. Mayer accepted the flag as a squad of Marines, commanded by Lon (in his sergeant's uniform) stood at attention. Sgt. H. H. Hopple commanded the color guard as the flag was raised and the bugler blew the appropriate call, "colors." (Sgt. Hopple actually appeared in the film, along with many other real-life Marines and their own mascot bulldog, Sgt. Jiggs.)

The Marine Corps base in San Diego along with the local train station and several streets in the city were used as a location for much of the film. The battleship USS California was an impressive set where the scenes at sea were filmed, with Lon, Haines, and Gribbon actually participating in the firing of one of the ship's 5-inch guns during target practice. The ship later fell victim to the Japanese during their attack on Pearl Harbor on December 7, 1941.

The climax of the picture takes place in China, as the Marines rescued the Americans from Chinese bandits. The sequence was filmed at Iverson's Ranch in Chatsworth, California, which for years served many studios as a location for such films as *The Good Earth* and *Fort Apache*, as well as a number of television series. During breaks in the filming at this location, Lon liked to sing songs from his old musical comedy days, accompanied by his close friends and set musicians, Sam and Jack Feinberg.

During the filming, Lon became good friends with General Smedley Butler, and when the General left in 1927 to take command of the Marine detachment in China, Lon presented him with a gift — of a 35mm DeVry camera. After Lon's death, Butler discussed his friendship with Lon:

> Lon was one of the most lovable fellows I ever had the pleasure to know. We met in 1926 when he was playing the leading role in *Tell It To The Marines*. There were things he wanted to know about Marine life, and we struck up an acquaintance which, under his magnetic personality, soon grew

into a warm friendship. We spent much time together. He was a very interesting character, wholly unlike the retiring Lon Chaney whom the public in Hollywood knew. Once you became his friend, you realized his was an entirely different personality.[116]

General Butler's son, Thomas, recalled in 1991 what it was like at the Marine base during the filming:

My dad was the commanding general of the base when the film company came down in mid-1926. Dad held a welcoming reception for everyone the following night at our home on the base. I remember that on more than one occasion Lon Chaney came over for dinner at our house. He and my dad became very good friends, and got along well. The movie was one of my dad's favorites. One time, Lon Chaney came over to our house with his 16mm film camera and had dad shoot some film of the two of us on the front lawn. Everyone on the base wanted to watch the making of the film, and especially see Lon Chaney. I approached a lady one day on the set who I thought was Eleanor Boardman. I asked for her autograph and it turned out to be her stand-in.[117]

Tell It To The Marines premiered at the Embassy Theatre in New York on December 23, 1926, where it had a successful run for 13 weeks. The film became M-G-M's second highest grossing picture for that year, earning $1.6 million dollars in box-office receipts world-wide. Upon its release to the general public in January, 1927, Major General John A. Lejeune, Commandant of the Corps, held a private screening of the film at the Department of the Interior auditorium.

Lon Chaney

The well-received picture was attended by President and Mrs. Coolidge, Cabinet members and a score of senators, representatives and the National Press Club.[118]

Motion Picture Magazine, in its March 1927 issue, called *Tell It To The Marines*

> Lon Chaney's first appearance 'au naturel' for many years and it makes one plead for more like it. He is a great actor and lifts himself out of the make-up artist class into real drama. This picture will be as popular as any we have had in many a day, and will go down on record as one of Chaney's greatest.

That same month, *Photoplay* voted the film, as well as Chaney's and Haines' performances, as one of the month's best picks, pointing out in their review:

> Lon Chaney, *sans* grotesque make-up for a change, proves himself an excellent actor by his playing of O'Hara. Indeed, his O'Hara has all the authentic earmarks of a real, honest-to-Tunney Marine.

The United States Marine Corps' own magazine, *Leatherneck*, stated,

> *Tell It To The Marines* wins by a wide margin the all-time laurels of movies which have our service as their backgrounds. . . . In his [Chaney's] portrayal of the part lay the composite picture of a thousand Marines we had known. Every look, every action, every gesture rang true as steel to the type familiar to us all. Few of us who observed Chaney's portrayal of his role were not carried away to the memory of some sergeant we had known whose behavior

matched that of the actor in every minute detail. . . .
Scores of Marines praised him, and never heard an
adverse criticism. After all, what better judges could
there be than the Marines themselves?[119]

In their year-end review, the *New York Times* mentioned *Tell It
To The Marines* as one of many outstanding films of that year even
though it did not place on their Top 10 list. "Lon Chaney's acting as
Sergeant O'Hara in *Tell It To The Marines* rivals that of Noah Berry in
Beau Geste or [Victor] McLaglen in *What Price Glory*. *Tell It To The
Marines* itself is a worthy production which gives an excellent idea
of the discipline and courage of the men who are 'soldiers and
sailors, too'," the reviewer said.

Lon's character of Sgt. O'Hara was the forerunner of the typically
tough military officer with a heart of gold. While Chaney's O'Hara
can bark out orders and instill fear in his recruits, he shows a softer
side to his character by allowing him to share his thoughts with the
Marine bulldog or his affection for the Navy nurse, Norma Dale. He
also exhibits a sense of humor when, after the new recruits have
been drilling very hard, he asks if any of them would like to drive
"the general's car." Chaney is smiling, rubbing his hands and
appearing not at all like the tough officer the recruits are use to.
When one of them volunteers, Chaney smiles broadly and gestures
for the recruit to follow him. By now the audience is aware that
Chaney plans to pull a stunt on the unsuspecting recruit, and "the
general's car" turns out to be a wheel-barrow filled with rocks.

Because Lon does not wear any make-up in this film, his
performance seems more real, giving the audience the feeling they
could reach up to the screen and touch him. Chaney's acting in the
scene between O'Hara and the Navy nurse, Norma, in the Chinese
tea garden is amazingly subtle and natural. Norma shares her feelings
for Skeet with O'Hara, unaware that the sergeant is in love with her.

Lon Chaney

All through this scene Chaney's emotions are torn between his love for the girl and his own code of honor. When Norma pointedly asks him if she should forget Skeet, Chaney looks off, lost in his thoughts. As he battles with his conscience, his fist hits his open palm, conveying his anguish over his dilemma.

Norma really strikes a chord when she tells the sergeant she wishes Skeet was more like O'Hara. In a tight close-up, Chaney laughs at the irony of this statement, and tears well up in his eyes. He dismisses her wish by saying she should have known O'Hara when he was young, and then, making up his mind once and for all, he tells her she is giving up on Skeet when he needs her most. After Norma leaves, Chaney stands solemnly in the doorway, watching her go. He tosses a coin onto their table and as he is about to leave, he adjusts the bottom of his dress coat, straightens up and walks off. This parting gesture helps to express to the audience O'Hara's accepting the resolution of this matter.

This film and *The Unholy Three* did a lot to increase Lon's reputation as a dramatic actor, since he dispensed with the use of make-up or other disguises. Despite the fact that some critics tended to view him as an actor who hid behind make-up, and many considered him more of a make-up artist than an actor, Chaney put a great deal of thought into his characters. The natural evolution of his interpretation of a character resulted in the final make-up, but his characterizations went much more than skin deep.

Lon and Hazel made one of their rare public appearances at the movie's Los Angeles premiere on February 24, 1927, at Sid Grauman's Million Dollar Theatre. Lon later claimed he made the appearance as a favor to his friend, General Smedley Butler, who was in attendance, along with other military officials and movie stars. Lon accepted the highest praise he'd ever received for his work when the Marine Corps bestowed upon him an honorary life membership, the first time any actor had ever received such an honor.

Lon and Hazel at the premiere of *Tell It To The Marines*., February 24, 1927.

He Who Gets Slapped (1924).
(Below) Lon is given his own chair by the crew of *He Who Gets Slapped*.
Victor Seastrom (hands in pants pockets) stands behind Lon.

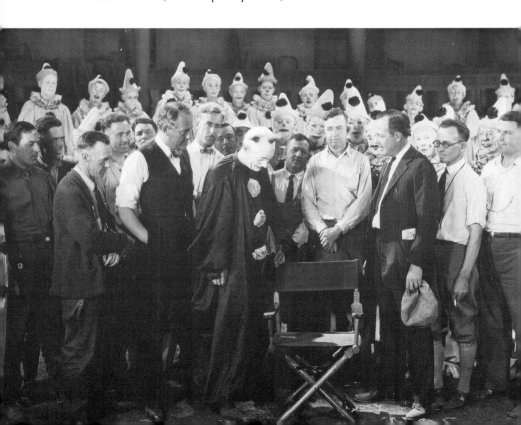

Director Rupert Julian attempting to get his point across to Lon during the
making of the problem-plagued film, *Phantom of the Opera*.
(Below) Rupert Julian (holding megaphone) introduces Carl Laemmle to
Mary Philbin and Norman Kerry during filming of the Masque Ball sequence.

164

(Left) *The Monster* (1925)
(Right) As the ventriloquist-crook masquerading as the old woman in Tod Browning's *The Unholy Three* (1925).

The three ages of Jan in *Tower of Lies* (1925)

The Blackbird (1926) *The Road To Mandalay* (1926)

Lon and Tod Browning on the studio backlot during production of *The Road to Mandalay.*
(Below) Lon's home in Beverly Hills at 604 Linden Drive. In 1986 it was sold for $800,000 and demolished.

Opening day ceremonies on the M-G-M lot celebrating the start of *Tell It To The Marines*, June, 1926.
Lon stands at attention with the squad of Marines. In foreground, left to right, Major J. P. Wilcox,
USMC; Louis B. Mayer; Irving Thalberg; Harry Rapf; and director George Hill.
(Below) On location at the Marine Recruit Depot in San Diego. Left to right: Lon; Thomas Butler;
Eleanor Boardman; General Smedley Butler, USMC; and his wife Ethel.

George Chaney visit his brother on the set.
(Below) Lon shows his 16mm Filmo camera to the Prince of Sweden and
Prince of Denmark during their visit to the M-G-M lot.

The Master Of Make-Up

_____

"It's an art, but not magic."
—*Lon Chaney discussing the use of makeup*

A rare shot of Lon and his famous make-up case,
photographed for a layout in *Photoplay* magazine (1922).

The origins of motion picture make-up date back to the legitimate theatre. However, the colors actors were able to use on stage were not easily transferred to the black-and-white screen. When this new notion of moving pictures began to catch on back in the first years of the 1900's, the film stock used to make these pictures was called Orthochromatic. This film stock was crisp but very slow in exposure and made natural skin tones appear darker than normal. Thus, if an actor applied his "stage" make-up as he normally would for a play, or if he were filmed without any make-up at all, his coloring would appear unnatural and almost grotesque. In order for the new movie actors to appear natural on screen, special make-up was an immediate necessity.

With Orthochromatic film stock, reds, oranges, and browns photographed black or very close to it. Even freckles came off darker than in real life, at times appearing almost black. Blue, pink, yellow and mauve photographed white. Therefore, a pink make-up base with a bluish tone to it looked more natural on film. The use of these strange base colors is why actors and actresses of early silent films appear to present-day audiences to have stark white faces.

Also, true black eyeliner or shadow appeared too harsh on film, so red, gray-green, blue or violet, which photographed a dusky black, were used instead. In the early years, lips, eyes and eyebrows were made up for both actors and actresses with these colors. Today, when we see this effect on screen, it looks "overdone;" however, at that time it was necessary in order to make facial expressions register on screen. No wonder the conservative residents of early Hollywood were aghast at the invasion of "picture people," particularly if they were seen in their film make-up, which must have looked quite odd indeed.

Because colors registered so differently on this new Orthochromatic film stock, actors could no longer rely on simply looking in the mirror. Instead, they had to relearn their make-up techniques for this new medium, and rely on a screen test for the final decision to determine the success of their efforts.

As if color distortions of movie make-up were not enough, actors faced yet another problem that their brothers and sisters of the stage did not: maintenance. Stage actors wore their make-up for only a few hours under a more or less controlled environment. Actors in motion pictures had to deal with all types of weather conditions, strenuous activity, perspiration, and a ten- to twelve-hour working day. Consequently, the movie actor's make-up tended to "break down," requiring more touch-ups than their counterparts on the stage.

There became a definite need for a longer-lasting, lighter-feeling make-up that would not require touching up as frequently. Max Factor developed a new greasepaint that came in a jar; it was messy but still an improvement over the stick form which always felt heavy on the skin. In 1921, Factor came up with greasepaint in a collapsible tube, which was even easier to apply. However, even these new greasepaints still felt very thick on the face, no matter how skillfully they were applied. They also required heavy powdering with powder a shade lighter than the base because the powder would darken when dry.

The advent of Panchromatic film stock once again changed the art of make-up. Panchromatic stock allowed colors to be photographed in a more accurate relationship to each other than was possible with Orthochromatic. For instance, light blue came across as light grey, dark blue as dark grey, yellow as a pale shade, and red somewhere in between. In 1928, Max Factor came out with a line of make-up called Panchromatic Make-Up to be used exclusively with the new film stock. This make-up allowed an actor to use a base color closer to his own skin tone and forgo gray-green, blue or violet for lining eyes and lips. Once again, actors could use realistic colors like red and brown for shading and lining. Face powder now needed to match the make-up base exactly, overall shadings and hues became more natural, and the eye was again a reliable judge of how successful a make-up would be on film.

This new Panchromatic make-up was equally helpful under the new incandescent lights the studios began using in 1928. Compared to the old Arc lights, incandescents were lighter to mover around, allowed the cameraman to place them in small areas of the set to get unusual effects, and gave a more accurate color rendition. Actors preferred the steady reliability of the new lights to the Arcs, which tended to sputter and flicker in the middle of a scene, ruining the shot. The introduction of incandescent lights also meant the elimination of "Klieg eyes." This was an inflammation of the eyes common to actors on a motion picture set, caused by the emission of carbon dust when the Arc lights were "fired up." (The term came from the Klieg Company which originally manufactured the lights.) The only remedies for "Klieg eyes" were to either wear dark glasses on the set between scenes, or place wet tea bags over the eyes to reduce redness and swelling.[120]

As wonderful as the new incandescent lights were, however, the changeover from one lighting system to another posed challenges to all studio departments. In the April, 1928, issue of *Academy Digest*, the Academy of Motion Picture Arts and Sciences published a report on the light's effects on everything from wardrobe to sets to make-up. In addition, an open meeting was held at the Academy Lounge on April 18, 1928, to discuss the problems these new lights posed for the actor in applying his make-up. Lon, who was not in attendance due to production on *While the City Sleeps*, wrote a paper analyzing the make-up implications of the lighting change. The entire article appears in that *Academy Digest* issue, and later was re-printed in the *New York Times* on October 14, 1928.

> So radical an innovation as the new incandescent light in studio practice must of necessity, for some time remain more or less in the state of experiment, and, naturally, draw into this same experimental field all details of photography connected with its use. Wherefore any discussion of make-up in connection with the lights and Panchromatic film must at this early day be developed more to broad essentials and primary principles. There is much to improve on the lights to date, and, naturally, much to learn in the practice of make-up under them.

> As compared to the arc lights, the incandescent have several striking differences. The most important is probably the matter of heat. They generate a far greater heat; in fact, in close-ups this heat becomes terrific, so that grease paint, nose-putty, glue, or other foreign substance on the face soon runs and melts. This, to a character make-up especially, is very dangerous.

> They are much more penetrating, which involves the matter of using make-up more sparingly, as a more natural appearance is necessary. For instance, in former practice one used powder a shade lighter than the base grease paint. Under the new lights this

cannot be done, as the penetrating quality of the light would disclose the subterfuge.

One important change in make-up brought about by the new lights has simplified the whole art of disguise. Under the new lights and Panchromatic film, the make-up that looks most nearly perfect to the eye is most nearly perfect to the camera. Under the old arc lights we had many tricks to learn, by using colors to compensate for light, and thus the eye, the most natural guide, was not reliable. The new lights will enable the actor to better judge his make-up by inspection without a screen test, and this, of course, will be a boon.

[Copyright © Academy of Motion Picture Arts and Sciences. Reproduced with permission.]

Lon was undoubtedly asked to write this report as he was considered one of the foremost experts on make-up at this time. Studios did not have full time make-up artists until the formation of the Motion Picture Make-Up Artists Association in September, 1926. By 1929, all major studios had at least one make-up artist on staff to oversee all productions, and by the early 1930's, every film had someone doing the make-up.[121] Make-up artists, along with other behind-the-scenes craftsmen, eventually formed the International Alliance of Theatrical Stage Employees (IATSE) Union which still exists today. Since Lon was a staunch supporter of unions and was already a member of the stagehands' union that later became the IATSE, it's probable he would have continued to apply his own make-up anyway.

Lon Chaney

Even after he was a star, Chaney was often asked to apply make-up to other actors. During the production of *Thunder*, Lon made-up actor James Murray's face to make him appear sweat-streaked and coal-dust-stained. Supposedly, Chaney even gave Will Rogers some pointers on make-up when he entered films.

One other well-known personality Chaney helped was boxing champion Jack Dempsey. In 1919, Dempsey signed with Pathe Pictures to star in a 15-part serial entitled *Daredevil Jack*. Lon portrayed the lead villain and also served as Dempsey's make-up artist. Lon did a complete "straight" make-up on him, including fixing his disfigured nose with putty, giving it a straight appearance. Unlike another make-up artist who applied make-up to Dempsey's face as if he were a boxing opponent, Dempsey said Lon had a feather-like hand.[122]

Fred Phillips, whose father formed the Motion Picture Make-Up Artists Association, was a make-up artist for over 50 years, with credits like *The Wizard of Oz* and the original *Star Trek* television series to his name. He started as an assistant to Cecil Holland, M-G-M's Director of Make-up, in 1926, and in a 1988 interview recalled working with Chaney:

> I was assigned by Cecil Holland to help Lon out
> whenever he had an elaborate make-up, but actually
> I was his 'hand me, get me, do me man.' Lon did
> everything himself, but I'd have to hand him things
> or run and get something if he didn't have it, and
> God help you if you were slow. He was very
> friendly, but he'd get nervous and pretty upset if he
> didn't get something right away because he was
> worried about holding up production. When he'd
> go to the set, I'd carry his make-up case for him and
> would be his eye behind the camera to make sure

everything was okay. There was never any truth to the story that if he needed a touch-up, he'd go back to his dressing room to do it in secret. He would do it right there on the set and I'd hold his mirror for him.

It was Lon who taught me how to use cotton and collodion for a number of things. The thing I remember the most about him doing his make-ups, was the amount of spirit gum he used in putting on beards, nose putty, and other things, because he wanted to make sure everything stayed in place and didn't have to worry about it on the set. When he passed away, his wife told me I could have anything out of his make-up case, but I declined and now I wish I hadn't. It would have been nice to have had something to remember him by and to remember those days.[123]

Chaney's make-up case, donated in 1931 to the Natural History Museum in Los Angeles by Mrs. Chaney, is still on display there today. The leather-covered case opens with metal shelves that fold out like an accordion. On the top it reads:

Lon F. Chaney
Hollywood, CA

In the case, one can see boxes of Miner's Thes-Paint, Max Factor nose putty, assorted brushes, a set of gutta percha false teeth, two glass shields (in their original cases) that Lon used for the dead eye in *The Road to Mandalay*, assorted powder puffs, several hair pins, a mirror, Lichetner grease liner pencils, and the eye glasses he wore as the old woman in *The Unholy Three*. Also on display are his stumps and costume from *The Penalty*, and a wax head that bears a strong resemblance to Lon. Lon would use this head to prepare in advance his cotton and collodion pieces, beards, moustaches and the like. They could then be quickly applied to his own face to create his different characters. Although no longer on display, the wig from *The Unholy Three* used to be part of the exhibit as well.

Lon explained his philosophy of make-up in the October 1927 issue of *Theatre Magazine*:

> All during the time I was traveling about the country with repertory and one night stands, the thing that interested me the most was make-up. It was not merely the applying of grease paint and putty noses to the face, but mental make-up as well . . . I felt there was a greater field in characterizations; nor was it the stereotyped characterizations that interested me. If I played the role of an old man, I tried to crawl into the old man's mind rather than merely build up a putty nose and don white whiskers. Even in the make-up I attempted to avoid the conventional. For example, whenever I was given an old man's role to play, I tried to inject into it some distinctive mannerism; a limp perhaps, or a drawn arm, or maybe just a slight nervous twitch of the face; anything, in fact, to take the character out of the lesson-number-52-in-make-up-old-men class.
>
> Grotesqueries as such do not attract me; it is vivid characterizations for which I strive. I want my make-

up simply to add to the picture, to show at a glance the sort of character I am portraying. But I want my role to go deeper than that. I want to dig down into the mind and heart of the role. But, as a man's face reveals much that is in his mind and heart, I attempt to show this by the make-up I use, and the make-up is merely the prologue.

Most of the procedures and materials used in Chaney's day have been replaced with new, up-to-date products that look more realistic when used with the film stocks and camera lenses available to today's filmmakers. Gone are the days of using nose putty or cotton and collodion to build up facial features. Today's make-up artists use foam rubber and plastic appliances which appear much more life-like on film, and do not require as much maintenance after application. However, non-flexible collodion continues to be used for scars, and crepe-wool hair is still used for moustaches and beards. Adhesives have been developed that are much stronger than those available in Lon's day, but almost every make-up artist still carries a bottle of spirit gum as "the old stand-by" when all else fails. Greasepaint has been replaced with a new thinner, creamier make-up base, and even liquid make-up bases are popular with some make-up artists. Facial powder no longer needs to correspond with the make-up base, and translucent powder is often used over any base color. Gone too from the make-up case is the rabbit's foot. While many thought it was merely a "good luck charm," it was actually used in the old days as a brush to dust off excess face powder.

One thing that has definitely not changed since Lon's era is the enormous amount of time it takes to apply a character make-up to an actor's face! Lon once said that the time he spent applying his make-ups was tiresome and he often envied actors who merely spent fifteen minutes or so applying their "straight" make-up.[124]

Lon Chaney

Chaney's knowledge of make-up prompted Max Factor to approach him to see if he would endorse the Factor make-up line. While Lon did use Factor's make-up (along with Miner's and Lichetner's) he declined the request, preferring to keep the public guessing about how he created his famous faces.[125] "There are tricks in my peculiar trade that I don't care to divulge any more than a magician will give away his art," Chaney once told *Colliers Weekly*. "I'm supposed to have evolved some magic process of malforming my features and limbs. It's an art, but not magic."[126] He did give the public a brief glimpse into how make-up could be used in film when he was asked by the *Encyclopedia Britannica* to pen the chapter on "Motion Picture Make-Up" for their 14th Edition in 1929.

In fact, the *Britannica* was not the first to take advantage of Lon's combination of make-up expertise and clear writing style. Cecil Holland, M-G-M's Director of Make-up, asked Lon to write the preface to his 1927 how-to book, *The Art of Make-Up for Stage and Screen*.

Lon was always eager to experiment with every new make-up product that came on the market. Sam Kress, who operated a drug store at the corner of Hollywood Boulevard and Cahuenga Avenue in the mid-teens through the early 1920's, was the only person in Hollywood to sell make-up supplies, and therefore his shop was a popular hangout for actors. In a 1934 *Photoplay* article, Kress recalled how Lon wanted to be kept informed when any new make-up material arrived. "When he found something he had never used, he was in a glow of excitement, opened it right there, and went back of the counter to put it on. I kept a mirror in a certain spot where the light was good just for Chaney," Kress said.

One make-up Lon was said to have done, but which few people ever got the chance to see, was his characterization of Jesus Christ. In his book *The Faces Of Hollywood,* Clarence S. Bull, a still photographer at M-G-M Studios, describes Lon's private portrayal of Christ — as well as its extraordinary outcome. During a photo session, Bull reputedly told Chaney that he had seen a vision of Christ in Lon's face while Lon was in his clown make-up for *HE Who Gets Slapped*. This inspired Chaney to pose for photographs made up as Jesus Christ. The finished prints were somehow lost. However, during the Christmas season of 1929, Bull and two other studio employees were making stops at homes of the needy with food and gifts when he saw the missing photo in one of the houses he visited. The young boy of the house told Clarence that his late father worked as a janitor in the studio and found the photo in the trash. Clarence said he meant to pass the story along to Lon, but never got the opportunity before Lon's death.[127]

Tim McCoy, who was MGM's cowboy star in the late 1920's, had a dressing room next to Lon. One day he saw Lon coming out of his dressing room made up as Grandfather Wu and remarked how great his make-up looked. Lon told him it was basically nothing but the aid of shadows and a dark cowl over the head and along the sides of the face. "But to wear your real face and make it look presentable — now that's a job and a half," Chaney remarked.[128]

Lon shows some of his false teeth he used in playing various characters. The wig on the wig block is the one he used for the ape-man in *A Blind Bargain* (1922).

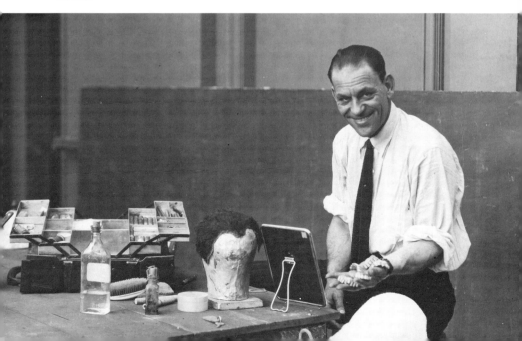

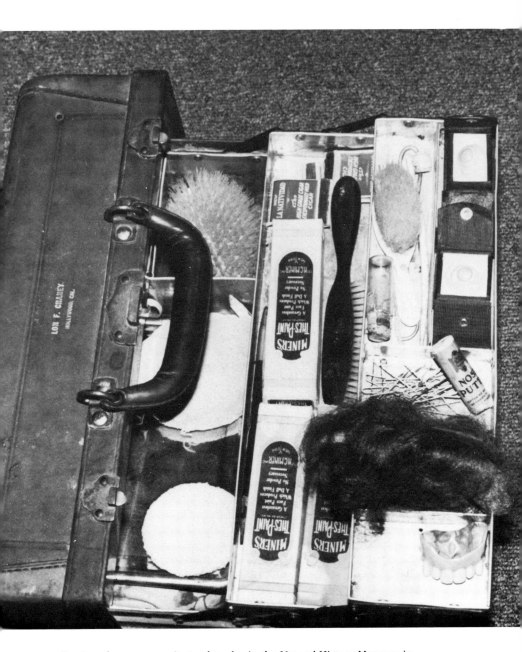

Lon's make-up case as it stands today in the Natural History Museum in downtown Los Angeles. The small black cases hold glass-eye shields that he used to simulate blindness in *The Road To Mandalay.*
(Left) Lon carrying his make-up case on the Goldwyn studio lot (1921).)

This wax head was used by Chaney to make his cotton and collodion pieces ahead of time. Note the dark discoloration around the cheekbone area from spirit gum used in preparing the pieces. The cap and costume are from *The Penalty*, on display at the natural History Museum..

(Below)Lon applies glycerin to James Murray's face during production of *Thunder* (1929). Glycerin gave the appearance of sweat.

Between Pictures
There Is No Lon Chaney
(1927)

---

*"Actors should pay more attention to
their work and less to their fan mail."*
                                              —*Lon Chaney*

Lon played both the 100-year-old grandfather and the revengeful grandson in
Mr. Wu (1927).

on's second release of 1927, *Mr. Wu*, was adapted from a New York stage play. Chaney played the dual roles of Mandarin Wu and his Grandfather. As the film begins, an elderly Chinese gentleman agrees to allow his grandson to be taught the ways of European society. The grandson becomes a wealthy mandarin and marries a woman who dies giving birth to their only child, a daughter, Nang Ping. The mandarin, Mr. Wu, devotes himself to his daughter, who grows up and prepares to marry according to the Chinese custom. However, Basil Gregory, a young Englishman, falls in love with Nang Ping. Soon Nang Ping reveals to the young man that she is carrying his child. Mr. Wu learns of this and, according to Chinese custom, he has to take the life of his daughter. Unhinged over this tragic turn of events, he plots revenge on the young man and his family. He invites Mrs. Gregory and her daughter to his palace where he confronts her with what her son has done, and forces Mrs. Gregory to choose between the life of her son or her daughter. When Mr. Wu tries to strike the gong to signal the execution of her son, Mrs. Gregory stabs the mandarin, freeing both her son and daughter.

This was a demanding role for Lon, requiring him to play the role of Mr. Wu as a young adult and at middle age, as well as his elderly grandfather who ages from his eighties to one hundred years old. In the opening credits of the picture, a separate title card read:

Lon Chaney

The Characters of
Grandfather Wu
and
Mandarin Wu
are both played by
Mr. Chaney

To portray the hundred-year-old Grandfather Wu, Chaney used his old fishskin technique to obtain the Oriental look of the eyes. He blocked out his own eyebrows and built up his nose with putty. Cotton wool was used under his eyes to create eyebags, while cheekbones and lips were built up with cotton and collodion. He placed the ends of cigar holders into the nostrils (as he did for the ape-man in *A Blind Bargain*). Hollow cheeks were created with a coat of light-colored greasepaint accentuated with many highlights and shadows. Finely painted wrinkles applied with a liner color helped to emphasize the character's age. Grey crepe hair was applied in a Fu-Manchu style moustache and goatee, while a cap made of fine muslin, glued down onto the forehead with spirit gum and covered with grease paint, gave the effect of a balding head. A black cowl was worn over the head and along the sides of the face; this, along with the built-up cheekbones, gave the gaunt, withering look to the face. His hands were made up with strong use of highlights and shadows and the long mandarin fingernails were made out of strips of painted film stock.

While the film was a success at the box-office (earning a world-wide gross of over $1 million), it received mixed reviews. *Photoplay* called it "Madame Butterfly with variations — most of them gory ones. Lon Chaney is swell, but Renee Adorée is even more so."

Variety said:

"From an artistic standpoint *Mr. Wu* cannot miss.
But from a commercial standpoint, it looks as
though this Lon Chaney starring vehicle, even
though the star is calculated to get them in, will not
be a big box office attraction. It is too gruesome and
draggy an epic to make the folks out front want to
say, "Here is another Chaney natural, don't miss it.".
. . . Chaney started by playing the grandfather of Mr.
Wu in the initial scenes. Then Mr. Wu grew up and
became a mandarin with Chaney changing
appearance and characterization in accord. It was a
walk-away for him.

Tod Browning took up the megaphone to direct Chaney in *The Unknown*, which was one of their strongest and most lurid films. In the film Lon played a circus performer named Alonzo, who wears a tightly laced straitjacket to conceal his arms so he can pose as an armless knife thrower in a Spanish circus. His apparent deformity prevents the police, who are searching for a criminal with two thumbs on one hand, from giving him a second glance. (Alonzo, of course, is that criminal.) Alonzo secretly loves the circus owner's daughter Nanon, who has a phobia about men's arms around her. Alonzo believes she can never truly love him as long as he has arms, so he has a doctor amputate them, only to find Nanon has overcome her fear of men's arms and has fallen for the circus strongman, Malabar.

The strongman has a new act in which he uses his arms to hold back two horses on treadmills, pulling in opposite directions. Nanon tells Alonzo her fear that if one of the treadmills were to stop, Malabar's arms would be torn from his body. This gives Alonzo an idea for revenge. During a performance, Alonzo engages the brake on one of the treadmills, causing one of the horses to rear up and jerk Malabar's arm. Trying to help, Nanon darts into the path of the horse. Alonzo, fearing for her safety, runs up and pushes her out of the way, but is struck by the hoofs of the horse and killed.

The film began its six-week shooting schedule on February 7, 1927, under the title *Alonzo the Armless.* Joan Crawford appeared as Nanon, with Norman Kerry as Malabar. In later years, Joan Crawford said that while working with Lon she first became aware of the difference between standing in front of a camera and acting. She said Chaney's concentration, the complete absorption he gave his character, filled her with such awe that she never considered addressing him with the usual pleasantries until he addressed her first.[129]

Bobby Mack and Polly Moran were cast as a gypsy and a landlady respectively, but their roles were cut from the final release print.

Photoplay picked the film as one of the month's best and said, "A fine sinister plot, alot of macabre thrills and great acting by Lon Chaney. Also Joan Crawford helps a lot. Don't go if you're easily scared."

Variety commented,

> A good Chaney film that might have been great.
> Chaney and his characterizations invite stories that
> have power behind them. Every time Browning
> thinks of Chaney, he probably looks around for a
> typewriter and says "let's get gruesome." In this
> instance he has again outlined strongly for the
> character actor. Possibly as brilliantly as in 'The
> Unholy Three,' although what momentum he has
> gained on paper has been lost in discretion. . . .
> Another Chaney-Browning program release that will
> reinforce the value of this combination.

It was widely publicized (but completely fictitious) that Chaney learned to throw knives, light cigarettes and even sign autographs with his feet. In some wide-angle scenes Lon does use his own feet, but Browning did use a double's feet for the medium and close-up shots. The double was a man by the name of Dismuki who was born without arms and worked on the film for seven weeks at a salary of $150 a week. He later toured with the Al G. Barnes Circus and Sideshow, billed as "The Man Who Doubled For Lon Chaney's Legs in *The Unknown*."[130] For two weeks, the film also employed the use of a real knife thrower.

Despite the "gruesomeness" of the theme, Lon wears little unusual make-up for this picture; his armless effect was achieved by wearing a straitjacket, and the double thumb he used was made out of wax and affixed with spirit gum. Much of the film's effectiveness lies in Chaney's characterization of Alonzo. In a particularly gut-wrenching scene, Alonzo returns from having his arms amputated and goes to see Nanon at the local theatre. Chaney's face is aglow as he fantasizes of winning her love. When she hugs and kisses him on the cheek Chaney interprets her excitement as love, especially when she says she is glad he has returned so that *they* can be married. Chaney's hopeful look further propels his character to his dramatic upheaval.

When Nanon goes to call Malabar from an upstairs dressing room, Lon looks perplexed. As the strongman greets him, Chaney clenches his teeth and forces a smile as it slowly dawns on him that Nanon is planning to marry Malabar and not him. At this point Chaney begins to build his emotional intensity. While the strongman holds Nanon in his arms, Chaney's taut face twists into a mad, contorted smile. When Nanon tells him she is no longer afraid of men's arms, Alonzo's lips begin to quiver as he realizes he has maimed his body for nothing. His maniacal laugh escalates to a fevered pitch, even without sound!

When Malabar tells Alonzo how he took his advice and put his arms around Nanon, it stops his laughter cold. Shock registers on his face as he realizes how his plan has backfired. His face contorts even tighter, and he suddenly lets out an agonizing scream. This entire scene is shot close-up, preventing Chaney the use of any body gestures. Because of this, Chaney must communicate his emotions entirely with his face.

Overcome, Alonzo slumps to the floor, and Malabar and Nanon gently help him up. As he slowly regains his composure, he wipes his face with a handkerchief, using his foot (actually his double's foot).

Hoping to engage Alonzo's interest in a less upsetting topic, Malabar explains his new act. Alonzo listens, slowly looking from the strongman to the horse and then to the treadmill. When Nanon expresses her fear that if the treadmill were to stop suddenly Malabar's arms would be torn from his body, Chaney's eyes widen; his character has a plan. When they leave, Chaney glances towards the brake lever of the treadmill, telegraphing his idea to the audience. Burt Lancaster called this scene "[one of] the most compelling and emotionally exhausting scenes I have ever seen an actor do."[131]

Lon once said that since he and Tod Browning worked together so often, some people called Browning "The Chaney Director."[132] Browning himself claimed that when he was working on a story for Chaney, he conceived the character first and the plot would follow. He said that when he started working on *The Unknown*, he merely came up with the idea of an armless man and then thought what kind of startling situations would there be for such a man's deformity. The final plot of the film grew from there.[133]

In retrospect, much of Browning's success outside of the Chaney/M-G-M films seems a bit overblown. Between 1924 and 1929 Browning made 11 films for the studio, eight of them with Chaney who had already proven his star stature before teaming up with

Browning. The other three films, *The Mystic*, *The Show* and *The Thirteenth Chair* did not equal the box-office or critical success of his films with Chaney. After Chaney died, Browning seemed to lose much of his inspiration. His later success in films was moderate at best, with the exception of *Dracula* and possibly *Freaks*. Working with an actor like Chaney gave Browning the chance to let his imagination run wild when it came to the story. Lon in turn probably felt challenged to come up with an absorbing and powerful character. It was as if they had a friendly rivalry between each other that challenged them to "top this one." Browning probably did not direct Chaney in the true sense of the word; rather, it is likely the director let Lon play the scene according to his emotions, guiding him only if he felt Chaney was going off in the wrong direction in his performance. It is a shame no film historian ever interviewed Browning before his death in 1962. He retired from making films after *Miracles For Sale* in 1939. He lived in seclusion in Malibu until his death, reputedly working as a "script doctor" for several studios and writers.[134]

During production of the film, Lon posed for a photo with the crew and gave copies to everyone. While he was basically a retiring person and rarely made the rounds at Hollywood social functions, he remained very close to the crew and office workers on the studio lot. Gestures such as the photo of Lon with the crew were typical of him, and upon completion of *The Unholy Three* in 1930, he had photos given to the crew of all of them together. He knew every worker by his or her first name and refused to be called "Mr. Chaney" by any of them. His generosity was legendary as well; many workers on the lot were directly or indirectly helped by Lon. One studio electrician's mother was in need of an operation and was helped out financially by Lon who refused repayment.[135] If a laborer on the lot received a bum rap from his bosses, Lon went to bat for him. On the set of *He Who Gets Slapped*, the crew presented Lon with a personalized director's chair, autographed on the back by all the grips, electricians and prop men. Lon used the chair for the rest of his career.

Clarence Locan said that Lon objected to having his charities publicized, since he generally refused to help such organizations as the Community Chest Fund. His brother George said that Lon felt those types of organizations couldn't help those who really needed it.[136] Yet he was a member of the Motion Picture Relief Fund which was established to help those employed in the motion picture industry, and the fund still exists today. He mainly helped crew members and old-time bit players and stage actors, either directly or indirectly.[137] One struggling actor who was given encouragement by Lon was an English actor named Boris Karloff. One day, as Karloff walked off the M-G-M lot in a dejected state of mind, Chaney pulled up beside him in his car and offered to give him a lift. During the course of the ride, Lon gave Karloff advice he never forgot. "The trick in this business," Lon told him, "is to do something totally different from the rest so they'll take notice of you."[138]

Karloff said he'd spot Chaney at the weekly Friday night fights at the Hollywood Legion Stadium. Lon was quite a fight fan and he even once admitted to *New York Times* reporter Lewis L. Nichols that he was a fighter's manager but in a more uncommon way:

> There used to be a little Italian boy fighting around
> Los Angeles. He was strong, but had no punches
> save a terrific wallop with a side arm swing. If it
> landed it was fine, but the trouble was that everyone
> knew the trick and kept out of the way. I arranged
> with him one day to sit just beneath the ring, and,
> when I saw a good opportunity, to call out Up!
> When he heard it he was to give over the side-
> wheelers and send out an uppercut.

The first night we tried it he was going along about as usual, swinging away at a great rate. I watched intently and saw what appeared to be the moment. I yelled Up! and he did. The other fellow was expecting a blow from the side, and was quite unprepared for the one from beneath. He was knocked cold. Before the season ended we had won two more fights that way.[139]

Lon had regular seats at the fights and usually attended them with his friend and family chauffeur, John Jeske. Jeske, who was a Polish immigrant, worked at the garage where Chaney brought his cars to be serviced. The two men hit it off and he came to work for the Chaney family as the chauffeur, soon becoming Lon's constant companion on the studio lot, at the fights, and on fishing trips in the Sierras.[140] Harry Earles said Jeske bore a strong resemblance to Lon [141], while George Chaney once described him as "a tough." George was not very fond of Jeske and felt his brother might have had him around as a sort of bodyguard.[142]

Lon's absence from Hollywood social functions was well known and helped to further his mystery with the public. When he did make an appearance with Hazel, it was news, and photographers and fans alike clamored for a glimpse of him. Lon was rarely accessible to the public to sign autographs, but he did autograph pictures for many people in the industry such as comedian Harold Lloyd, director Herbert Brennon, Dr. Hugo Keifer (the eye doctor who made the glass lenses for *Road to Mandalay*), and even the wardrobe women at M-G-M. Chaney's autographs sell for a minimum of $3,000 today, when one can be found.

Disliking Hollywood society as he did, Lon made few public appearances. At the M-G-M Studio Christmas parties, Lon stayed around just long enough for the greetings and then left.[143] Yet on occasion he and Hazel did attend social functions in Hollywood. On May 11, 1927, they attended the Organization Banquet at the Biltmore Hotel for the Academy of Motion Pictures Arts and Sciences. Lon and Hazel were seated at a table with Delores Del Rio, Ralph Forbes, Lew Cody, and directors William Nigh and Clarence Brown. Lon became the 75th member to join the Motion Picture Academy that night.[144]

Aside from appearing in movies, Lon was occasionally featured in the newsreels of the day. One of the better ones, called *Life In Hollywood,* is a tour of Universal Studios shot about 1923-24. Lon appears wearing a three-piece suit and cap, guiding another gentleman around the set of the cathedral of Notre Dame. Lon pantomimes how he climbed down the face of the church set and offers to demonstrate to his guest. The guest demurs, but Lon gestures it's okay and hops up on the church building. When he climbs down, he lurches up to his guest as Quasimodo. Lon then straightens up, offers his guest a cigar, and they walk off to Lon's car and drive away.

This "full treatment" is quite a contrast to his appearance in the 1925 M-G-M studio tour newsreel. As the camera pans across the row of stars standing on the lawn in front of dressing room row, Lon appears with his back to the camera, holding an overcoat and cap in his arms and wearing glasses. He is engaged in a very spirited conversation with another actor and quickly turns to the camera and then away from it, just giving the audience enough of a glimpse to know it was he.

A third newsreel appearance shows Lon and Hazel at the ground breaking ceremonies for Grauman's Chinese Theatre. They stop briefly in front of the camera, Lon smiling but seemingly somewhat uncomfortable being shot as is. His only other known newsreel clip is a brief shot at the M-G-M backlot in his khaki uniform from *Tell It To The Marines,* holding his 16mm Filmo camera, filming a group of men as he walks towards them. The newsreel then shows Lon holding the camera and pointing things out to two men who turn out to be the Prince of Sweden and the Prince of Denmark!

The parties Lon and Hazel gave at their home were for their own group of friends — the Clinton Lyles, Sam and Jack Feinberg (Lon's set musicians), Millard K. Wilson (an assistant director and former actor), Eddie Gribbon, Mr. and Mrs. William Dunphy (a San Francisco business man), Phil Epstein and his wife Fay Parks. Fay Parks had worked with Lon in several musical comedy companies in California, and after Lon was successful, he had her husband, Phil Epstein, become his business manager.

Lon was noted for some interesting dishes that came out of the Chaney kitchen. He was quite fond of steak tartare and raw spinach with caviar, as well as a tasty roast duck. Hazel was also busy in the kitchen, but not creating as many unusual recipes as her husband. Her specialty was Italian dishes, something Lon mentioned to *Photoplay* writer Ruth Waterbury, joking that, "Being part Italian she eats too much spaghetti."[145]

Even when he was not doing make-up, Lon loved to work with his hands. When his first grandson was born, Lon carved wooden animals and made clay figures for the child. One day Lon and Hazel were entertaining their old friends Clinton and Florence Lyle, and Hazel remarked that some time before Lon had promised to build her a bird house for the back yard. Clinton Lyle told her not to expect something like that from the now famous Lon Chaney. Lon paid no attention to the conversation but on their next visit to the Chaney home, Lon made a point of it of showing his old friend the new bird house in the back yard made by the 'Man of a Thousand Faces' himself.[146]

Chaney was never really comfortable with his success, even though it allowed him to play the unique roles he loved and earn him a handsome salary. In order to sustain his star status he was required to be in the public spotlight, something he never wanted and made him uncomfortable. More than anything, Lon hated the ever-present "yes men" that filled Hollywood studios, and in a 1930 article in *Motion Picture Magazine* he told Gladys Hall why he disliked their attention:

> It isn't success that kills us, that spoils us. It isn't having a great deal of money. It is the parasitism that goes with success and with money. It is the effect upon us of the 'yes men'—and women. The effect of the men and women who fawn upon us and tell us we are greater than we really are or ever could be. I have seen more than one screen celebrity tumble from real ability to a sickening complacency and from there to failure and oblivion for no other reason than an inflated ego. It is the most dangerous foe we have. It is what makes us believe that we are so good, so infallible, that we no longer have to strive. I wouldn't trust myself not to be affected by this thing. And so, I stay away from it. So far, I have discovered, money has not affected me. Success hasn't changed me. I am the man I started out to be as a boy.
>
> Vanity is a personal parasite that must be fed until it is gorged and renders its victim a failure. I care nothing whatever about fame. The less I have of it, the better for me personally. I work for money and I work because I am interested in the things I do. If I were not, I wouldn't do them.[147]

As he shunned vanity, Chaney paid little attention to fan mail. He considered fan mail an inadequate representation of public opinion. He felt only certain classes, types, and ages wrote to stars, while many older, mature people did not, although they were equally faithful movie-goers. He maintained that the only true guide to a star's popularity was box-office receipts, not fan mail.[148] "Actors," he once stated, "should pay more attention to their work and less to the fan mail."[149] Even though he dumped large amounts of fan mail every week into a near-by trash can outside his dressing room, which he jokingly referred to as his "high-priced secretary"[150], his countless fans remained loyal.

After completing *The Unknown* on March 18, 1927, Lon went to the mountains for a vacation, but his stay was cut short when his father suffered a stroke just a few days after his 75th birthday. Frank Chaney died on April 11, 1927, as a result of complications from his stroke. The funeral at Forest Lawn Cemetery in Glendale was attended by a large contingent from the Los Angeles deaf community.

On May 19, Chaney began work on *Mockery* for Danish director Benjamin Christensen. Originally titled *Terror*, the story takes place during the Russian Revolution. Lon played a dim-witted Russian peasant, Sergei, who is befriended by the Countess Tatiana. She disguises herself as Sergei's peasant wife in order to get past the Bolsheviks and deliver a message to a Russian military stronghold. Because Sergei helped her, she arranges a position for him with the rich profiteer with whom she is staying. There Sergei is exposed to the political speeches of Ivan the cook, who tells Sergei everyone is equal and he should have the Countess in his arms if he desires. The Revolution heats up and as the city is being ransacked by the Bolshevik army, the Countess finds herself alone in the house with Sergei. He attempts to attack her only to be interrupted by the storming Bolsheviks. The Countess' lover rescues her and orders all of the revolutionaries shot, but the Countess asks that Sergei's life be spared. Sergei cannot believe her generosity, and when the revolutionaries attempt to attack the Countess a second time, he almost loses his life defending her.

Variety felt that

> Lon Chaney is put through a routine of pug-ugly mugging, but even this flops, as somehow he hardly achieves the ferocious power of facial characterization he has often managed to convey in other productions. . . . The picture may be figured to draw on the strength of Chaney's box-office value the first half of the week. It lowers the star's batting average considerably.

Motion Picture Classic magazine had a different opinion:

> Chaney makes "Sergei" into an effective character. This star is the only film luminary who can play dumb gents minus sex appeal and ring the gong at the box-office. "Sergei" is a big blunder and harelip man from the steppes with nothing to recommend him but Chaney's fine performance.

Lon's make-up for Sergei was fairly simple; he grew his own beard, pencilled in heavy brows to the bridge of his nose, and widened his nostrils with the use of cigar-holder ends. A low forehead wig completed the look. The greasy texture of the face was accomplished by applying very little powder to the heavy greasepaint base.

What is now considered one of the most sought-after lost silent films, *London After Midnight*, was made under the working title *The*

Hypnotist. It started production on July 25 and was released shortly before Christmas, 1927. Lon again worked under the direction of Tod Browning who later remade the film in 1934 as *Mark of the Vampire;* Lionel Barrymore and Bela Lugosi played the dual roles Chaney performed in the original. The story concerns Scotland Yard Inspector Burke (Chaney) who believes that a criminal under hypnosis will recreate his crime. He puts his theory to the test in the unsolved murder case of Roger Balfour. Vampires also figure in the solution of the mystery, and at the end of the film the vampire turns out to be none other than the inspector himself. When Burke removes his make-up at the picture's climax, Chaney's own make-up case can be seen in the shot.

The review in the *New York Times* read,

> "It is a somewhat incoherent narrative, which, however, gives Lon Chaney an opportunity to turn up in an uncanny disguise and also to manifest his powers as Scotland Yard's expert hypnotist . . . Mr. Chaney is sound and sure in his acting, but this detective character does not give him anything in the way of a big opportunity. His other role is shrewdly made-up and portrayed.

Photoplay wrote,

> Lon Chaney has the stellar role in this mystery drama and the disguise he uses while ferreting out the murderer is as gruesome as any he has ever worn. . . . Chaney plays a dual role, and, when conventionally clad, is a little less convincing than usual. In the other role, perfect.

Lon Chaney

Incredibly, Lon's characterization of the vampire in this movie was so chilling that it may have inspired a murder. Robert Williams was a carpenter in London who claimed that after seeing *London After Midnight*, had visions of Chaney's vampire character. These visions terrified him so much that he went into an epileptic fit and killed an Irish housemaid. The English court accepted the possibilities of the story and Williams was found not guilty by reason of insanity.[151]

As Inspector Burke, Chaney simply grayed his hair and wore long sideburns to give his character the no-nonsense look of a Scotland Yard man. The vampire, referred to in the script as The Man In The Beaver Hat, is described in the July 16th version of the script as being "as strange a creature as the eyes ever beheld. He wears a black beaver hat and a black Inverness coat and his face has on it the pallor of death. There is, indeed, something not of this earth in his appearance." For this role Lon wore a straggly, shoulder- length wig along with a light-colored base. His eyes were shaded and his eyebrows darkened, while a thin wire ring was placed around the outside of his eyes (like a monocle) to give the hypnotic, hollowed-eye look. The upper and lower sharply pointed false teeth were made from guttapercha with small dental wires placed in the upper plate to keep his mouth open. This fixed grin was further emphasized by shading in the upper corners of the mouth with a liner color.

During production of the film, *Photoplay* writer Ruth Waterbury interviewed Chaney, and in her article she hinted at the fact that Lon was in pain from the wire rings around his eyes. "Yet in this visible suffering," she wrote, "Lon was plainly an artist in the exquisite travail of creation. To endure pain for his work brought him strange joy."[152] Over the years, this quote has been used by writers to imply that Chaney might have been something of a masochist. This type of speculation has been fueled with reports that he used a 70-pound rubber hump for *The Hunchback of Notre Dame* or inserted celluloid discs in his cheekbones for *Phantom of the Opera*, regardless of the obvious impossibility of these feats.

True, he did endure discomfort and pain in some of his roles, but nothing to the extent some writers have claimed. Many actors over the years — Boris Karloff in *Frankenstein*, Charles Laughton in the 1939 *The Hunchback of Notre Dame*, Roddy McDowell in the *Planet of the Apes* series, John Hurt in *The Elephant Man* — experienced and endured some pain and discomfort in their make-ups. Yet no one has ever hinted that they might be masochists. If Chaney did endure the sufferings writers claim he did, he would have been risking his health, and possibly causing production to be halted, thereby putting friends, as well as himself, out of work — a risk he would never have taken.

During this period Chaney was at the apex of his career. His 1927 releases were among M-G-M's most popular. *Tell It To The Marines*, *Mr. Wu*, and *London After Midnight* each posted a world-wide box-office gross of over $1 million dollars. These three films, along with *Laugh, Clown, Laugh* and *While The City Sleeps* were Chaney's top profit making pictures at M-G-M.

But October, 1927 brought a sweeping and dramatic change to the entire motion picture industry. Movies had learned to talk, and it was quite obvious the silent era had come to an end with the release of Warner Bros.' *The Jazz Singer*. While this film is routinely considered to be the first all-talking picture, it was released with the sound-on-discs system called Vitaphone and actually had only two talking sequences. The rest of the film was silent accompanied by a synchronized musical score. Warner Bros. originally intended that this concept of presenting silent films with synchronized discs (looking like over-sized records) would allow movie-goers to hear a full orchestra in any size theatre that had a Vitaphone sound system installed. It was not until Al Jolson talked and sang in *The Jazz Singer* that the full implications of "talking pictures" caught the audience's attention.

Most studio executives were hesitant to charge head-on into the making of all-talking pictures because of the expensive outlay to refurbish not only studio lots, but theatres as well. By 1928 it was apparent to the studios that the public now wanted films to speak, and studios quickly added "partial dialogue" scenes to several silent films. Paramount studios was the only facility in Hollywood that had stages with a sound system already installed and could shoot these newly added talking sequences. M-G-M hastily built two primitive sound stages which were in constant use for several months, each film shooting in eight hour shifts, seven days a week.[153]

In those early days of panic, Irving Thalberg honestly felt that silent and talking pictures could exist together, and the studio continued to make silents as well as all-talking pictures. After all, theatre exhibitors voted Lon Chaney and Clara Bow the most popular box-office stars of 1928 and 1929. But box-office receipts for silent pictures in 1929 showed the producers that lush green lawns, beautiful flower beds and glass stages of the studio lots had to give way to concrete boxes now known as "sound stages."

Cameraman John Arnold and Director William Nigh watch Lon and Louise Dressler act out the climax scene from *Mr. Wu.*

As the "armless" knife thrower in Tod Browning's *The Unknown* (1927).
(Below) Norman Kerry, Lon, and director Tod Browning pose for Joan
Crawford during production of *The Unknown*.

This picture shows Dismuki, not Lon, playing the guitar. Dismuki doubled Lon's feet and legs in *The Unknown*.

(Below) Lon poses with crew members on the set of *The Unknown*.

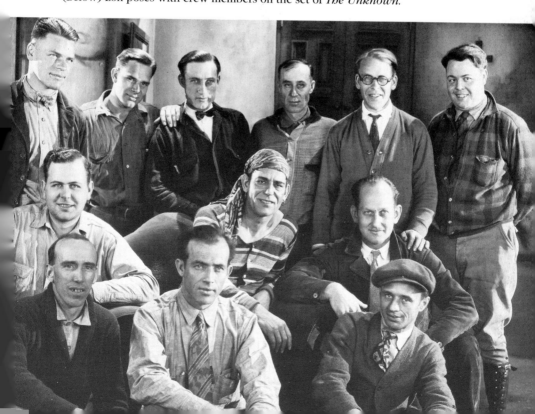

Lon as would-be vampire and the Scotland Yard Inspector in *London After Midnight* (1927).

Tod Browning, Marcelline Day, and Lon appear a bit surprised by something in the book. The only time Lon used his make-up case as a prop in a motion picture was in this film, seen lower right.
(Below) Tod Browning throws a little light on the subjects, Lon and Edna Tichnor on the set of *London After Midnight*.

(Above) As the Russin peasant in *Mockery* (1927)
Actor Charles Puffy (leaning on stairs) and director Benjamin Christensen(white shirt, behind camera) watch Lon during production of *Mockery*.

Lon Chaney's Gonna Get You If You Don't Watch Out! (1928-1929)

"He was a very interesting character, wholly unlike the retiring Lon Chaney whom the public in Hollywood knew. Once you became his friend, you realized his was an entirely different personality."
—*Gen. Smedley Butler, U.S.M.C.*

Lon as the gangster in Tod Browning's *The Big City* (1928)

In *The Big City*, Lon's first release of 1928, he played crafty gangster Chuck Collins in "straight" make-up. Director Tod Browning started filming on October 27, 1927, with Lon's former co-star of *The Miracle Man*, Betty Compson, playing his "moll" Helen.

As the story opens, Chuck Collins' gang has developed an elaborate ruse to cheat another gangster, Red Watson, out of a night club robbery. Collins' gang, posing as dancers, wear black hoods as part of their costumes, so they can rob the club's patrons unrecognized. Believing the crooks are members of his own gang, Red Watson willingly parts with his own cash and jewels. Collins returns with his loot to a clothing store he and Helen use as a front and hides the jewels in boxes mixed with fake jewelry. Employed at the store, however, is the innocent Sunshine, a girl so exasperatingly naive that she sews real pearls into a dress for display, thinking they are fake. Sunshine eventually persuades the crooks to reform. Collins tells Helen he will quit his life of crime and marry her, and as she rushes to him, overwhelmed at his proposal, he barks back: "Listen! I ain't buying you nothing. I'm just gonna marry you."

Variety said,

> Chaney as Chuck Collins, one of the crook leaders,
> is a consummate actor, in this as well as in character
> or otherwise. And at least in *The Big City*, Chaney

> accepted a story he knew he'd fit. . . . To insure
> attention to *The Big City*, the heavy publicity should
> be placed upon Chaney as himself, without disguise,
> just to see the difference. It's quite a different
> Chaney, and finely supported.

Photoplay commented, "Lon Chaney and Betty Compson [are] re-united in a crook story in which Lon proves that he needs no trick make-up to make him a fascinating person."

Taking advantage of his relative freedom from grotesque make-up, harnesses, glass eyes and the like, Lon often relaxed between scenes by dancing to tunes played by Sam and Jack Feinberg, Lon's set musicians since *The Hunchback of Notre Dame*. Between scenes, Sam, Jack and Lon also enjoyed playing impromptu musical games. Lon would name a song, mostly from old musical comedies, and Sam and Jack would try to play it. They, in turn, would play a song and Lon would have to name it, and the loser bought lunch in the studio commissary.[154]

The Feinbergs were not just on the set for Lon's entertainment; set musicians were essential to the making of silent pictures. They provided the actors with music to fit the scene's mood; generally there were two or three musicians, playing a small portable organ, violin and sometimes a cello. In the early 1970's, Sam Feinberg accompanied silent films shown at the Encore Theatre, a revival house in Los Angeles. After screening Chaney's *The Monster*, Sam told the audience that when he and his brother worked with Lon Chaney, the actor would tell them what the mood of the scene was like and what kind of music he wanted to hear.[155]

Jack Feinberg's violin was his most treasured possession. On this violin anyone who was a star, director or featured player in Hollywood signed his or her autograph. Among those providing signatures are Lon Chaney, Greta Garbo, Douglas Fairbanks, Mary

Pickford, Tod Browning, Fred Niblo, Jack Conway, Buster Keaton, Roscoe Arbuckle, Joan Crawford, Jean Harlow, Tim McCoy, John Gilbert, Norma Shearer, Charles A. Lindberg, Einstein, Ripley (of *Believe It or Not* fame), Herbert Hoover and Franklin D. Roosevelt, to name a few. When former President Coolidge visited the M-G-M lot with his wife, Jack couldn't bring himself to ask for this formidable signature, so he recruited his very reluctant friend Lon Chaney to perform the task.[156] The violin recently was up for sale at a price of $50,000.

Jack and Sam Feinberg both appeared in films; Jack played his violin in an orchestra in Joan Crawford's 1927 *Taxi Dancer*, and in Lon's *While The City Sleeps*, both Sam and Jack can be glimpsed as passers-by.

Lon's next picture, *Laugh, Clown, Laugh*, had been a successful play on Broadway with Lionel Barrymore in the lead role. The play was purchased as a Chaney vehicle, and its screen version began a seven-week filming schedule on December 19, 1927, under Herbert Brennon's direction. The cast included 14-year-old Loretta Young as Simonette, the young girl Lon adopts and eventually falls in love with, and Nils Asther as Lon's rival, the Count.

Chaney played Tito, a popular clown of Italy. While camping in the woods, Tito and his partner, Simon, find an abandoned girl whom Tito adopts and names Simonette. Years later, when she has grown into a beautiful woman, Tito trains her to do a wire walk act. He realizes he has fallen in love with the young woman and cannot control his crying. He seeks out a doctor who suggests he sees the circus and laugh at the famous clown, Flick. "I *am* Flick," he replies. Another patient, Count Luigi, is there to see the doctor because of his uncontrollable laughing. Luigi and Tito conclude that each might help the other's problem. Unfortunately when the Count meets Simonette, he falls as deeply in love with her as Tito had. Tito finally realizes, even after Simonette pledges her love to him before a statue of the Virgin Mary, that he is standing in the way of the young couple's happiness. In a fit of despair, he yells at himself "Laugh, Clown, Laugh!" and sacrifices himself in his slide-for-life high wire act so Simonettte may marry the Count.

Photoplay said, "This is the best work of Lon Chaney since *The Unholy Three*, and it is a great relief to have him minus his usual sinister make-up. His characterization of Tito Flick is perfect."

Variety agreed:

> Another romantic play with a semi-tragic finale, the fortunes of which are always anybody's guess. In this case, Lon Chaney as the star should be almost an insurance of a draw. Star's name value is the film's best asset. . . . Chaney does some splendid acting as the clown who makes the world laugh while his heart is breaking with a vain love. Sentiment sometimes gets a bit sloppy, but this actor always has the situation in hand and carries through some passages that call for dainty treatment and nice judgment.

The movie received a nomination at the first ceremony of the Academy Awards in the field of "Best Title Writing" for 1927-28. This was the only year this category would be given an award due to the birth of sound.

Laugh, Clown, Laugh was accompanied by a theme song of the same title, written by Ted Fiorito with lyrics by Lewis and Young. The song, one of Lon's personal favorites, went on to become one of the biggest hits of 1928; it was recorded by many artists, most notably Fred Waring's Pennsylvanians.

Lon appeared on the sheet music in his clown make-up, termed by circus clowns a "grotesque whiteface" (more elaborate) make-up, as compared to the "neat whiteface" he wore in *He Who Gets Slapped*. In the early scenes of the film, Lon used a lighter base make-up to help soften his face and give a more youthful look. Throughout the rest of the film, he is seen as an aging man of middle years with his hair grayed; the use of highlights and shadows give the impression of age.

Probably because of his early mastery of screen tests, Chaney knew almost as much about the technical points of cinematography as the men behind the camera. James Wong Howe, a cameraman on *Laugh, Clown, Laugh* recalled in 1974, "[Chaney] was the only actor I knew that could stand in front of the camera, and no matter what lens I told him I put on the camera, he could give me the sidelines at any distance from the camera. He knew exactly."[157]

In February of 1928, M-G-M and Chaney hammered out an agreement to do a fifth picture during his yearly contract. As a result of this new arrangement, Lon received not only his weekly salary, but also a $25,000 bonus. Three weeks later the studio also agreed to exercise another contract renewal option, with his weekly salary raised to $3,500.[158]

Easy Money, a police drama, began shooting on April 12 under Jack Conway's direction. When the film was released in October of 1928, the title had been changed to *While the City Sleeps* and boasted synchronized sound effects and a musical score for theatres equipped to handle the new sound pictures.

In the film, Chaney played Dan, a tough New York City detective who is always swearing he is going to quit the force. "You go through life with fallen arches, and wind up with your name on a brass plate," he complains to fellow officers. He suspects a gang led by a crook named Skeeter to be responsible for a jewelry heist and murder, and becomes even more determined to arrest Skeeter when he learns that the gangster has eyes for Myrtle, a naive flapper whom Dan admires from afar. Skeeter plans to murder Myrtle's boyfriend

Marty, so he can make his move on the young flapper. Dan saves the boy's life and defeats the gangster's plan. Meanwhile, Skeeter tries to seduce Myrtle at a night club, but is thwarted in his attempts when Dan and other officers arrive to arrest him. In escaping, Skeeter kills a police officer in front of Myrtle and plans to kill her so she cannot finger him. Dan hides her at his apartment until Skeeter is caught, and while staying with him, Dan proposes to her. She accepts his offer out of gratitude but she still loves Marty. Acting on a tip, Dan and other officers catch up with Skeeter and his gang in a fiery shoot-out, killing Skeeter and most of his mob. When Dan returns to his apartment, he realizes that Myrtle truly loves Marty and re-unites the two young lovers.

Although today *While The City Sleeps* is considered one of Chaney's best films at M-G-M, *Variety* didn't like it at all:

> To begin with, Lon Chaney doesn't do at all in the
> semi-heroic role. You can't disassociate him from
> something monstrous and all the bizarre characters
> he has ever played come up to confront the
> spectator. Good judgment ought to have barred
> Chaney from the role in the first place. Therefore, a
> misplaced star turns what might have been a stirring
> meller into second grade quality program output,
> wholly dependent on Chaney's name.

While *Variety* didn't care for the film, business at the box-office was brisk (earning over $1 million dollars in world-wide receipts), and other magazines voiced different thoughts. *Time* said, "Lon Chaney as a very plainclothes detective with bunions strides painfully through a convincing picture about bad men and a good girl." *Photoplay* quipped, "Now and then Lon Chaney tosses his make-up kit over the fence and acts like a human being . . . proving that an occasional straight role is fine balance for big character actors. He gives a remarkable characterization of a tough dick. A well-knit story, exceptionally cast and directed."

The Film Society of Screen Actors Guild held a special screening of the film in September of 1992 with co-star Anita Page (accompanied by actor Randal Malone) as the guest of honor. Shortly after the event, Miss Page recounted her memories of working with Lon:

> Lon had seen my performance in *Our Dancing Daughters* and recommended me for the part of Myrtle in *While the City Sleeps*. He later told me he was so impressed by the use of my eyes to express my emotions in the film and that was why he requested me. I was so busy going from one film to another I didn't realize at that time what an honor it was to be requested to work with Lon Chaney.

> I remember once Lon and I talked about how your facial features had to be beautiful photographically, but your 'story' was told with your eyes. He once said 'the eyes are windows of the soul' and he was so right in that. His eyes had a very sharp look, very startling — you found yourself looking at them.

> Lon was as fascinating with his own face as he was with some of his make-ups. The real Lon Chaney was one fascinating man. I thought he was fantastic in *The Hunchback of Notre Dame* and in *Phantom of the Opera*. Look at today—look at the big hit musical play. Part of its popularity goes back to Chaney's performance. He was the original. Of

course, *he was an original*. Who else do you know who could play the roles like he did?

I don't recall Thalberg ever coming down to the set during production. He didn't have to on this one. I remember he came down to the set alot on *Broadway Melody* [the first all-talking musical] because it was a new venture. Chaney knew what he was doing, as we all did and it [the production] pretty much ran itself. My favorite scene in the film is when Lon asks me to marry him and we both have different reactions. [Chaney's being one of happiness, while Anita is heartsick over the offer.] He was a marvelous, fine, kind man but I think if you [as a director] tried to steer him wrong in a picture, he could take care of it like that! [and here she snapped her fingers for emphasis.]

Jack Conway [the director] was a real clown on the set, he loved to have fun. I don't recall Lon ever trying to tell Jack how to direct. The set was very relaxed and had a lot of comradery and I think he [Lon] had one heck of a good time on that picture. I don't remember any fussing or anything on the set. I enjoyed working with Lon and he never made me feel uncomfortable. He never stayed in character in between scenes on the set. He could go right into his scene without having to get worked up. He never gave me any advice on my make-up but he did approve of what I did in applying it. I found him very interesting to talk to. We'd talk about things that were of interest to him, especially acting. He

was so easy to work with. He was a natural born
actor. I admired him a lot.

When I saw him the other night in the film, I
thought "You know, he wasn't so bad looking!" He
was attractive in his own way — he had a certain
ruggedness. When I worked with him I didn't
appreciate him as much as I do now. I mean I
appreciated his work and art, but as for looks I
thought he was a nice older man. But then I was
going out with people like Bill Haines and Roman
Novarro and never gave Lon Chaney a second
thought to how handsome he was. But now after
seeing the film again I'm struck by how attractive he
really was![159]

In a 1970 interview, Carroll Nye, who portrayed Marty, had
similar recollections of Lon at the time:

I found him to be a modest, rather quiet man who
always strove for complete perfection in his roles.
He was most helpful to me, but not the type of man
you'd get chummy with. He kept pretty much to
himself, and didn't stand around telling jokes or
making up lies. He commanded your respect
because of his skills and obvious sincerity.[160]

Lon was coached for his role in *While The City Sleeps* by Lt. Roy
Harlacher of the Los Angeles Police Department, who showed him
every aspect of police work from fingerprinting to firing a police-
issue shotgun. It was a role that suited Lon perfectly. He was an
honorary member of many police departments as well as a strong

advocate of prison reform and fair and humane treatment of those "inside the walls." His interest in prison inmates may have stemmed from the obvious affection prisoners had for him. Many men behind bars wrote to him, and here Lon broke his long-standing rule regarding answering fan mail. He replied to every letter he got from a convict, and often helped ex-cons find work when they were released from prison. For five years, each Christmas and birthday, a box of stationery with Lon's name engraved on it came from Chicago. There was no name or return address on the box and Lon believed it might have come from a fellow who did a term in stir, and had since found an honest trade.[161]

In January of 1930, Lon wrote a lengthy article that appeared in *Island Lantern* magazine published at the U. S. Penitentiary at McNeil Island, Washington. Entitled "Wanted: New Medicine," the article discussed the need for better rehabilitation programs for prisoners and reads in part:

> We are proud of our rehabilitation, such as it is, of
> our wounded soldiers, but we have done nothing
> toward rehabilitating our lawbreakers. I believe that
> the state should support a form of rehabilitating
> bureau to help men leaving prison to useful work, a
> chance to make good, and thus give each and every
> prisoner an incentive to avoid lapses from the law. It
> is a basic fact that in every man is an inherent desire
> to be a respected member of society. Shown the
> opportunity and the means, in nine cases out of ten
> he'll do so. But our present system of turning a
> prisoner out with a small bill, a suit of prison clothes
> — and a tip to the police that he's at liberty again,
> certainly can't be said to help that prisoner along
> the "straight and narrow."

To sum up, my idea, as an observer, of effective
prison work leading to better observance of laws,
would embrace the following points:

Segregation of prisoners, and corrective education.

Indeterminate sentences, coupled with an effective
scheme for state rehabilitation, furnishing a goal
toward which each man should work.

Educational work in prisons, trades instruction and
interesting labor. Give the jute mill and the stone
pile to him who deserves it, for instance; give
constructive work to the man who will profit by it.

Administration of prisons by specialists, trained for
this important work, and not fettered by politics.
Like our schools, our prisons should be entirely
removed from the influence of politicians.

And don't class any man as a permanent danger to
society until all efforts at rehabilitation have failed —
and then, I think, you'll find that the "failure" is a
case for a psychiatrist rather than a penologist — or
the real subject for the jute mill and rock pile.

Underlying it all is just one thing — a square deal.

The Golden Rule is still a splendid old idea that
doesn't get old-fashioned. And man still is his
brother's keeper.

Lon Chaney

Filming on *While the City Sleeps* was completed on May 19, and a week later Lon and Hazel left Los Angeles Central Train Station for a visit to New York City. At this time, Herbert Voight was working at the M-G-M offices in New York, and part of his job included arranging hotel rooms, transportation and escorting the studio stars to interviews, parties, or shows. In 1985, Voight recalled the Chaneys' trip:

> Lon was courteous enough to inform me in advance of when he was arriving and told me what he wanted to do. He and his wife arrived at Grand Central station and when we got out of the limo at the Warrick Hotel where they were staying, a passing taxi driver saw Lon and yelled "Hey, step on him! It's Lon Chaney!" I had first met Lon in the summer of 1926 when I visited the studio in Culver City and he was making *Tell It To The Marines*. He was a very gentle man, no pose about him. When he was working, there was a no-nonsense attitude about him. That's where he might have given the impression that he was hard to direct, but from my personal viewpoint he wasn't that way at all. He was a very intelligent actor and was respected by everyone on the lot. While he was never very chummy with Garbo, they shared a nice comradery with each other.
>
> When we were driving in the limo to go to meet New York's Mayor [Jimmy] Walker, we were at a traffic light and next to us was another limo with a very stuffy-looking man in the back seat, who just happened to be U. S. Supreme Court Judge Charles

Evans Hughes. When he looked over at us and saw Lon Chaney in the car next to him, he waved and yelled like a kid, telling Lon how much he liked his films. Lon got a great kick out of it and laughed like hell.

He and his wife were a delightful couple and one night I took them to Texas Guinan's nightclub where she and the Chaneys spent a lot of time recalling their days in musical comedy troupes. Lon was never a heavy drinker but, my God, he was a constant smoker.

One of Lon's requests was to sit in the night court in the Tombs, which was the city prison outside of Greenwich Village. City Police Commissioner Enright, who knew Lon, offered him a chance to sit with the judges, but Lon declined and preferred to sit in the audience virtually unrecognized by the crooks and whores and other criminals. He was terribly fascinated by watching them and studying them for a possible characterization.[162]

While Lon was visiting New York, he and Hazel attended ten stage shows and on June 3, 1928, he told Lewis L. Nichols of the *New York Times* that he was letting "Mrs. Chaney spend some of my money." He gave the reporter probably one of his most engaging interviews, including his thoughts about retirement, which in retrospect seem somewhat ironic:

"But I don't know," he remarked just a shade mournfully. "I'm afraid that when the time comes I will never be able to do it. There is something about this that is like a disease, and I suppose I never will be able to stop. I would like to retire and get away, but probably won't."

Regarding the "disease" of work, he cited an example of the picture he had just made, *While the City Sleeps.* A detective of the old school is the hero, a cantankerous man who goes to work each day vowing that he will quit at night. He does nothing but curse the Police Department — yet he sticks to his job. Life is like that, Mr. Chaney thinks, and the things you are most derogatory about you like the best.

In his article, Nichols also mentioned Lon's hobby of taking home-movies with his 16mm camera. Aside from the traditional family records, Lon had amassed tremendous footage of wildlife from his trips to the mountains. (He claimed that humming birds were the hardest wildlife subject to photograph.) Of greater interest to the historian are the many reels of film Lon shot of the various guests who visited M-G-M yearly. He liked to capture these guests off-guard. In a profile article, Lon told the *American Cinematographer* that famous visitors came to the studio and he wanted to have a personal record of them.[163] One celebrity he was particularly proud of catching on film was Prince William of Sweden.

Some of Lon's home movies still exist in the collection of William Dunphy's grandson. In one vignette, Lon, Hazel, and the Dunphys are shown vacationing at Saboba Springs and Saratoga. Lon playfully picks up his wire-haired terrier Sandy by the tail, kisses Hazel while hiding behind his cap and then, in a very hammy fashion, picks a bud from a tree and pretends to eat it. Another sequence shows the Chaneys and Dunphys at Lon's home, playing with Sandy in the backyard. Lon tickles Hazel and playfully slaps her on the behind, taking off her shoes to show her tiny feet to the camera. Hazel then tries to enlist the aid of Sandy to "attack" Lon but the dog fails to even get up from where he sits. Lon used title cards in these home movies to help tell the viewer what was going on. In one shot we can see Lon preparing to film some of these title cards, showing them off to a visiting friend. Even in these films, Lon Chaney the actor upstages Lon Chaney the man.

On their return trip from New York, Lon and Hazel stopped in Colorado Springs on the afternoon of June 11th and registered at the Antlers Hotel. They spent the rest of the day visiting old friends like Harry Hughes before returning to Los Angeles the following day.[164] This was to be Lon's last trip to his hometown.

On June 25, 1928, Lon started production on *West of Zanzibar*, based on the stage play *Kongo*. Lionel Barrymore, Warner Baxter (in a role originally intended for Owen Moore) and Mary Nolan supported Chaney in the ninth — and one of the best — of the Chaney-Browning collaborations. In 1932, M-G-M remade the film under its original title, *Kongo*, with Walter Huston reprising his Broadway role. The film used some footage from *West of Zanzibar*, including a scene where Lon (wearing a witch doctor mask) crawls out to officiate at a native ceremony.

Chaney plays Phroso, an English music hall magician who is paralyzed after a fight with Crane, his wife's lover. A year later his wife returns with a child, dying before Phroso can reach her. He works his way to Africa, where Crane has gone to trade for ivory. Phroso hates Maizie, the little girl, whom he believes to have been fathered by Crane, and has her raised in the worst dives in Zanzibar. Eighteen years later Phroso, known to the natives as "White Voodoo" because of his ability at magic, puts his plot for revenge into action.

Maizie, now an adult, is brought to Phroso's jungle compound to meet the father she never knew, and Crane is summoned as well. Phroso plans to have Crane killed by the natives, and according to their customs, when a father dies and is cremated, his first born daughter or wife must meet the same fate. At the climactic moment, however, Crane relates that Maizie is actually Phroso's daughter, not Crane's. The natives carry out the execution of Crane and Phroso must use one of his old magic tricks, at the expense of his own life, to save his daughter.

Variety was not impressed:

> Weird atmospheric effects will get this by as a straight one or two-day program attraction. Lon Chaney's name must do the rest. . . . *West of Zanzibar* indicates an over-worked Chaney. The star is there, but the rush of getting his quota on the release schedule is taking its toll in the most important phase of production — preparation. In this respect, Chaney's latest impresses as having exhausted the property men and the casting director and allowing Tod Browning to follow religiously one of those cuff scripts.

Motion Picture Classic was a little more positive:

> Lon Chaney is back at his old gruesome habits. This time he's a thing that crawls, dragging himself around on the palms of his hands with his useless legs behind him. And very convincing, too.

During production, Lon was outfitted in a "duck suit," giving the appearance of a half-man, half-duck. The scene of Lon as this bogus "duck-man" at a sideshow was cut from the film. Browning used the "duck suit" for the chilling climax of his 1932 feature *Freaks*, where the circus freaks turn Olga Baclanova into a "duck woman." Also cut from the final print were several scenes showing how Chaney and his group get to Africa. In one such sequence, Chaney crawls into a bar on a wheeled platform begging for handouts. When Doc, played by Warner Baxter, tells the panhandler to beat it, Chaney ignores him. Doc and another man, Babe, pick up Chaney and throw him through a glass window of the saloon, replying they don't like cripples. This brutal response on their part instills sympathy from the other bar patrons who toss Chaney money. The next scene showed Chaney, Doc, and Babe counting and splitting up the money their ruse had collected.

In late December, 1928, Lon started work on *Where East Is East*, the tenth and final picture made with director Tod Browning. The film, Lon's first release for 1929, is considered to be the poorest of their collaborative efforts.

Set in Indo-China, Lon played Tiger Haynes, a wild animal trapper for the circus, with the scars and claw marks on his face to prove it. Tiger's daughter Toyo, (played by Lupe Velez) is about to marry Bobby, the son of an American circus owner who often employed Tiger. Happiness abounds in the family until the return of Tiger's ex-wife, who had deserted her daughter and husband years earlier. After seducing Bobby, she is finally done in by a gorilla Tiger set free. At the urging of his daughter, Tiger tries to save his ex-wife, but he is too late. He himself is mortally wounded, living only long enough to see his daughter and Bobby happily married.

The film is a great disappointment to the record of successes the two men had racked up over the years, especially considering their previous hit, *West of Zanzibar*. One has to question the studio's judgement in producing this film. With the transition to talking pictures causing such an upheaval, studio executives may have felt that any picture with Chaney's name on it would make money. Additionally, Tod Browning's films were generally produced on schedule with a relatively economical budget.

However, reviews at the time weren't all that bad. "Gather round, folks, for another Chaney bedtime story — something with a touch of Kipling and Poe. . . . Chaney is excellent and Lupe Velez lends fiery aid," commented *Photoplay.*

And *Variety* wrote,

> Most of these Chaneys [pictures] make money, some, of course, being better than others. *Where East Is East*, despite its trite title confusingly like many others from the Chaney factory, is one of the better efforts. But you must like Chaney to like his pictures. This one is silent besides. . . . Chaney himself is rather subordinated, with the picture belonging to Estelle Taylor and Lupe Velez."

Variety's implication that *Where East Is East*'s silent format lowers its box-office appeal seems to have been lost on Lon. While other actors and actresses rushed to the recording booth to see if they would be able to make the transition to talking pictures, Lon publicly refused to make the change. Rumors began to fly about his steadfast refusal, one of the cruelest being that Lon was deaf like his parents.

In late February, 1929, with the studio making more than half of their films as "all-talking pictures," Chaney started work on what was to be his last silent film. In *Thunder* he portrayed "Grumpy" Anderson, a veteran Chicago-Northwestern railroad engineer who is determined to bring his train in on time no matter what. This single-mindedness alienates him from his son Tommy, a train fireman who blames his father for the death of his brother who was killed in the railyards after working an overly long shift. While driving the train that carries his son's coffin, Grumpy and Tommy get into a heated argument and do not see another train crossing their path until it is too late. The resulting wreck relegates Grumpy to the locomotive machine shop where he gets a chance to oversee the repair of his old engine. Meanwhile, heavy rains in the South have caused tremendous flooding and stranded hundreds of people, including Grumpy's daughter-in-law, grandson, and Tommy's new girlfriend, Zella. The Red Cross puts out a call for trains to run relief, and Grumpy and his engine are drafted into action. With Tommy as his fireman, Grumpy plows ahead, even when told the train tracks are under four feet of water. "Well, any place there's a track, pardner. . . I ride!" he tells them, and drives his train through the flood waters to rescue the stranded people.

In his role as Grumpy, Lon came up with a simple yet very effective make-up to portray someone in his 60's. He grew his own moustache and then grayed it (and his eyebrows) using either aluminum powder or a hair-whitener called Masque. Masque came in cake form and was applied with a toothbrush moistened with either water or brilliantine (a hair-styling gel). Aluminum powder had a better look to it on film, but was very difficult to wash out of the hair. Also, if any of the powder got on the make-up, it would darken and could not be brushed off.

Lon used the basic principles of highlights and shadows to age himself, drawing fine lines and wrinkles with either an eyebrow pencil or a fine-tip brush and liner color. This gave Lon an enhanced appearance of aging and a certain amount of texture to the face. This procedure, along with the basics of highlights and shadows, is still used by make-up artists today. Lon also shaved the front of his own hairline to accommodate the lace-front white wig which blended into his own hair just above the ears, and he then greyed the rest of his hair to match the color of his wig.

Filming began on March 3 at the Chicago and Northwestern Railroad yards in Green Bay, Wisconsin. On March 9, the studio sent a telegram to Lon at Hotel Northland, notifying him that they were picking up the third yearly option on his contract for $3,750 a week.[165]

While on location, Lon caught a cold which progressed into walking pneumonia. Pictures taken behind the scenes show that filming in Green Bay was extremely cold compared to the spring-like climate of Southern California. Lon kept working despite his illness, even after returning to finish filming at the M-G-M studio. "He would keep working even if he was sick," Anita Page said referring to Lon's trouper spirit.[166] By April 28, Lon's fever was so high that his physician, Dr. John C. Webster, ordered him to cease work and go to bed to rest. Four days later, newspapers reported his fever had broken and he was on the road to recovery.[167] Lon went back to work May 13 and finished the film ten days later. The picture required two additional days of retakes (May 29 and June 3) before it was released on July 8, 1929.[168] While no prints of the film are known to exist, the synchronized musical tracks are stored in the M-G-M film vaults.

The train rushing through flood waters was filmed with model trains in a miniature set. Lamar D. Tabb said that when he saw the film in its original release in Dayton, Ohio, the audience jumped up and cheered when Chaney drove the train through the flooded tracks and saved the people.[169] Railroad workers were equally enthusiastic; Lon was presented with an honorary membership in the Brotherhood of Locomotive Engineers for his performance in *Thunder*.

The film received mixed reviews, with *Variety* commenting, "Second Lon Chaney picture lately with that player of bizarre roles doing a straight character old man. Poor stuff from all angles . . . Chaney fans don't want him as a semi-comic, semi-heroic old man."

Photoplay wrote,

> Don't be skeptical. Lon Chaney actually drives that
> engine and, if you don't believe it, he'll show you
> his honorary membership in the brotherhood. His
> only disguise is grey hair and a moustache. As usual,
> he turns in a sturdy performance. . . . Snow storms,
> train wrecks and floods. Good entertainment.

Just before his doctor ordered him to go home to rest, another
Chaney vehicle was being prepared, possibly as a talking picture. A
memo to Louis B. Mayer, dated April 29, 1929, from studio manager
M. E. Greenwood read,

> One of the things Lon Chaney was extremely
> concerned about yesterday was why Stallings should
> be writing dialogue on the Foreign Legion, when
> nothing has been said to Lon as to whether he
> would consent to talk. His contract does not provide
> for his talking. I avoided this by telling him that so
> far as I knew, Stallings was working on the
> continuity only.[170]

The script of the Foreign Legion picture mentioned in the memo
was based on a novel entitled *The Bugle Sounds* by Major Linovi
Pechkoff who had written about his exploits with the Legion during
the North African campaigns. Laurence Stallings, who had written the
play *What Price Glory?* and the screenplay of *The Big Parade* was
under contract to the studio and may have contributed to the script,
but A. P. Younger, writer of *While the City Sleeps*, was given credit
for "continuity writing" when *The Bugle Sounds* received script

approval in June, 1929. During the silent era, writers were referred to as "continuity writers;" in the early days of talkies, they became known as "continuity and dialogue writers."

The Hollywood Revue of 1929 was released by M-G-M in June, and every star and feature player on the lot — excluding Lon and Greta Garbo — appeared in the film, which consisted of musical numbers and skits to show off their vocal talents. The balcony scene from *Romeo and Juliet* was shot in Technicolor, with John Gilbert and Norma Shearer. The film was made during the "graveyard shift" of 7 p.m. to 7 a.m., since most of the stars were working on other films.[171] A possible reason Lon did not appear in this film, aside from his contract not requiring him to talk on screen, is that his appearance might have constituted one of his four-pictures-per contract year. If that was the case, the studio obviously would make more money on a regular Chaney feature instead of a brief appearance in this production. While Lon did not appear in the film, Jack Benny introduced a musical number called *Lon Chaney's Gonna Get You If You Don't Watch Out* in which Gus Edwards performed. Ann Dvorak, who later became a popular actress in the 1930's, was one of the dancers in this number.

In reviewing the film *Variety* noted,

> Ditty devoted to Chaney has Gus Edwards lyrically
> warning a dozen bedtime girls with as many boys
> entrancing wearing hideous masks, picking up the
> girls and the entire ensemble disappearing below on
> a big trap door, through which clouds of steam
> ascend. Finish of this was a perfect spot for Chaney
> to have appeared immaculately dressed to take a
> bow if nothing more, but report is he refused to
> appear in the picture. He muffed a great bit.

Lon's refusal to make the jump to talking pictures continued to fuel the rumor fires. The latest gossip in Hollywood fan magazines was that Lon Chaney was too ill to make another film. Unfortunately, this was proving to be all too true, for while he recovered enough to be able to finish *Thunder*, the bout with pneumonia had depleted his strength. "When I worked with him I had no idea he would be so sick a year later. He seemed so strong," Anita Page recalled.[172] On July 25, 1929, the studio suspended Lon's contract — and his paycheck — until he could return to work. [173]

The next year was to be a trying time for everyone — including Lon Chaney.

(Overleaf) "Lon Chaney's Gonna Get You" number from the *Hollywood Review of 1929*. Gus Edwards stands in the center.

(Above) Lon is introduced to Irving Berlin by director Herbert Brennon,
during a visit to the set of *Laugh, Clown, Laugh*.
(Right) *Laugh, Clown, Laugh* (1928)

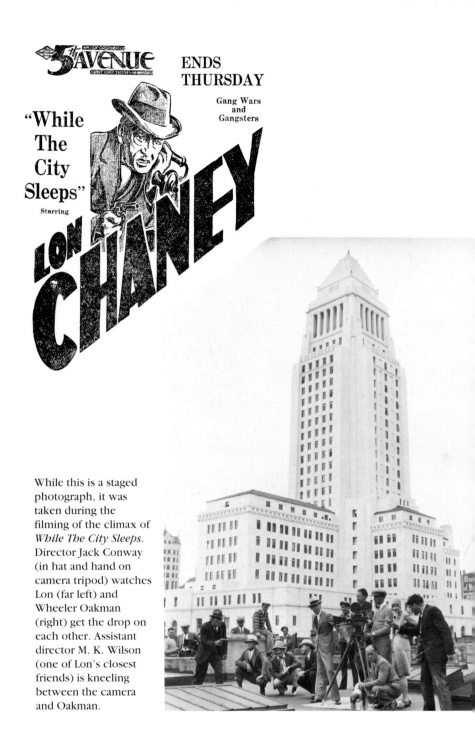

5th AVENUE

ENDS THURSDAY

Gang Wars
and
Gangsters

"While
The
City
Sleeps"

Starring

LON CHANEY

While this is a staged photograph, it was taken during the filming of the climax of *While The City Sleeps*. Director Jack Conway (in hat and hand on camera tripod) watches Lon (far left) and Wheeler Oakman (right) get the drop on each other. Assistant director M. K. Wilson (one of Lon's closest friends) is kneeling between the camera and Oakman.

244

(Right) As the tough detective in *While the City Sleeps.* (Below) Left to right, director Edward Sedgwick, Anita Page, Lon, Polly Moran, Buster Keaton, and director Jack Conway. Sedgwick and Keaton were visiting the *While The City Sleeps* set during production of their film *The Cameraman.*

(Above Left) Lon arriving in Los Angeles, June 14, 1928, from his trip to New York City.

(Above Right) *West of Zanzibar* (1928)

(Right, top picture) Tod Browning with Lon in the "duck suit" costume. This sequence was cut from the final release print of *West of Zanzibar*. Browning later used the costume in the finale of his 1932 film *Freaks*.

(Right, lower picture) Tod Browning (kneeling) directs Lon in a scene from *West Of Zanzibar*. Sam and Jack Feinberg can be seen to the right.

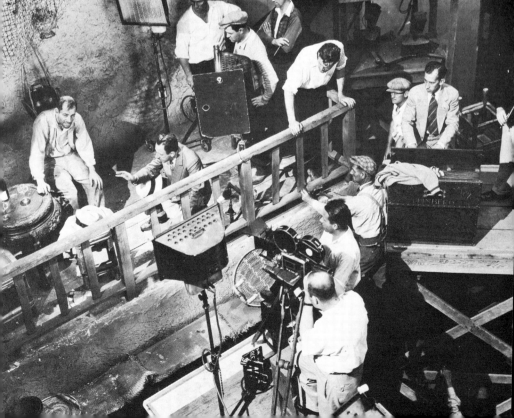

Where East Is East (1929)

Lon with cameramen Henry Sharp and Charles Strummar on location for *Thunder* in Green Bay, Wisconsin.

(Below) This picture shows just how cold it was on location for *Thunder*. During this film Lon caught a cold which later developed into walking pneumonia.

Thunder (1929)

Lon Chaney Talks!

(1929-1930)

"The chief thing for any actor to remember is that it wasn't his brains that got him to stardom, it was only his acting."
                                        —*Lon Chaney*

Even with his contract suspended, silent films were still being planned for Lon. Aside from *The Bugle Sounds*, another script, *Brother Officers,* was also in the works. The story would feature Lon as Sgt. Major John Hinds of the British Army 10th Lancers, who forms a close friendship with a younger officer. One of the script's writers was Lt. Commander Frank "Spig" Wead who held many flight records in the early days of naval aviation. When he was left paralyzed from a freak fall at home, he turned to writing scripts, mostly with military themes, and later became close friends with director John Ford for whom he wrote the script for his 1945 film, *They Were Expendable*.

All film projects, however, had to wait until Lon recovered. In 1929 Lon and Hazel spent the summer months with William and Mabel Dunphy in a rented cabin at Brook Dale Lodge near Boulder Creek in the Santa Cruz mountains of Northern California.

William Dunphy's grandson said his mother remembered Lon as "not feeling well physically but taking his condition without complaining." He said his mother and Lon often played a card game called "Russian Bank," either one-on-one or in a group. She said Chaney occasionally drank hard liquor but never to excess. When the Chaneys visited the Dunphys in San Francisco, they stayed at the city's best hotels (usually the St. Francis) and they often went to a Columbus Avenue night club called The Bal Tavern. She recalls that Hazel, whom she described as "very friendly and outgoing," took a

Lon Chaney

Hawaiian vacation with Mabel Dunphy, leaving San Francisco by ocean liner the day the stock market crashed.[174]

Adela Rogers St. John said that in September, Lon went into a Los Angeles hospital to have his tonsils removed.[175] He had a recurring cough and was evidently experiencing throat irritation which he hoped surgery would eliminate. Over the years it has been reported by various writers that Lon had his tonsils removed and then went directly into production of *Thunder*, where, during a snowstorm scene, a piece of artificial snow lodged in the unhealed portion of his throat, causing his death. However, the facts at hand do not support this story.

An October 1, 1929, memo to Thalberg from M. E. Greenwood stated:

> On account of incapacity, Lon's contract has been suspended since July 25, 1929. We have the right to extend for the time of his incapacity.
>
> Lon saw me Saturday morning and said that he had notified you that he was still sick and not ready to work; and that he was leaving on a trip to be gone for possibly six weeks.
>
> If the above coincides with his notice to you, will you please initial this memorandum so that there may be no question whatsoever about the term of his incapacity?

Thalberg's reply to the memo: "He told me 4 weeks."

According to Lon's death certificate, about this time Lon's illness became much more serious than originally thought. The diagnosis was cancer of the upper and lower right bronchus, no doubt from his years of smoking.

Lon had been scheduled to be a master of ceremonies at a November 23 benefit at the Los Angeles Philharmonic Auditorium The special event, entitled *The Deaf Mute Howls*, was organized to help author Albert Ballin raise funds for the publication of his book making sign language available to both the deaf and the hearing public. This obviously would have been a cause dear to Lon's heart, but because of his health, he had to cancel his appearance.

Milton Cohen, Lon's attorney, and Louis B. Mayer reached an agreement in early November, 1929, that Lon return to work as of January 2, 1930, to continue the fulfillment of his contract. It had been suspended for a total of twenty-three weeks. The two men were also working on a new contract which called for Lon to make talking pictures. This deal was called off because Lon demanded a cash bonus of $150,000 to speak on film.[176]

The studio took the position that they would not pay any bonus until they had proof Lon's voice would register successfully. Because contract negotiations were called off, M-G-M decided to have Lon continue making silent films and notified him of their decision.[177] This might have been a negotiation tactic used by the studio; however, they were no doubt aware that making silent films was a losing proposition, regardless of the strength of Chaney's box-office draw.

Although Lon's contracts seem surprisingly generous for the 1920's, they contain a number of clauses that might strike the modern reader as strange. All of Lon's contracts stipulated he would only work reasonable hours, but if an emergency came up, he could be compelled to work however long the studio deemed necessary. He also had to furnish his own wardrobe (a common clause in most contracts of actors in that era) if it were modern dress; the studio would supply the wardrobe if it were a character or period role. Also in this contract, the studio was not allowed to issue photographs of him without make-up unless he appeared that way in a film. However the contract did not state Lon had photograph approval.[178]

Unlike many stars of his day, Lon never asked for, nor received, script approval on any of his films. He was of the opinion that if the studio gave him a bad picture it would cost them money, so he trusted their judgement. In an interview with Ruth Waterbury, he said:

> People seem to have the impression I study scripts
> all the time. I don't. I don't even try to find stories
> for myself like some stars. I wouldn't know where to
> look for them and I probably would not recognize
> them if I found them. I trust my
> producers to look out for my good. All I want to
> know is what the character is like and what
> emotions rule him. It takes me two to four weeks to
> work out a make-up for a new picture. That set, I
> don't worry.
>
> The chief thing for any actor to remember is that it
> wasn't his brains that got him to stardom. It was
> only his acting. He isn't paid to think about
> production plans and when he starts he usually sinks
> his whole career.[179]

Despite Lon's stated intention to stay out of "production planning," one of the reasons he resisted making talking pictures was his feeling that the problems connected with recording sound had not yet been properly worked out. No doubt another reason may have been that make-ups such as *The Hunchback of Notre Dame* or

Phantom of the Opera would now be literally impossible for him to implement; he would not be able to put anything in his mouth that would restrict his ability to speak.

A third advantage of silents over talkies was their universality; no matter what language picture-goers understood or even whether they were able to hear at all, silent films could be enjoyed by people all over the world, including, of course, deaf people. No doubt Lon was aware that with the advent of talking pictures, the deaf would once again be shut out from this form of entertainment which the hearing world took for granted. There has been much speculation that this might have been a particular reason he was a hold-out when it came to making talking pictures.

In addition, Lon was concerned that dialogue would spoil the illusion of mystery he had built up. It made no sense to him to make up a face for a character and then use his own voice; rather, he wanted to speak as the character would speak, which was an even more demanding job.[180] Reading Lon's interviews even after he had made his first "talkie," one senses that he was trying to make the best of the situation, but he was not at all happy about it. His feelings are best summed up by his comments in "Chaney Talks!" by Harry Lang, which appeared in *Photoplay* in May, 1930:

> I hope they [the public] like my first talkie. If they
> do, that will be fine. But if they don't — well, it will
> do something to me. It will make me what I've
> never been since I went into pictures — a man
> whose sole interest is the money he's being paid.
> I'll just go ahead, making the required talkies under
> my contract terms, and collect my pay. And at the
> end of five years, I'll step out of the picture, and that
> will be all. I'll probably retire then, anyway. I'll have
> enough to take it easy.

M-G-M and Chaney's attorney resumed contract talks in late December. The new offer gave Lon a cash bonus of $25,000, plus salary increase options for five years, ranging from his current $3,750 a week to $11,250 a week. The studio also insisted that Lon submit to a voice test to satisfy their concerns before they would sign the contract.[181]

Lon agreed to all the conditions except the cash bonus. For that, he wanted $50,000. Louis B. Mayer countered with an offer to advance Lon $75,000, of which $25,000 would be considered a bonus and the balance repaid over a two-year period. If the studio failed to exercise the option for the second year, they would forfeit an additional $25,000.[182]

On January 11, 1930, Lon and his attorney met the studio manager, M. E. Greenwood, to sign the new contract. However, Lon was still holding out over the bonus clause, insisting that the $75,000 be considered a cash bonus and not be repaid. Greenwood, Louis B. Mayer, Lon, and his attorney held another conference, and Lon said that if he did not get the cash bonus, the deal was off. Mayer refused to budge, and Lon left the office with his attorney, saying he would never agree to the deal. That night, Lon received a telegram at his home on 203 North Mansfield Avenue, instructing him to report to the studio on Monday to director Jack Conway regarding wardrobe for *Sgt. Bull*, which indicated that the studio had reverted to their contingency plan of making silents.[183]

In *Sgt. Bull*, Lon was to play the title character, an officer in Her Majesty's Army, opening in 1912 India and climaxing in the trenches of World War I. The movie never went into production because of Irving Thalberg's intervention into Lon's contract negotiations. Louis B. Mayer usually did all of the negotiating of contracts at the studio, and this mediation on Thalberg's part was highly unusual. Thalberg had a great respect for Chaney's talent, and, no doubt, he realized

Chaney's value to the studio, not only because of his talent but because of his box-office draw.

Lon and Thalberg reached an agreement and signed the new contract on January 23. Lon would get a $50,000 bonus and another bonus of equal amount if the studio picked up the first of five yearly options. His salary in the first year remained at the current $3,750 a week, and he would receive yearly increases to $4,000, $7,500, $9,375 and $11,250 a week between 1931 and the expiration of the contract in 1935. He would make no more than four pictures a year, excluding foreign versions.[184] In the early days of sound, pictures were often filmed in Spanish and German for overseas distribution with many stars speaking their lines phonetically in a foreign language.[185] When Lon signed the contract, he and Thalberg shook hands on the agreement that if Lon's voice did not record well he would refund the $50,000 cash bonus.[186]

Lon took his voice test in February, and if he was worried about passing it, he needn't have been; his stage-trained voice reproduced beautifully, and now Irving Thalberg had to decide on a vehicle for Chaney's talking picture debut. He selected a remake of Lon's 1925 silent success *The Unholy Three*. The sound version allowed Lon to use not only his own voice, but also that of an elderly woman, a ventriloquist's dummy, a parrot, and a girl in the sideshow audience. Lon actually learned to do ventriloquism for the opening scenes of his act in the sideshow, and if the viewer watches carefully, he will see his lips move occasionally.

The father-and-son team of J. C. and Elliott Nugent were assigned to write the screenplay and Elliott Nugent played the role of Hector MacDonald, the innocent victim framed by the gang. Film historian Leonard Maltin said Nugent told him that they had a moviola (a screening device used by film editors to view the film) put in their office and simply went through the silent version scene by scene while they wrote the new script with dialogue.[187] Lila Lee played Rosie and Ivan Linow was cast as Hercules, the strongman. Harry Earles revived his role of the midget, Tweedledee.

Lon began production of the film on April 1, his 47th birthday. He completed filming on April 24, but during production he was out sick for two days. Harry Earles said that Lon was not feeling very well during filming, and at times seemed to be struggling just to get through the day.[188] Upon viewing photos from the film, Lon does appear to have a haggard look and certainly seems older than his 47 years.

The major differences between the silent version and the remake occur in the ending and in the courtroom scene which was was rewritten to show off Lon's vocal talents. Unlike the silent version where Echo (Chaney) jumps up from the courtroom audience and, by confessing, saves Hector, this time Echo takes the witness stand in his disguise as the elderly Mrs. O'Grady. During the intense questioning by the prosecuting attorney, Echo's voice cracks from the old lady to his natural voice. They attorney rips off the wig, exposing Echo who makes a full confession.

The ending of the film was originally copied from the silent version; Rosie goes back to see Echo at a sideshow and says she is willing to come back to him in gratitude for saving Hector's life. Echo, realizing she truly loves Hector, laughs off her offer. As she leaves, Echo throws his voice as the dummy in saying good-bye, then sits on the stage broken-hearted. As the crowd gathers around him, Echo recomposes himself and goes into his old act. He ends it by saying, "That's all there is to life — just a little laugh, a little tear." However, this ending was scrapped and a new one shot on April 30. In the new version, Hector and Rosie see Echo off on a train bound for prison. Rosie tells Echo she will wait for him to return, but he declines her proposal. As he boards the train, he calls out to Hector, "You better come over here and take care of this girl of yours!" As the train pulls away from the station, Echo stands on the back of the platform, waving good-bye as the screen fades to black.

In early June, the film had a sneak preview in the Pasadena area and was well received. Lon attended this preview and, as the theatre patrons were exiting the theatre, they spotted him with his wife in a limo and rushed toward him, cheering and applauding. It was reported that Lon smiled and waved at the crowd as the limo pulled away.[189]

The Unholy Three's official premiere took place on July 3 at the Capitol Theatre. While some critics preferred the silent version for its drama and suspense, Lon's performance and voice were praised. Mordaunt Hall of *The New York Times* said,

> Mr. Chaney has made a further contribution to the modern motion picture — although it may be a bit indelicate to mention it here. Like the two dozen students who swam the Hellespont and so ruined the beautiful legend forever, he has destroyed the effect of the phrase, "See your favorite actor; he speaks." For while others were loudly proclaiming the finding of a forgotten note, he quietly went fishing and came back with five. The industry will never be the same again.

On May 19, 1930, Lon signed a notarized affidavit swearing that all vocal reproductions of his voice in the film were really his, and at no time did anyone else substitute or double his voice. This document was used in connection with the film's publicity, to refute any suggestion that those widely differing voices could not possibly have issued from the same person.[190]

Photoplay picked the film, as well as Lon's performance, as one of the best of the month and reviewed, "The finest thing about this picture is that it discloses Lon Chaney's natural voice just exactly as it should be — deep, vibrant and perfectly poised. You'll get thrills-a-plenty." *Motion Picture Classic* magazine wrote, "Lon Chaney proves once and for all that his popularity is based upon skillful acting and not grotesque make-up." The film did well at the box-office even after Lon's death, earning over $980,000.

With the talking version of this film, Chaney proved he could now use his voice as well as facial and body gestures to convey emotions. Lon still used his face and body to make his characters work and with the addition of his voice, everything blended into a harmonious mixture that allowed Chaney, unlike some other silent screen actors, to make a very successful transition to talking pictures. When one considers the film projects M-G-M had planned for Chaney, or other pictures in which he could have appeared (such as *Grand Hotel*), it's tragic that his career was cut short and he was never able to do more than one talking picture.

Chaney plays the part of Echo with more of an edge than he had in the silent version. This is due in part to additional dialogue which allowed Chaney to give his character texture. In the sideshow scene at the beginning of the picture, Chaney plays Echo as an engaging, likeable performer. Later, in his dealings with the midget and strongman, he is curt and not afraid to give them a verbal lashing. Unlike the silent version, he does not treat them as his equals. At one point in the film Chaney says to them, "That's the trouble with you guys; you try to think."

Lon portrays Mrs. O'Grady as a loveable and kindly old grandmother. His uncanny ability to use his whole body to get into his character shines in a scene where Chaney stands behind a closed door, dressed as Echo, and speaks to Rosie and Hector as the old woman. Even though he is not in the Mrs. O'Grady disguise, he uses her facial and body gestures when he speaks in her voice. Lon said he discovered the best way to imitate the female voice was not by speaking in falsetto, but by speaking quietly and enunciating carefully.[191]

Lon Chaney had become the next-to-the-last star to make a talking picture, with Charles Chaplin being the sole hold-out. Critical and box-office success of *The Unholy Three* assured Lon's status as a star. M-G-M announced that his next project would be *Cheri-Bibi*, based on the novel by Gaston Leroux, author of *Phantom of the Opera*. *The Bugle Sounds* was also formally announced as an upcoming project for Lon.

Many writers have speculated that before his death, Lon was slated to do *Dracula* for Tod Browning at Universal. This is highly unlikely due to Lon's star status at the studio, as well as his new success in talking pictures. Universal made a request for Lon's services in 1929 to do some dialogue scenes for a part-talking reissue of *Phantom of the Opera*, but Louis B. Mayer turned them down. M-G-M's only options would have been to either buy the rights to *Dracula* from Universal or to simply loan out Chaney and count it as one of his four pictures per his contract. It is improbably that M-G-M would have done the latter unless Universal paid them much more than Chaney's weekly salary of $3,750.

But as fate would have it, Lon never made another picture for any studio. Following *The Unholy Three*'s sneak preview in June, his health took a dramatic turn for the worse, and he began suffering from pulmonary hemorrhages brought on by his bronchial cancer. A June 30 memo from M. E. Greenwood to one of his assistants said Lon was examined on Saturday, June 21, and diagnosed as being incapacitated. However, Lon's business manager Phil Epstein contended that Lon had met with producer Hunt Stromberg on June 25 to review the script of *Cheri-Bibi*.[192]

On June 23, 1930, two days after being examined by Drs. Frank Dolley, Simon Jesberg, and Leon Shulman, Lon Chaney made out his Last Will and Testament. After his death, many newspapers stated that Lon was unaware of how seriously ill he was. In an article by his friend Clarence Locan for *Photoplay* magazine, Locan stated that after completing *The Unholy Three*, Lon said to M. E. Greenwood that he had a hunch he would never make another picture. Greenwood laughed the comment off, but Locan said that despite every effort to keep the severity of his illness from him, he honestly felt that Lon knew all along and said nothing.[193] It is hard to imagine that anyone as seriously ill as Lon was, could not have known the desperate state of his health.

During the last week of June, Lon and Hazel left Los Angeles for New York City to see Dr. Burton J. Lee. He was chief of surgery at Memorial Hospital in New York City and a surgeon specializing in cancer cases. After examining Lon, Dr. Lee had him stay at Memorial Hospital for radium treatments. The hospital since its very beginning specialized in the treatment of cancer. The July 4 edition of the *Los Angeles Times* carried a report that Lon was in New York seeing a specialist for a throat infection.

In a July 10, 1930, letter to Lon, M-G-M notified him that they were suspending his contract again until he could report back to work.[194] Lon's physical condition continued to deteriorate after his return from treatments in New York. During the last week in July, he and Hazel went up to their cabin outside of Big Pine, California, where Lon always felt his best.

The cabin, which still stands today, is located in the Inyo National Forest on a half-acre of land in a lodgepole pine forest along the northern fork of the Big Pine Creek. It was built at a cost of $12,000 by Russo Contractors of Owens Valley during 1929 and 1930. The cabin was the only one ever designed by the famous black architect Paul Williams, who was also designing Lon's new home at 806 Whittier Drive in Beverly Hills. The cabin is a one-story structure made out of granite stones set randomly in mortar. The two-foot-thick walls keep the cabin cool in the summer and also make it able to withstand the harsh winters of the High Sierras. The fireplace, also made out of granite stones, has a six-inch wooden mantel. When Lon owned the cabin, there was a mounted deer head above the mantel, a bear rug on the floor, and a kerosene lamp rigged to a pulley which ran the length of the one-room living quarters to the kitchen area.[195]

Upon visiting the area today, it is easy to understand why Lon loved the mountains. Aside from the natural beauty, it is very similar geographically to the Pike's Peak region where he grew up. To many residents of the Big Pine area, Lon was not known as an actor, but simply as someone who had a cabin there. But according to Jim Nikolaus, others in town knew who Lon Chaney was, and it was big news whenever he arrived. At the age of 16, Nikolaus worked in the town's only gas station and remembers that Lon would drive up in his Lincoln and get gas, then head up the mountain. He said Lon was friendly, but never engaged in much conversation.[196]

Lon's cabin was built under what the government called a "special use permit," taken out in 1929 and expiring in 1980. This permit allowed Lon to own the actual structure, while leasing the land from the government. Lawson Brainard was the district ranger at the time, and said Lon and Hazel had an argument about exactly where on the lot the cabin should be built.[197] In Lon's time, as well as today, the only access to the cabin is to either hike up the 1¼ miles from the end of the vehicle road, or take a pack train.

Henry Kurth, a resident of the area for over 60 years, said that Lon and his family always went up to the cabin by pack train:

> He always gave the pack guide a $20 bill as a tip and upon his arrival, the packers would clamor for his business. That kind of money went a long way back then. He always held out an invitation to me to stop by and visit him at the cabin when he was there. He

Lon Chaney

was a very nice man, but you never hung around
long as you respected his privacy.[198]

Kenneth Partridge, another resident of the Big Pine area, said Lon used to camp out in that area before he built his cabin. Just above his cabin site, the Big Pine Creek takes on a horseshoe shape and is reported to be one of the best locations for trout fishing in the area. According to Partridge, it was here that Lon did much of his fly fishing.[199] After catching his limit, Lon continued to fish using barbless hooks and throwing back whatever he caught. He once said he found no sport in catching more fish than he could use.[200] He once told Ruth Waterbury, "Tonight I start out for the High Sierras. No shaving, no make-up, no interviews for four long, lazy weeks. We take a stove along and the wife cooks the fish I catch. We sleep under the pines and I try to climb high enough to reach the snows. Camping's the biggest kick in life for me."[201]

Pictures from Lon's personal photo album show just how much the outdoors was a part of his life, and how truly different he was from the man Hollywood knew. In one snapshot, he clowns around by a creek bank with his dog Sandy. Another shows him eating lunch beside his tent with Creighton and one of his friends. There are several pictures of Lon the fly fisherman, or of Lon the hunter, holding his shotgun while hunting for quail. On the pages of this album Lon has sketched horses, trees or mountainscapes between the pictures. There is one photo of Lon wearing his traditional cap, rough clothes and calf-length hiking boots, sitting astride a horse, while a particularly comical shot shows him sitting in a portable outhouse!

"He prefers — a little defiantly, in case anyone starts to contradict — Royal Coachman and Black Gnat flies for giving the trout what they desire. In Grass Lake there are also larger fish, so he has bought a rubber boat and expects to get some of them 'to take me for a ride in it soon'," wrote *New York Times* reporter Lewis L. Nichols.[202]

However, Lon's rapidly deteriorating health made even such simple pleasures impossible. Adela Rogers St. John said that Lon was so weak on his last trip to the cabin that he could not even enjoy his hobby of fly fishing.[203] Eventually the combination of high altitude (9,200 feet) and the continuing hemorrhages forced Lon to return to Los Angeles.

Before the Chaneys left for New York, they moved out of the Mansfield Avenue duplex and placed their furniture in storage. Upon their return, the house on Whittier Drive was almost finished, and the Chaneys took an apartment at the Beverly-Wilshire Hotel while waiting for the completion of their new home.[204]

The first of three serious hemorrhages forced Lon to enter St. Vincent's Hospital in Los Angeles on Wednesday, August 20. He developed a serious case of anemia and was given the first of three blood transfusions that Friday, August 22, and nearly a quart of blood was used to combat both the anemia and hemorrhages. "Critical Illness Grips Lon Chaney" read the headline of the August 23, 1930, edition of *Hollywood Daily Citizen*. Newspapers across the country carried the first news of Lon's being critically ill. The switchboard at M-G-M was swamped with more than a thousand phone calls from people offering to donate blood. The calls became so overwhelming that the studio was forced to hire extra switchboard operators.[205] Among the people offering their blood was Fred J. Stocker, general manager of the Chicago Northwestern railroad, who became friends with Lon during the production of *Thunder*.

The San Francisco Call-Bulletin in their edition of August 23, 1930, reported that Lon "emphatically denied" any rumors to his ill health when he visited San Francisco in July, after his treatments in New York. At the Hotel St. Francis, Lon told a reporter, "I feel fine. I have undergone no operation. I absolutely am not suffering from cancer of the throat or any other ailment." When the reporter asked Lon for a third time if he denied he was seriously ill or had undergone an operation, Lon replied: "The weather is certainly fine in San Francisco."

Lon, reported to be near death that Saturday, was given two additional blood transfusions which seemed to restore some of his strength. The following day, St. Vincent's Hospital issued this statement: "The patient has passed the crisis and is on the mend and unless unexpected complications occur, he should improve from now on." Reports issued on Monday, August 25, said that Lon had spent his most restful night since his arrival at the hospital. They said he had awakened on Sunday in good spirits and spoke briefly with his wife. But the same day this report was released, Lon slipped into a coma. One of the last telegrams he was able to read was from his friend, General Smedley Butler of the United States Marine Corps. "Get well old boy. Every Marine in the world is pulling for you."[206]

Lon Chaney died at the age of 47 at 12:55 a.m., Tuesday, August 26, 1930, from a hemorrhage of the throat.

Lon's sudden death came as a shock to his fans, as well as to his associates and friends. Many of them praised Lon and his work.

Irving Thalberg:

> Lon Chaney leaves behind him a beautiful memory
> in the hearts of the world and particularly in the hearts
> of his close friends and associates. He was a great
> artist and his passing leaves a void no one can fill.

Wallace Beery:

> Besides being gifted with his great artistry, Lon had
> fundamentally, a sense of humor that permitted no

self pity, yet his great sympathy with others was an outstanding trait. He was the one man I knew who could walk with kings and not lose the common touch.

Cecil B. DeMille:

Chaney carved for himself a niche in motion pictures of so unique a chapter that it is doubtful if it will ever again be filled. He was a sincere artist and a splendid gentleman. The loss suffered by the industry is that of a very important and constructive force.

Will Rogers:

When Lon Chaney passed away the whole amusement world lost a great asset, and our profession lost its most outstanding character actor and a man that brought the movies credit. His art was understood the world over regardless of language or titles and to have known him personally was a privilege. He was a fine fellow and would have been an honor to any profession.

Probably one of the most moving tributes came from his fans in the mining center of Rock Springs, Wyoming. Over 1,500 theatre patrons of various nationalities rose and stood silently for five minutes as *The Unholy Three* flashed onto the screen. This tribute was repeated at every performance of the picture.[207]

Louis B. Mayer issued the following memo on August 27 to all studio departments:

Lon Chaney

> To honor the memory of our beloved friend Lon
> Chaney, whose untimely passing has been a severe
> blow to us all, this studio will observe a period of
> silence tomorrow, Thursday, at three o'clock.
>
> At this time the remains are to be lowered to their
> final resting place and in respect to our departed co-
> worker everyone at the studio is requested to
> maintain complete silence at his post between
> signals of the siren.

The day before his funeral, hundreds of people filed by his silver and bronze casket at the Cunningham and O'Connor funeral home in downtown Los Angeles to pay their respects. Many mourners were from the Los Angeles deaf community. Frank McCloskey, the former Marine who Lon befriended, kept a vigil beside Lon's casket in his Marine dress uniform.

The funeral service was held on Thursday, August 28, in the funeral home chapel. Throughout the service, five members of the U. S. Marine Corps, in full dress uniform, stood at attention beside Lon's casket. Lieutenant-Commander H. S. Dyer, the chaplin of the Marine Corps base in San Diego, gave the eulogy. While there was no traditional religious service, several passages of I Corinthians were recited. Lon had once said that even though he was not religious in the church-going sense, he did have his own faith. "I believe that we desert God, but God never deserts us," he said.[208]

As the eulogy ended, Lon's set musicians and close friends, Sam and Jack Feinberg, played a selection of Lon's favorite tunes, including "Let the Rest of the World Go By" and "Laugh, Clown, Laugh." Lon's pallbearers consisted of his close friends John Jeske, Clinton Lyle, Phil Epstein, R. L. Hinckley (Creighton's father-in-law), William Dunphy, and Claude I. Parker.

As the funeral procession with its motorcycle-police escort arrived at Forest Lawn Cemetery in Glendale, a plane flew overhead and dropped wreaths of flowers. After circling the cemetery several times, the plane disappeared.[209]

Lon's casket was escorted by the Marine Honor Guard to the Dahlia Terrace section of the main mausoleum, where his body was laid to rest next to his father's. A large collection of roses and lilies-of-the-valley with a streamer reading "Lover, Darling" was placed on the floor in front of the crypt by Hazel, who was nearly hysterical with grief.[210]

All studios in Hollywood observed two minutes of silence at three o'clock in Lon's memory. At the M-G-M studios, a squad of Marines lowered the studio flag and blew taps. On the day of Lon's death, almost every customer in the studio commissary ordered a "Lon Chaney Sandwich," a combination of bacon, cheese, and tomato, from the menu in memory of their former co-worker.[211]

The evening of Lon's funeral, the Fox-Colorado Theatre in Pasadena held a memorial service for Lon in which theatre manager Max Bradfield gave a eulogy, and in the silence that followed, a bugler sounded taps. Lon's brother John, and Hazel's brother Charles Bennett were members of the theatre's stage crew.[212] The Hollywood Legion Stadium also held a memorial service for Lon, the first fight night after his death. The ring announcer called attention to the vacant ringside seat that Lon had always occupied, then the lights went out and Alan Hale climbed into the ring and, with a flashlight illuminating his face, read a poem in memory of Lon. According to a reporter, the response from the crowd of fight fans "was a touching tribute from men to the memory of a man's man."[213]

Filming an outdoor scene with Lila Lee standing behind Lon. Note the
"blimps" on the cameras. This was done to prevent the noise of the camera
being picked up by the microphone. Today they are called "barney's" and are
made out of a padded canvas material.

(Below) This is supposed to be the last-known picture taken of Lon Chaney.
Clarence Locan said that Lon had copies made of this picture and gave one to
each crew member. Sitting in the judge's chair is director Jack Conway
(pointing finger). Lila Lee (right) and John Miljan (next to lamppost) look on.
Actor/screenwriter Elliott Nugent (standing right, with pipe in mouth) co-
wrote the screenplay with his father.

(Right) Masquerading as the old woman in his talking picture debut *The
Unholy Three* (1930). Note the difference in his appearance between this
portrait and the 1925 silent version.

(Left) Lon Chaney, fly fisherman. (Courtesy of the Chaney Family Collection)
(Below) Lon's cabin in the Eastern Sierra Nevada Mountains in California. The structure, originally built at a cost of $12,000, still stands today.

(Above) Lon's casket arriving at Forest Lawn Cemetery in Glendale, California.

(Overleaf) A grief-stricken Hazel is escorted from Forest Lawn by Creighton and nurse Zina Luckenbach after Lon's funeral. (Courtesy of Lamar Tabb Collection)

That's All There Is To Life–
Just A Little Laugh,
A Little Tear
(Epilogue)

"He was the one man I knew who could walk with kings and not lose the common touch."

—*Wallace Beery*

LON CHANEY RESIDENCE

Newly Completed: The Late Mr. Lon Chaney's Luxurious Home at
806 WHITTIER DRIVE, BEVERLY HILLS

Designed by Paul R. Williams leading Residential Architect to conform to Mr. Chaney's most exacting requirements and built from the finest materials by O'Neal & Son, Contractors. This charming home that was never intended for the market, must be sold at a price worthy of the attention of those who appreciate the best in architecture and construction. Shown by appointment. Call DRexel 6575 or WHitney 4723 evenings or Sundays.

(Also Mr. Chaney's 1929 Lincoln Judkins coupe may be seen at the property.)

An ad for Lon's home in Beverly Hills shortly after his death. The house still stands today, having recently been up for sale at the price of $1.3 million dollars. (Courtesy of Lamar Tabb Collection)

L on's Last Will and Testament was probated on September 4, 1930, leaving an estate valued at $550,000. While this may seem to be a small amount for a movie star by today's standards, one has to remember that this was during the Depression. Lon's probate papers showed that he had invested in stocks of corporations like Davidson Chemical, Goldman Sachs Trading Company, Anaconda Cooper Company, Kinner Motor Corp., as well as real estate, leaving him financially better off than many of his colleagues who were wiped out in the 1929 stock market crash.

Hazel, who was named executrix, received the bulk of the estate. Lon's son, his brothers and his sister were all provided for by his life insurance policies which were said to total some $275,000. John Jeske received $5,000, and Cleva (now known as Cleva Creighton Bush) was left the sum of one dollar.[214] While many have thought over the years that this was Lon's way of retribution, it is probable that this was done at the time so that Cleva could not put a claim against the estate. A few months after the will had been probated, Hazel discharged Milton Cohen as legal counsel and hired Claude I. Parker and Ralph W. Smith. Probate was finalized on May 13, 1938.[215]

In October of 1930, Louis B. Mayer consulted with the studio's lawyer to see if they had any legal recourse to recover any or all of the $50,000 cash bonus Lon had received. The attorney advised Mayer that he had no grounds whatsoever to recover any of the bonus money.[216]

Hazel exchanged the four crypts in the Dahlia Terrace at Forest Lawn Cemetery on November 30, 1931, for a five-tier crypt in the Sanctuary of Meditation Terrace of the main mausoleum. The caskets of both Lon and his father were moved to this new location, their present resting place.[217] Hazel and her mother were also interred there as well as Frank's second wife Cora, who died in 1937. To this day none of the Chaney crypts bear name plates.

Hazel never moved into the Whittier Drive house, and it was sold in 1931. She resided in the west section of Hollywood until her death from lung and liver cancer on October 31, 1933.

Lon's cabin at Big Pine was sold by Hazel to Mr. and Mrs. Ruluff Slimmer in 1932, and then purchased in 1955 by Mr. and Mrs. Charles Strickland and Mr. and Mrs. Laurence Fuller. They shared in its ownership until the special use permit expired in 1980 when the U.S. Forest Service took possession. The Forest Service considered destroying it, but fortunately the cabin was so well built that the only way to knock it down would have been to dynamite it, so the structure still stands. In 1982, a proposal was made to place the Lon Chaney Cabin on the National Register of Historic Places, but at the time of this writing, no action has been taken in this regard.[218]

John Jeske stayed on as family chauffeur after Lon's death, and on October 17, 1933, he made an attempt to marry Hazel while she was bedridden in St. Vincent's Hospital. Family members, her attorney, and her physician, Dr. William P. Kroger, protested, and Jeske abandoned his marriage plans. Jeske, who was presenting himself to newspapers as Lon's "make-up man,"[219] may have been hoping that he could use the community property laws of California to his advantage by marrying Hazel on her death bed. As it was, Jeske received a total of $25,000 from her estate.[220]

In a bizarre twist of events, Jeske nearly lost that inheritance as well. Nine months after Hazel's death, Jeske married Elaine Bula, and in July, 1934, they were honeymooning in Big Pine, California, near

Lon's cabin site, when they were kidnapped by two men and a woman. After being driven back to Los Angeles, the kidnappers released Jeske, but held his wife until Jeske turned over his inheritance money from Hazel's estate. The following day, July 27, police arrested the kidnappers and freed Jeske's bride. The three kidnappers, Floyd Britton, D. R. Russell, and Ida May Alameda, were sentenced to life imprisonment on September 14, 1934.[221] John Jeske divorced his wife the following year, and died on May 11, 1944, at the age of 55. At the time of his death, Jeske was working as a truck driver for the County of Los Angeles.

Lon's older brother, John, continued to work as a stagehand until his death at the age of 66 in Shell Beach, California on June 15, 1946. Carrie, Lon's only sister, spent most of her life in Berkeley, California, until she and her husband moved to White Bear Lake, Minnesota. She died there on September 5, 1960, at the age of 74. Both John and Carrie were cremated, and their remains were interred in their mother's plot in Colorado Springs at Evergreen Cemetery. George Chaney, the youngest of the family, lived in California, working as an editor of a small newspaper in Paso Robles, then later running a hotel near Sacramento before his death on December 26, 1984, at the age of 91. He was cremated and buried in Pacheco, California. Cleva Creighton Bush died at the age of 78 as a result of a stroke in a Sierra Madre, California, rest home on November 21, 1967, and is buried at the Live Oak Cemetery in Monrovia, California.

In 1932, Creighton Chaney gave up his job at his father-in-law's plumbing company to pursue an acting career. He was under contract to RKO Studios and was billed as "Creighton Chaney" until the studio forced him to change his name to Lon Chaney, Jr. This was a move Creighton would long regret, not only because of the inevitable comparisons to his father and his inability to compete with him, but because he was given only mediocre roles which caused him a great deal of personal frustration throughout his life.

Lon Chaney

In 1936 he divorced his wife Dorothy, and the following year married model Patricia Beck. He appeared in many films, among them *High Noon, Northwest Mounted Police, My Favorite Brunette,* and *The Defiant Ones.* But he will probably be best remembered as "Lennie" in *Of Mice And Men,* and in the title role of *The Wolf Man.* Creighton worked steadily in many "B" pictures of the 1950's and 1960's as well as guest appearances in numerous television shows, even appearing as a regular in the comedy-western series *Pistols and Petticoats* for Universal.

In the early 1970's, he announced his intention to publish a picture book about the careers of his father, mother and himself entitled *A Century of Chaneys.* (His great-grandson Ron Chaney Jr., is currently planning to pick up where Creighton left off, and the book should be of enormous interest.) By 1973 Creighton had been treated for throat cancer, but despite this diagnosis, he made plans to tour with a dinner theatre circuit in Ohio doing *Arsenic and Old Lace.* Unfortunately, those plans never materialized because, on July 12, 1973, at the age of 67, Creighton Chaney died from a heart attack. There were no funeral services, as he donated his body to the USC School of Medicine.[222]

Creighton's two sons, Lon and Ronald, never entered the motion picture business. Lon was president of a company that manufactures parts for the aerospace industry in Southern California until his death in 1992. His brother Ronald, who died in 1987, was an alfalfa farmer in northern Nevada.

In 1936, Lon's old dressing room at M-G-M, along with others, was torn down to make room for the studio's new make-up department, which remained at that location until the mid-1960's.[223]

Hollywood in the 1950's and early 1960's found an audience for biographical films of Hollywood stars. *Valentino, Perils of Pauline, The Buster Keaton Story, Jeanne Eagles, The Will Rogers Story, The Jolson Story* and its sequel *Jolson Sings Again, The Eddie Cantor*

Story, The George Raft Story, as well as two versions on the life of Jean Harlow were some of the films that came out of various studios during this period. Most of these films were more fiction than fact and rarely stayed with the true subject matter.

The April 5, 1956, edition of *The Hollywood Reporter* announced Universal had acquired the screen rights to *Man of a Thousand Faces*. The story, originally written by Ralph Wheelwright, a publicist at M-G-M during Chaney's era, first came to James Cagney's attention when he worked with Wheelwright at M-G-M on *These Wilder Years*.[224] Ivan Goff and Ben Roberts (who had written scripts for Cagney films like *White Heat* and *Come Fill The Cup*) and R. Wright Campbell were signed to write the screenplay. Cagney himself wrote the music for his two dance numbers in the film, *Vagabond Waltz* and *Eccentrique*. When it was revealed that Cagney would play Chaney, Hollywood watchers shook their heads, saying it was another typical example of mis-casting. But in the end, James Cagney proved the nay-sayers wrong with his moving and thoughtful performance.

(Years later, Creighton Chaney said he had written a story and screenplay on his father's life and sold it to Universal. According to him, the studio promptly hired writers to redo the entire screenplay.[225] Creighton's claim has never been proven one way or the other.)

Producer Robert Arthur signed Joseph Pevney to direct the film, casting Dorothy Malone as Cleva, Jane Greer as Hazel, and Jim Backus as Lon's publicist friend Clarence Locan.

Many of the featured players in the film had real connections with Lon. Marjorie Rambeau, who played the role of Gert, a fictional extra player who helps Chaney enter films, was actually playing in Los Angeles with her own touring company at the same time the then unknown Lon Chaney was performing with Fischer's Follies. Clarence Kolb played himself while Danny Beck played his partner

Max Dill (the real Max Dill died in 1948). John George, who co-starred in four films with Lon, worked as an extra at the time and can be glimpsed in the scene where Cagney makes himself up as an East Indian sailor for a job as an extra. Robert J. Evans was chosen by Norma Shearer, who had casting approval, to play her late husband Irving Thalberg. (In the early 1970's, Evans became head of production at Paramount Studios, overseeing such hits as *Love Story* and *The Godfather*.) In a bit of nepotism, James Cagney's sister, Jeanne, played Lon's sister Carrie; it also marked the last time the brother and sister would play opposite each other in a film. This author's father, Larry J. Blake, appears early in the film as theatre manager David Stone who fires Cleva (Dorothy Malone) when she is late for her appearance on stage.

The studio obtained the approval of George Chaney and Lon's sister Carrie Keyes, as well as Cleva Creighton Bush.[226] Lon Ralph Chaney said that the studio arranged a private screening for his family, his brothers, Creighton's family and Cleva's family. He later asked Cleva how true to life was the film, and Cleva said it was "fairly accurate."[227]

The film was shot entirely at Universal, even making use of the theatre set from Lon's *Phantom of the Opera*, the front entrance of the studio, and other locales on the studio lot. In the opening of the film, a plaque memorializing Lon appears on the side of the stage where *Phantom of the Opera* was made. That plaque was made solely for the picture; however, in the mid-1940's a small plaque was placed on the stage to honor Chaney, but it has long since disappeared.[228]

Bud Westmore, who had replaced Jack Pierce as head of the studio's make-up department in 1946, was given the task of recreating several of Chaney's famous make-ups. Unfortunately these recreations are tremendously inferior to the originals; even with the use of foam rubber pieces, they were unable to come close to

Chaney's make-ups. Westmore's version of *The Hunchback of Notre Dame* bears no resemblance to Chaney's and the *Phantom of the Opera* version is a very pale imitation. Cagney's face was also much rounder than Chaney's, which added to the difficulty of recreating Lon's original look.

However, upon its release on August 14, 1957, the film received generally favorable reviews. Bosley Crowther of the *New York Times* said "Thanks to a dandy performance by James Cagney in the role of the great silent-film star Lon Chaney, there is drama and personality in *Man of a Thousand Faces*. . . . Joseph Pevney's direction has a curious affection for cliches, but Mr. Cagney rises above it. He etches a personality."

Variety added:

> "As everyone old enough to have lived through the silent film era is well aware, Chaney was one of the stalwarts of the period and any history of the motion picture industry would be woefully incomplete if it did not include this talented, tortured man, excellently portrayed by James Cagney in the present telling. . . . As Chaney, Cagney gives one of his most notable performances."

The film received an Academy Award nomination for best screenplay of 1958. It was also selected by the Department of Health, Education and Welfare to be captioned for the deaf. *Man Of A Thousand Faces* is considered one of the better film biographies of a Hollywood star, even though it occasionally strays from the facts. For example, at the end of the film Lon dies in bed after adding "Jr." to the name on his make-up case and passing the case on to his son! The biggest criticism of the film is that it tended to play up the unhappy marriage between Lon and Cleva rather than focusing more on

Chaney's talent and career. However, many of the up-and-coming make-up artists in the film industry credit this movie as sparking their interest in their current craft.

In 1983, the centennial year of his birth, the Academy of Motion Picture Arts and Sciences hosted a tribute to Chaney moderated by author Ray Bradbury, with appearances by co-workers Patsy Ruth Miller and Jackie Coogan. That summer, the UCLA Film Archive held a much-anticipated ten-week retrospective of Chaney's performances. Admirers of Chaney, new and old alike, were able to view several films that hadn't been screened since their original release.

On August 26, 1983, the 53rd anniversary of Lon Chaney's passing, ceremonies were held before the weekly film presentation at the UCLA Melnitz Theatre. Lon Ralph Chaney, Lon's grandson, and Ron Chaney, Jr., his great-grandson, accepted an award from the Hollywood Make-Up Artists and Hairstylists Union, in centenary tribute for Lon Chaney's "outstanding achievements in Motion Picture Make-Up." It was the first time the union had honored anyone outside of their own membership.

While Lon was alive, Colorado Springs' newspapers always referred to him in their movie ads as "Our Own Lon Chaney," or as "Colorado Springs' Own Great Actor." Such ads can be found as far back as 1916. In the years following Lon's death, several proposals were made to rename a street or school or erect a statue in Chaney's memory. Unfortunately, these proposals were never acted upon and Lon Chaney seemed all but forgotten by his hometown.[229]

While researching material for this book in early 1985, this author wrote to the mayor and other city officials, urging that Colorado Springs do something to honor their native son. Under the guidance of Sterling Campbell of the City Public Relations department, Mary Jane Rust of the Park and Recreation Department, and Beverly Diehl, a proposal was drafted to rename the 225-seat Little Theatre in the City Auditorium as the "Lon Chaney Theatre."

Both the Park and Recreation Department and the Colorado Springs City Council voted unanimously to approve the proposal in December, 1985. On a bright sunny morning of May 31, 1986, with Pike's Peak looming in the background, the Lon Chaney Theatre was officially dedicated and Lon Chaney was finally honored by his hometown 103 years after his birth.

In the lobby of the newly renovated theatre are several displays of photos and movie memorabilia of Lon Chaney from several of his films. The Lon Chaney Theatre has its own resident theatre company, the Star Bar Players, who perform four plays a year, and is in also constant use for seminars and children's theatre events.

In his twenty-eight year career on stage and in films, Lon Chaney carved a unique place for himself in the annals of motion picture history. Today he is generally remembered as a "horror actor," or one who could do anything with make-up. But Lon Chaney was more than that. He was an incomparable performer, a gifted artist who always managed to rise above his material. His work has been an inspiration to actors, writers, and make-up artists alike. Lon Chaney's performances have managed to stand the test of time, a prime example of a star's enduring quality.

It is true that talent and art are gifts from God. But it is what we do with those gifts that is important. How we use them, how we shape them — that is the test. Lon Chaney not only used his gifts as an accomplished actor, but a compassionate human being.

(Above) James Cagney and make-up artists Jack Kevan (left) and Bud Westmore discuss how Cagney will be made up to look like Chaney's *Phantom of The Opera*.
(Right) James Cagney as Lon Chaney in *Man Of A Thousand Faces* (1957).

The Lon Chaney Theatre, Colorado Springs, Colorado. (Photo courtesy of Patrick Wood)

Appendix

THE WRITINGS OF LON CHANEY

A. Wanted: New Medicine

B. Effects of Make-up Under Incandescent Lights

C. Preface to The Art of Make-up
For Stage and Screen

WANTED: NEW MEDICINE

(The Island Lantern; U. S. Penitentiary,
McNeil Island, Washington; January, 1930)

When a physician visits an ailing patient, and prescribes a medicine, his work has just begun. He watches the sufferer carefully, to note whether or not the treatment is obtaining results. If no improvement is apparent, he changes his prescription. He doesn't blindly cram more of the ineffective remedy down the sick man's throat.

But, paradoxically enough, that's exactly what society does, under our present system of jurisprudence. When prison fails as a cure for crime, we double the dose.

Lon Chaney

The law itself admits that prison, as a crime deterrent, is a failure. The passage of the Baumes and similar "habitual criminal" laws is prima facie evidence that prison terms cannot be relied upon to return lawbreakers to society as law-abiding individuals. True, the excuse for this type of law is usually that "habitual criminals can't be cured, and should be incarcerated for the safety of society." But, regardless of any theories woven around these laws, the one fact stands out: prison, in its present form, and aided and abetted by the multiplicity of unnecessary laws that legislatures delight in putting on the books, does not deter lawbreaking. And I do not think I am making too broad a statement when I say that in many cases prison returns a prisoner to society probably more accomplished in crime, and surely more bitter against society, than when he entered the institution.

Accepting as a postulate the fact that prison at present is ineffective as a crime deterrent, let us examine the details of the problem, and try to ascertain why.

The population of a prison includes as many classes as the population of a city. We have precocious youngsters, with minds not already formed by maturity. We have a class of lawbreaker such as the young bank clerk who embezzles, under the lash of some desperate need and an impulse born largely of panic. I class him as a lawbreaker, rather than as a criminal, and I think there is justice in this classification. We have other cases parallelling this type.

Then, too, in the same prison we have the experienced criminal, often perpetrator of many crimes, perhaps having served more than one term. And all these offenders, regardless of degree of offence, experience, or age, are herded together. The youth, inexperienced in lawbreaking, hears tales of older men who have "gotten away" with it. Often this youth is released from prison well grounded in the lore of the lawbreaker; oftentimes with the feeling that, thoroughly educated in the fine art of crime, he can "beat the rap" next time.

292

Often, too, he may feel that society is against him, he will be hounded as an "ex-convict," and that his only choice is crime. Self-pity is oftentimes at the bottom of this self-justification of the criminal.

It seems obvious that the remedy lies in segregation of classes of prisoners. Criminals and lawbreakers should be separated: an institution for first offenders, and grading as to nature and circumstances of the offence, with regard, too, to environment, education, and mental condition of each individual, would remove the present problem of prison as a school for crime. Intelligent analysis of every case in such an institution would enable a properly equipped prison administrator to return most of these cases to society as useful citizens.

The present argument against this plan is that prisons are overcrowded, but a very small tax would solve this. I think, too, that the best efficiency in such a system would be in small first-offence prisons in different districts. Large prisons are unwieldy to manage, and so highly specialized a work as equipping prisoners to rejoin society can't be accomplished by mass production methods. This is, however, a detail. The basic principle should be gone into first.

Another very important reform, applying to all prisons, would to my mind be this: some form of incentive to the man leaving prison to "go straight." We are proud of our rehabilitation, such as sit is, of our wounded soldiers, but we have done nothing toward rehabilitating our lawbreakers. I believe that the state should support a form of rehabilitating bureau to help men leaving prison to useful work, a chance to make good, and thus give each and every prisoner an incentive to avoid lapses from the law.

It is a basic fact that in every man is an inherent desire to be a respected member of society. Shown the opportunity and the means, in nine cases out of ten he'll do so. But our present system of turning a prisoner out with a small bill, a suit of prison clothes — and a tip to the police that he's at liberty again, certainly can't be said to help that prisoner along the "straight and narrow."

And — a man must eat. The average man in such a situation feels that crime is his only resort. Perhaps he's misguided — that's beside the case in point. The fact is that this is the psychology of the ex-prisoner. There's no use theorizing over it, or examining motives, and so forth. Something ought to be done about it.

Any plan for rehabilitation should be coupled, I also believe, with an intelligent administration of the indeterminate sentence. Let the man who has broken the law realize that by his own efforts he can cut down his time — and be backed up by the state in his attempt to make good on the outside — and he'll leave prison with a far different viewpoint from that usually seen today. Give him a chance to study in prison, if his education has been neglected — in fact — encourage it. Universities have excellent correspondence courses always available; trades can be taught, and often the teachers can be found in the very prison population. Thus a prisoner can, if need be, receive equipment for earning a lawful living. The man who becomes interested in being an electrician, it might also be pointed out, is going to lose interest in, say, picking pockets. The old saying that a man is never too old to learn, is, to my mind, true, and I think the most erroneous of proverbs is the one which proclaims that one can't teach an old dog new tricks.

Apparently there must be prisons, but in them, I think, the idea of punishment will be ultimately replaced with the idea of rehabilitation. When my auto ceases to perform, I send it to the repair shop to be repaired—not punished. When a tooth acts up I go to the dentist, not to ask him to punish me (though I know of no more exquisite punishment than the dental chair), but to ask him to find the seat of the trouble and correct it.

The man who runs afoul of the law has something that needs to be repaired, and, like the man in the dentist's chair, he has to face some suffering in the process. Perhaps it's a moral stamina that needs repairing—perhaps the result of environment—perhaps he lacks the necessary equipment to live within the law.

I believe that to punish, harden, and educate this man in crime only returns him to society more dangerous than before. Other crimes follow; perhaps more prison terms and then the "habitual criminal" conviction. He just gets the limit dose of the medicine that didn't do him any good in the first place.

Among medicines, we are largely addicted to the use of cathartics in these modern days. One takes a preparation of this kind, and finds that the dose has to be increased to get results, as the system becomes inured to it. Finally the cathartic is ineffective entirely. Solitary confinement, and some other methods of prison "discipline" can be likened to this — custom renders the prescription ineffective in time.

Why not, instead of such superficial attempts at correction, find the real seat of the trouble, and a real corrective?

To sum up, my idea, as an observer, of effective prison work leading to better observance of laws, would embrace the following points:

  •Segregation of prisoners, and corrective education.

  •Indeterminate sentences, coupled with an effective scheme for state rehabilitation, furnishing a goal toward which each man should work.

  •Educational work in prisons; trades instruction and interesting labor. Give the jute mill and the stone pile to him who deserves it, for instance; give constructive work to the man who will profit by it.

  •Administration of prisons by specialists, trained for this

important work, and not fettered by politics. Like our schools, our prisons should be entirely removed from the influence of politicians.

•And don't class any man as a permanent danger to society until all efforts at rehabilitation have failed — and then, I think, you'll find that the "failures" is a case for a psychiatrist rather than a penologist — or the real subject for the jute mill and rock pile.

Underlying it all is just one thing — a square deal.

The Golden Rule is still a splendid old idea that doesn't get old-fashioned. And man still is his brother's keeper.

Lon tending to his wardrobe on the set of *All the Brothers Were Valiant* (1923). Note his open make-up case in the foreground.

EFFECTS OF MAKE-UP
UNDER INCANDESCENT LIGHTS

So radical an innovation as the new Incandescent light in studio practice must of necessity, for some time, remain more or less in the state of experiment, and, naturally, draw into this same experimental field all details of photography connected with its use. Wherefore any discussion of make-up in connection with the lights and Panchromatic film must at this early day be devoted more to broad essentials and primary principles. There is much to improve on the lights to date, and, naturally, much to learn in the practice of make-up under them.

As compared to the Arc lights, the Incandescents have several striking differences. The most important is probably the matter of heat. They generate a far greater heat; in fact, in close-ups this heat becomes terrific, so that grease paint, nose-putty, glue, or other foreign substance on the face soon runs and melts. This, to a character make-up especially, is very dangerous.

The solution must, of course, be in lights that will be cooler, and this, I understand, engineers are working on with every promise of success, hence it may be classed as a temporary difficulty only.

They are much more penetrating, which involves the matter of using make-up more sparingly, as a more natural appearance is necessary. For instance, in former practice one used powder a shade lighter than the base grease paint. Under the new lights this cannot be done, as the penetrating quality of the light would disclose the subterfuge.

Because of this penetrating effect, shadows are more pronounced, and therefore objects tend to photograph with more contrast under Incandescent lights. The result is that shadings, linings and such details must be applied much more delicately, lest they "jump out."

In general then, considering straight make-ups, we have these basic rules: Make-up must be applied very naturally, and usually in a slightly darker shade than formerly. Lip rouges must be in the dark brown tones rather than the reds, as reds seem to photograph less accurately. Lining on the eyes, too, must be applied on the same principle; that is, reddish browns instead of the blacks, greens, yellows and blues of former practice under the Arc lights. Brown gives a soft effect, and when used it is difficult to realize, seeing it on the screen, that any grease paint has been used. Powders must harmonize with the grease paint, as, for instance, number 22 powder with a number 22 grease paint, to preserve this natural effect.

As before remarked, because of the excessive heat of the lamps, grease paint runs faster, hence it is fortunate that less paint is required.

At the same time this brings up many new problems; how this thinner make-up will photograph as regard certain disguises or effects where artificial material must be used on the face. Later I propose to touch on these problems more in detail. The thinness of the coat of make-up may in a measure compensate for the danger to the grease paint from heat. This I cannot accurately say, but eventually a balance must be found. It is one of the important problems at present.

It is possible that new and cooler lights will soon be developed, and possibly elaborate character make-ups will have to be filmed under the old lights until this is done, or improvements in make-up materials devised that will permit the use of the new illumination. Here, I think, are the two most important fields for experiment in connection with the lights, for either one problem or the other must be solved, before perfection can be reached.

It would hardly be possible to say at this early date that the new lights give a better quality of photography; cameramen differ widely on this point. But it is safe to say that they give as good, or the producers would have abandoned them from the start, and it certainly would appear that with experiment and improvement we will achieve better effects eventually. They are here to stay, because of the saving in time, labor and current, and minor details will have to be adapted to them.

One important change in make-up brought about by the new lights has simplified the whole art of disguise. Under the new lights and Panchromatic film, the make-up that looks most nearly perfect to the eye is most nearly perfect to the camera. Under the old Arc lights we had many tricks to learn, by using colors to compensate for light, and thus the eye, the most natural guide, was not reliable. The new lights will enable the actor to better judge his make-up by inspection without a screen test, and this, of course, will be a boon.

The above discussion applies primarily to the so-called straight make-up. Character make-up, or make-up for disguise rather than merely efficient photography, presents many different problems.

In the main, the principle of darker shades and brown lining will obtain. In shading, instead of red and gray we will turn to the browns, and any artificial applications such as plastic material, will have to be toned down in browns so as to eliminate lighter photography.

This means much experimenting. The lights are so new that practically none of a thousand devices in character make-up have been filmed under them, and each of these will, of course, have to be tested and experimented with to evolve necessary changes. Hence for a time we will have to experiment at length with every new character make-up, to learn which of the old principles to abandon and which to retain. It will evolve many new devices, it goes without saying. Again, as in straight make-up, colors and shades natural to the eye will appear most natural to the camera, which will often simplify these experiments.

Black is especially dangerous under the new lights and must be handled with the utmost delicacy wherever used, either on eyes or on linings. I venture to say that eventually the black pencils will be eliminated from the actor's make-up kit.

To recapitulate, the new lights are more penetrating and cast deeper shadows, hence contrast must always be toned down, and Panchromatic film, registering shades in relation to color more accurately, call for shadings and hues more nearly natural to the eye. Because of the tendency to photograph more rapidly and minutely, much less make-up, in point of quantity, must be used. Deep shadows and accented highlights must be avoided for fear of contrast.

These are all matters to be worked out by changing the technique of make-up. The heat problem is an engineering one that will doubtless soon be overcome. And with these worked out, cameramen will be in a position to go ahead on the problem of better photography under the new lights. I believe this will ultimately be achieved; in fact, possibly in a very short time. There are no insurmountable difficulties, so far as I can see.

These are my views from what limited investigations I have been able to make, and for the purpose of discussion I would like to ask a few questions which, I feel, are important. Perhaps they can be answered now; if not, we will have to experiment to find the answers.

What will be the photographic effect of putty or wax used in building up a character make-up? This is a dead substance, and prone to photograph as such, unless great care is used, even under the Arc lights. Suppose we apply this substance, tone it down with brown, apply linings, powders, and thus have several colors superimposed. Just what will be the result?

Consider the collodion scar. Just how will it be handled under the new lights, with their searching penetration? How can we make the scars now used appear genuine, rather than a film applied to the face?

What will be the effect of, say, a toupee, when dead hair is contrasted with live hair? Here, it seems to me, is a problem that will take considerable research, and I would be glad to hear some discussion of it.

Any foreign substance applied to the face, and then colored over will, I think, have certain distinguishing effects under the new make-up. How will we grapple with the cauliflower ear of artificial material, a wax protuberance, or perhaps a set of false teeth?

How will crepe hair photograph under the keener lights?

These are all questions that will come up many times in practice. Perhaps some of them have been already solved; if not, experiment along these lines will be valuable, I am sure.

Lon shows director Victor Seastrom how his clown make-up will look for the film *He Who Gets Slapped* (1924)

Lon Chaney

Preface to

THE ART OF MAKE-UP
FOR STAGE AND SCREEN

Undoubtedly the greatest single gift to the civilization of mankind is the printed word and, as a corollary, the most useful tool in the world is the text-book. It is the chisel by which the worker can carve out a structure of knowledge; by which he can inspect the experiences of others, go through these same experiences himself, and, with the knowledge gleaned during another man's span of life and activity, advance one step further on the road of progress.

This is as true of the stage and screen as of any other profession, but the student of stage and screen has had few such tools to work with. A practical compendium on makeup therefore fills a very important niche in the existing textbooks of the play. Cecil Holland has given the student such a textbook.

Mr. Holland approached the problem from the standpoint of an actor, for it was as an actor that he learned the art. In fact, his textbook is really a mirror of a lifetime of experience of an actor on the stage and screen; the problems he discusses and solves are the problems he met and solved by experiment in his own calling, and are the problems that the student actor is most likely to meet himself.

With these problems solved, the student of the technique of screen or stage will be equipped to strike out on his own — to advance further through adapting his knowledge to new experiences as they come up. As I said, the textbook is a tool, and, like any other tool, its usefulness depends on the way that it is used. One may create a masterpiece with a tool, another a slovenly piece of workmanship.

Therefore the student must bear in mind that no textbook can completely educate him in any art — but it can help him adapt his

302

own mind to problems that arise and thus help him make himself an artist. When a student has learned all there is in a textbook he has advanced just as far as the man before him — and from then on he must move forward as an original searcher. Thus everything progresses — engineers of today are moving forward beyond the heritage of knowledge left them by Faraday, Steinmetz, and Marconi; physicians beyond the experiences of Lister, Metchnikoff and Pasteur to new discoveries — and so must the actor of tomorrow tread across the experiences of those of us who worked today — to achieve a more advanced knowledge in the dim tomorrow.

Cecil Holland's book can help the student do this. It is crammed with practical hints on the modus operandi of makeup, and describes carefully the study of the face necessary to make a given disguise convincing. Mr. Holland is an expert in the reproduction of cuts, scars, and other forms of illusion. I have long watched his work in the studios with interest; the different disguises he worked out for Mary Pickford, Claire Windsor and others. Of course, makeup is a hobby with me, hence perhaps I was more interested than anyone else in Holland's work.

He created the office of staff makeup expert at a studio, and is acting in this capacity at the Metro-Goldwyn-Mayer plant, where it was found that such a functionary could save much trouble and time dealing with such problems as special disguises for principals — or wholesale disguises for extras, such as the crowds in "Ben Hur," etc. Holland knows both angles. He can dispense illusion wholesale or retail.

I trust that his attempt to dispense knowledge of this rather abstruse art fulfills his aim — which is to help the actors of the world solve a few problems. If this book can help the actor in at least one important emergency, I know that the actor will feel that Mr. Holland's effort was well worth while — and so will Mr. Holland.

Lon Chaney

And, if I may be permitted just a word of advice to the student who may peruse this book — remember that this textbook is a tool — and how you use it depends on yourself. Careful study of its facts, and careful application of them to original problems is your stepping stone to possible fame — at any rate to the joy of knowing, in your own heart, that you are, as an actor, a competent workman.

Lon Chaney

Lon sits on his make-up case on the Goldwyn Pictures studio lot (1921). Today make-up artists still use their cases as a make-shift chair while filming on a stage or on location.

Chronology

1852 Frank H. Chaney (Lon's father) is born in Carroll, Ohio, on April 3.

1855 Emma A. Kennedy (Lon's mother) is born in Lawrence, Kansas on October 13.

1874 John and Mary Kennedy (Lon's maternal grandparents) open a school for the deaf in Colorado Springs, Colorado on April 8.

1877 Frank H. Chaney arrives in Colorado Springs, Colorado.
On December 5, Frank H. Chaney marries Emma A. Kennedy.

1879 Jonathan Orange Chaney (known as John) is born to Frank and Emma on August 5 in Colorado Springs.

1882 Frank H. Chaney begins working at Phil Strubel's barber shop.

1883 Leonidas Frank Chaney is born to Frank and Emma on April 1.

1887 Earl Chaney is born to Frank and Emma Chaney on May 14 and dies on July 7.

1888 Caroline Emma Alice Chaney (Carrie) is born to Frank and Emma on December 20.

1893 George Leonidas Chaney is born to Frank and Emma on June 10. Shortly after his birth, Emma is stricken with inflammatory rheumatism which renders her bed-ridden. Lon is forced to drop out of the fourth grade to care for his mother as well as for his younger sister and brother. At this time Lon begins to develop his skill of pantomime by relating the day's happenings to his mother.

1897 Lon works as a tour guide during the summer months at Pike's Peak. He obtains work as a prop boy at the city's local Opera House.

1900 Lon is employed at Brown's Wallpaper and Paint Company in Colorado Springs.

1902 Lon becomes a full-time employee at the Opera House.
Lon makes his theatrical debut as an actor in an amateur play, *The Little Tycoon,* on April 19 at the city's Opera House.

1903 Lon appears in the play *Said Pasha* with the Casino Opera Company at the Opera House on June 8.
On July 13 Lon appears as the "Assessor" in *The Chimes of*

Normandy with the same company, now renamed the Columbia
Opera Company.

1904 Lon is listed as "Lon F. Chaney, actor" in the city directory.
After a brief stint in California, Lon rejoins the Columbia Opera
Company, about to embark on a tour of the mid-West.

1905 In the spring, the Columbia Opera Company arrives in
Oklahoma City, where Lon falls in love with a 16-year-old girl
named Cleva Creighton. Lon temporarily leaves the Opera
Company and gets a job in a furniture store.

1906 Lon and Cleva's only child, Creighton Tull Chaney, is born on
February 10.
According to city marriage records, Lon and Cleva are married on
May 31, by pastor Thomas H. Harper of the People's Temple
Church. In May, Lon rejoins the Columbia Opera Company.

1908 Lon, Cleva and Creighton move to Colorado Springs.

1909 In April, Lon and Cleva perform in Chicago with the
Cowpuncher Company.
In October, Lon and Cleva appear in Denver in *The Royal Chef*,
and play a one-night stand in Colorado Springs at the Opera
House.

1910 Lon and Cleva work in Los Angeles and throughout the state of
California.

1911 *The Los Angeles City Directory* lists Lon and Cleva as living at
826 East 7th Avenue.
In August, Lon appears with Max Dill's company in San
Francisco.

1912 Lon opens with Fischer's Follies in Los Angeles on March 17.
Fischer's Follies closes its run in Los Angeles on August 31.
Lon possibly works part-time as an extra in motion pictures.
Cleva makes her debut at Brink's Cafe in Los Angeles on August
28.
In September Lon returns to San Francisco to join Kolb and Dill.

1913 Lon is hired to stage musical numbers by the producers of *The
Talk of New York*, a George M. Cohan musical.
After completing her dinner show at the Brink's Cafe on April 30,
Cleva attempts suicide at the Majestic Theatre where Lon is
working. She is rushed to the hospital where her life is saved.

Lon and Cleva separate on May 26. About this time Lon officially enters motion pictures as an extra and bit player.

In July, he appears briefly and unbilled in *Suspense*.

Lon receives his first-known screen credit in a one-reel comedy, *Poor Jake's Demise,* on August 16.

Lon files for divorce from Cleva on December 19.

1914 Lon's divorce trial begins on April 1, Lon's 31st birthday. Lon is granted sole custody of Creighton.

Emma Chaney (Lon's mother) dies of a heart attack on April 8 in Colorado Springs.

Frank Chaney retires from barbering on June 9 after 37 years and moves to Berkeley, California.

Lon places Creighton in a private home for children of divorce and disaster.

Lon works with Joseph de Grasse and Ida May Park for the first time in *Her Bounty*, the first of 64 films for them between 1914 and 1918.

1915 Universal City Studios opens on March 15.

Lon directs the first of six films for the Victor Company at Universal starting with *The Stool Pigeon*, released on April 9.

On November 26, Lon and Hazel Hastings are married in the courthouse in Santa Ana, California. Creighton comes to live with them at 1607½ Edgemont Avenue in the east section of Hollywood.

On location in Chatsworth, California,for *Riddle Gwane*, Lon plays craps with some of the cowboys and crew members (1918).

Lon Chaney

1916 Frank Chaney moves from Berkeley to Los Angeles.

1917 Frank Chaney marries Cora Marker on February 6.

Lon receives good notices for his villainous portrayal of Sleter Noble in *Hell Morgan's Girl*.

1918 Lon quits Universal and decides to free-lance.

Lon plays the lead villain role in William S. Hart's *Riddle Gwane*.

1919 Lon works with director Tod Browning at Universal in *The Wicked Darling*, the first of ten films the two would make over a ten-year period.

Lon appears in *The Miracle Man* for Paramount Studios, released August 31.

1920 Lon plays the lead role in *The Penalty* for Goldwyn Pictures.

Lon and Hazel buy a bungalow at 1549 Edgemont Avenue.

1921 Lon appears in a dual role in hit *Outside The Law*.

The joke "Don't step on that spider! It might be Lon Chaney!" becomes popular.

1922 Lon is referred to as "The Man of a Thousand Faces" for the first time in connection with release of *The Trap*.

Lon and Hazel sell their home on Edgemont Avenue and move to 7152 Sunset Blvd.

Lon appears in his last film for Goldwyn Pictures, *A Blind Bargain.*

Production of *The Hunchback of Notre Dame* for Universal begins on December 16.

1923 Filming of *Hunchback* is completed on June 3.

Lon and Hazel attend the opening of *Hunchback* in New York on August 30

1924 Lon begins work on June 17 on M-G-M's first feature, *He Who Gets Slapped*. Filming is completed July 28.

Filming begins on October 29 for Universal's *Phantom of the Opera*, Lon's last film as a free-lancing actor.

1925 Lon signs a one-year contract on January 6 with M-G-M that includes two yearly option renewals. His weekly salary is $2,500.

The Unholy Three is released on August 16 and appears on 60 Top Ten Film Lists for the year.

Phantom of the Opera opens September 6 at the Astor Theatre.

Lon and Hazel move to 7166 Sunset Blvd.

September
28th,
1 9 2 3

Miss May Robson,
Wright Ave.,
Bayside, Long Island,
New York.

My dear Miss Robson:-

      Please accept my humble thanks and

appreciation for your wonderful letter of recent date

regarding my work in "The Hunchback of Notre Dame".

      Believe me it is very gratifying

to me and only hope you will enjoy my future work.

      With sincerest thanks, I beg to

remain,

      Yours reppectfully,

Lon Chaney

7152 Sunset Blvd.,
Los Angeles, Calif.

While Lon refused to answer fan mail, he occasionally broke his own rule.
May Robson was a famous stage actress before going into films and played in
the original *A Star Is Born*.

Chaney autographed this photo to the wardrobe women at M-G-M, a rare occurrence, which makes Chaney's autograph a sought-after collector's item.

Dr. Hugo Keifer, a prominent Los Angeles optician, designed the glass shield that Lon wore to simulate a blind eye in *The Road to Mandalay*.

Lon and his close friend Clinton Lyle on the set of *The Big City* (1928). The two men played together in musical comedy shows and Lon eventually persuaded Clinton to enter films. He appeared with Lon in this film and in *While The City Sleep*s.

1926 Lon's first option on his contract with M-G-M is picked up. His weekly salary is increased to $2,750.

Lon signs a new contract with M-G-M. His salary increases to $3,250 a week.

Lon and Hazel move to an English Tudor-style home at 604 Linden Drive in Beverly Hills.

Creighton Chaney marries Dorothy Hinckley on April 25.

1927 *Tell It To The Marines,* Lon's top profit-making picture for M-G-M, is released January 29.

Lon and Hazel make a rare appearance at the Los Angeles premiere of the film on February 24.

Filming of *The Unknown* begins on February 7.

On April 11, Frank Chaney dies in Hollywood at the age of 75.

Lon writes the preface to Cecil Holland's book on make-up.

London After Midnight is released on December 17. It is now one of the most sought-after "lost" films of the silent era.

1928 *Laugh, Clown, Laugh,* Lon's thirteenth film for M-G-M, is released.

Lon's essay on "The Effects of Make-up Under Incandescent Lights" appears in the *Academy Digest* in April and in *The New York Times* on October 14.

Lon's first grandchild (Lon Ralph Chaney) is born in July.

While The City Sleeps is released on October 20. This is the first Chaney film that boasts synchronized sound effects and musical score for theatres equipped to handle this new process.

West of Zanzibar, also with synchronized score, is released on December 24.

1929 Lon is asked by the *Encyclopedia Britannica* to write a chapter on the subject of make-up for motion pictures.

Lon appears in *Where East Is East.*

Lon refuses to make the transition to talking pictures, and rumors begin to circulate that he is actually deaf like his parents.

M-G-M sends Lon notice on March 9 that they are picking up the third option on his contract, boosting his weekly salary to $3,750.

In early March, Lon starts work on his last silent picture, *Thunder* in Green Bay, Wisconsin. He becomes ill with pneumonia during production and filming is suspended for two weeks.

Due to Lon's illness, M-G-M suspends his contract on July 25 until he can return to work.

In October Lon is diagnosed with lung cancer.

1930 Irving Thalberg enters Lon's contract negotiations; Lon is eventually offered a $50,000 cash bonus for agreeing to talk in motion pictures, refundable if his voice does not record well.

Lon passes his voice test and the studio decides on a remake of *The Unholy Three* as Lon's first all-talking picture.

Lon and Hazel purchase a building lot at 806 Whittier Drive in Beverly Hills and hire noted black architect Paul Williams to design their new house.

Lon's second grandchild (Ronald Creighton Chaney) is born in March.

Lon begins work on *The Unholy Three* on April 1, his 47th birthday.

On June 21 Lon is diagnosed as "incapacitated." He makes out his Last Will and Testament two days later. Lon leaves for New York in the last week in June to see Dr. Burton J. Lee.

The Unholy Three is released on July 3.

On July 10, M-G-M notifies Lon that they are suspending his contract until he is physically able to return to work.

Lon and Hazel make their last trip to their newly built cabin outside of Big Pine, California. He is too weak to fish and the high altitude and recurring hemorrhages force the Chaneys to return to Los Angeles.

Lon enters St. Vincent's Hospital on August 20.

On August 23, newspapers carry the first news of the seriousness of Lon's illness .

Lon falls into a coma on August 25.

On August 26 at 12:55 a.m., Lon Chaney dies from a hemorrhage of the throat at the age of 47.

Lon's funeral is held on August 28. He is laid to rest in the Forest Lawn Cemetery in Glendale, California.

1932 Creighton Chaney enters motion pictures billed under his birth name. While under contract to RKO Studios, he is forced to change his name to Lon Chaney, Jr.

1933 Hazel Chaney dies from lung and liver cancer on October 31 at St. Vincent's Hospital in Los Angeles.

1936 Lon's old dressing room at M-G-M, along with others, is torn down to make way for the new studio make-up department.

1946 On June 15, John Chaney dies at the age of 66 in Shell Beach, California.

1956 Production begins in November on a film biography of Lon's life, *Man of a Thousand Faces*. James Cagney is signed to star as Lon.

1957 *Man of a Thousand Faces* opens on August 14.

1960 On September 5, Carrie Keyes, Lon's only sister, dies at the age of 74.

1967 Cleva Creighton Bush, Lon's first wife, dies at the age of 78 on November 21.

1973 On July 12 Creighton Chaney dies at his home in San Clemente, California at the age of 67. There are no funeral services, as he donated his body to the USC School of Medicine.

1983 April marks the hundredth anniversary of Lon's birth. The Academy of Motion Picture Arts and Sciences holds a tribute to Lon in June, moderated by author Ray Bradbury, with appearances by Lon's co-workers, Patsy Ruth Miller and Jackie Coogan.

Starting on July 7, UCLA Film Archive holds a ten-week retrospective of Lon's pictures. Some films are seen for the first time since their original release.

On August 26, the 53rd anniversary of Lon's passing, the Hollywood Make-up Artists and Hairstylists Union, in tribute to Lon's "outstanding achievements in Motion Picture Make-Up", present an award to Lon's grandson, Lon Ralph Chaney, and his great-grandson Ron Chaney, Jr. It is the first time the union has honored anyone outside its own membership.

1984 On December 26 George Chaney dies at the age of 91, in Martinez, California.

1986 The Lon Chaney Theatre in dedicated on May 31 at the Colorado Springs City Auditorium.

Lon Chaney

Displays at the Lon Chaney Theatre, Colorado Springs, Colorado. (Photo courtesy of Patrick Wood)

Film Reference List

This list contains all known films in which Lon Chaney received screen credit. Where release dates of films are at variance, the earliest release date is used. Some information respecting his early films at Universal is scarce, and whatever information was available is what was used. An asterisk (*) after a film title indicates that a print of the film exists in partial or complete form, either in a private collection, film archive or university.

POOR JAKE'S DEMISE
IMP/Universal, 1 reel. Released: August 16, 1913. Directed by Allan Curtis. (No other information is available at this time. This is Chaney's first known screen credit.)
CAST: Lon Chaney.

THE SEA URCHIN
Powers/Universal, 1 reel. Released: August 22, 1913. Directed by Edwin August. Scenario by Jeanie MacPherson.
CAST: Lon Chaney (Barnacle Bill), Robert Z. Leonard and Jeanie MacPherson (The Lovers)

THE BLOOD RED TAPE OF CHARITY
Powers/Universal, 1 reel. Released: September 12, 1913. Directed by Edwin August.
CAST: Lon Chaney, Edwin August.

SHON THE PIPER
101 Bison/Universal, 3 reels. Released: September 30, 1913. Produced by Otis Turner. Photographer: William Foster.
CAST: Robert Z. Leonard, Marguerite Fisher, Lon Chaney.

THE TRAP
Powers/Universal, 1 reel. Released: October 3, 1913. Directed by Edwin August.
CAST: Lon Chaney, Cleo Madison.

Lon Chaney

AN ELEPHANT ON HIS HANDS
Nestor/Universal, 1 reel. Released: November 8, 1913. Directed by Al Christie.
CAST: Lon Chaney (Eddie)

ALMOST AN ACTRESS
Joker/Universal, 1 reel. Released: November 15, 1913. Directed by Allan Curtis.
CAST: Louise Fazenda (Susie) , Max Asher (The Director), Edward Holland (The Heavy), Lee Morris (Lee), Lon Chaney (Cameraman), Silvion de Jardins aka Bobby Vernon (Benny)

BACK TO LIFE
Victor/Universal, 2 reels. Released: November 24, 1913. Directed by Allan Dwan. Scenario by M. de la Parella.
CAST: Pauline Bush (The Wife), J. Warren Kerrigan (Destiny's Victim), William Worthington (The Gambler), Jessalyn Van Trump (The Charmer), Lon Chaney (The Rival).

RED MARGARET, MOONSHINER
Gold Seal/Universal, 2 reels. Released: December 9, 1913. Directed by Allan Dwan. Scenario by Jeanie MacPherson.
CAST: Pauline Bush (Red Margaret), Murdock MacQuarrie (Government Agent), James Neill (The Sheriff), Lon Chaney (Lon)

BLOODHOUNDS OF THE NORTH
Gold Seal/Universal, 2 reels. Released: December 23, 1913. Directed by Allan Dwan.
CAST: Pauline Bush (His Daughter),William Lloyd (The Embezzler), James Neill (The Refugee), Murdock MacQuarrie (A Mountie), Lon Chaney (A Mountie).

THE LIE
Gold Seal/Universal, 2 reels. Released: January 6, 1914. Directed by Allan Dwan. Scenario by Jeanie MacPherson.
CAST: Murdock MacQuarrie (Auld MacGregor), Pauline Bush (His Daughter), William Lloyd (Mac's Brother), Lon Chaney (Young MacGregor), Richard and Arthur Rosson (More Fortunate Youths), Fred McKay (Their Father), James Neill (The Gambler).

THE HONOR OF THE MOUNTED
Gold Seal/Universal, 2 reels. Released: February 17, 1914. Directed by Allan Dwan. Scenario by Arthur Rosson.
CAST: Pauline Bush (Marie Laquox), Murdock MacQuarrie (A Mountie), Lon Chaney (Jacques Laquox), James Neill (Post Commandant)

REMEMBER MARY MAGDALEN
Victor/Universal, 2 reels. Released: February 23, 1914. Directed by Allan Dwan.
CAST: Pauline Bush (The Woman), Murdock MacQuarrie (The Minister), Lon Chaney (The Half-Wit)

DISCORD AND HARMONY
Gold Seal/Universal, 3 reels. Released: March 17, 1914. Directed by Allan Dwan. Scenario by Arthur Rosson.
CAST: Pauline Bush (The Girl), Murdock MacQuarrie (The Composer), Allan Forrest (The Artist), James Neill (The Symphony Conductor), Lon Chaney (The Sculptor)

THE MENACE TO CARLOTTA
Rex/Universal, 2 reels. Released: March 22, 1914. Directed by Allan Dwan. Scenario by Lon Chaney (his first known scenario credit.)
CAST: Pauline Bush (Carlotta), William C. Dowlan (Tony), Murdock MacQuarrie (His Father), Lon Chaney (Giovanni Bartholdi), John Burton (The Vulture)

THE EMBEZZLER
Gold Seal/Universal, 2 reels. Released: March 31, 1914. Directed by Allan Dwan.
CAST: Pauline Bush (His Daughter), Murdock MacQuarrie (John Spencer), William C. Dowlan (Arthur Bronson), Lon Chaney (J. Roger Dixon), William Lloyd (William Perkins), Richard Rosson (The Penman).

THE LAMB, THE WOMAN, THE WOLF
101-Bison/Universal, 3 reels. Released: April 4, 1914. Director and scenario: Allan Dwan.
CAST: Pauline Bush (The Woman), Murdock MacQuarrie (The Lamb), Lon Chaney (The Wolf)

Lon Chaney

THE END OF THE FEUD
Rex/Universal, 2 reels. Released: April 12, 1914. Directed by Allan Dwan.
CAST: Murdock MacQuarrie (Hen Dawson), Pauline Bush (June), Lon Chaney (Wood Dawson), William Lloyd (Jed Putnam), William C. Dowlan (Joel)

THE TRAGEDY OF WHISPERING CREEK
101-Bison/Universal, 2 reels. Released: May 2, 1914. Director and scenario: Allan Dwan.
CAST: Murdock MacQuarrie (The Stranger), Pauline Bush (The Orphan), William C. Dowlan (Bashful Bill), Lon Chaney (The Greaser), George Cooper (The Kid), Mary Ruby (His Sweetheart), John Burton, Doc Crane, and William Lloyd (Prospectors)

THE UNLAWFUL TRADE
Rex/Universal, 2 reels. Released: May 14, 1914. Director and scenario: Allan Dwan.
CAST: Pauline Bush (Amy Tate), William Lloyd (Old Tate), George Cooper (Young Tate), William C. Dowlan (Neut Tate), Murdock MacQuarrie (The Revenue Man), Lon Chaney (The Cross Blood)

THE FORBIDDEN ROOM
101-Bison/Universal, 3 reels. Released: June 20, 1914. Directed by Allan Dwan.
CAST: Murdock MacQuarrie (Dr. Gibson), Pauline Bush (Mother/Daughter), William C. Dowlan (Prosecuting Attorney), Lon Chaney (John Morris), John Burton (Dr. Jarvis)

THE OLD COBBLER
101-Bison/Universal, 2 reels. Released: June 27, 1914. Directed by Murdock MacQuarrie.
CAST: Murdock MacQuarrie (The Cobbler), Richard Rosson (His Son), Agnes Vernon (Jess), Lon Chaney (Wild Bill)

A RANCH ROMANCE
Nestor/Universal, 2 reels. Released: July 8, 1914.
CAST: Murdock MacQuarrie (Jack Deering), Agnes Vernon (Kate Preston), Lon Chaney (Raphael Praz), Seymour Hastings (John Preston), E. Keller (Don Jose Praz)

HOPES OF A BLIND ALLEY
101-Bison/Universal, 3 reels. Released: July 4, 1914. Directed by Allan Dwan.
CAST: Pauline Bush (Pauline), Murdock MacQuarrie (Jean Basse), William C. Dowlan (The Unsuccessful Artist), Lon Chaney (Vendor)

HER GRAVE MISTAKE
Nestor/Universal, 2 reels. Released: July 15, 1914.
CAST: Murdock MacQuarrie (Roger Grant), Agnes Vernon (Isabel Norris), Seymour Hastings (Her Father), Lon Chaney (Nunez)

BY THE SUN'S RAYS *
Nestor/Universal, 2 reels. Released: July 22, 1914.
CAST: Murdock MacQuarrie (John Murdock), Lon Chaney (Frank Lawler), Seymour Hastings (John Davis), Agnes Vernon (Dora Davis), Dick Rosson (Bandit)

THE OUBLIETTE *
101-Bison/Universal, 3 reels. Released: August 15, 1914. The first of four 3 reelers about the adventures of Francois Villon; Chaney also appeared in the second episode *The Higher Law*. Directed by Charles Giblyn. Scenario: H. G. Stafford, from a story by George Bronson Howard. Photographer: Lee Bartholomew.
CAST: Murdock MacQuarrie (Francois Villon) Pauline Bush (Philippa de Annonay), Lon Chaney (Chevalier Bertrand de la Payne), Harry F. Crane (King Louis XI), Chet Withey (Colin)

A MINER'S ROMANCE
Nestor/Universal, 2 reels. Released: August 26, 1914.
CAST: Murdock MacQuarrie (Bob Jenkins), Agnes Vernon (Lucy Williams), Lon Chaney (John Burns), Seymour Hastings (Dave Williams)

HER BOUNTY
Rex/Universal, 1 reel. Released: September 13, 1914. Directed by Joseph de Grasse. Scenario by Ida May Park.
CAST: Pauline Bush (Ruth Braddon), Joe King (David Hale), Lon Chaney (Fred Howard) Beatrice Van (Bessie Clay)

THE HIGHER LAW
101-Bison/Universal, 2 reels. Released: September 19, 1914. The second episode of the adventures of Francois Villon. Directed by Charles Giblyn; based on a story by George Bronson Howard.

CAST: Murdock MacQuarrie (Francois Villon), Pauline Bush (Lady Eleyne), Harry F. Crane (King Louis XI), Lon Chaney (Sir Stephen)

RICHELIEU
101-Bison/Universal, 4 reels. Released: September 26, 1914. Directed by Allan Dwan. Technical direction by Frank D. Ormstron. Based on the play of the same title by Edward George Bulwer-Lytton.

CAST: Murdock MacQuarrie (Cardinal Richelieu), Pauline Bush (Julie de Mortemar), William C. Dowlan (Adrien de Mauprat), Robert Chandler (Sieur de Beringhen), Edna Maison (Marion de Lormer), James Neill (The King), Lon Chaney (Baradas), Richard Rosson (Francois), Edna Chapman (The Queen), William Lloyd (Joseph), Frank Rice (Huget)

THE PIPES OF PAN
Rex/Universal, 2 reels. Released: October 4, 1914. Picture Code #: 739. Directed by Joseph de Grasse.

CAST: Pauline Bush (Marian), Joe King (Stephen Arnold), Carmen Phillips (Caprice), Lon Chaney (Arthur Farrell)

VIRTUE ITS OWN REWARD
Rex/Universal, 2 reels. Released: October 11, 1914. Directed by Joseph de Grasse. Scenario by H. G. Stafford, from a story by John Barton Oxford.

CAST: Pauline Bush (Annie Partlan), Gertrude Bambrick (Alice), Tom Forman (Seadley Swaine), Lon Chaney (Duncan Bronson)

HER LIFE'S STORY
Rex/Universal, 2 reels. Released: October 15, 1914. Directed by Joseph de Grasse. Scenario by James Dayton, from a poem "The Cross" by Miriam Bade Rasmus.

CAST: Pauline Bush (Carlotta), Laura Oakley (Sister Agnes), Ray Gallagher (Don Manuel), Lon Chaney (Don Valesquez), Beatrice Van (The Wife), Felix Walsh (The Child)

SMALL TOWN GIRL
101-Bison/Universal, 3 reels. Released: November 7, 1914. Directed by Allan Dwan.
CAST: Murdock MacQuarrie, Pauline Bush,William Lloyd, Lon Chaney, Richard Rosson, Rupert Julian

LIGHTS AND SHADOWS
Rex/Universal, 2 reels. Released: November 29, 1914. Directed by Joseph de Grasse.
CAST: Pauline Bush (Mother/Daughter), Lon Chaney(Bentley)

HE LION, THE LAMB, THE MAN
Rex/Universal, 2 reels. Released: December 6, 1914. Directed by Joseph de Grasse.
CAST: Pauline Bush (Agnes Duane), Lon Chaney (Fred), Millard K. Wilson (The Brother), William C. Dowlan (The Reverend)

NIGHT OF THRILLS
Rex/Universal, 2 reels. Released: December 13, 1914. Directed by Joseph de Grasse. Featuring Lon Chaney.

HER ESCAPE
Rex/Universal, 2 reels. Released: December 13, 1914. Directed by Joseph de Grasse. Scenario: Lon Chaney.
CAST: Pauline Bush (The Girl), William C. Dowlan (Her Lover), Lon Chaney (Pete), Richard Rosson (Dope Fiend)

THE SIN OF OLGA BRANDT
Rex/Universal, 2 reels. Released: January 3, 1915. Directed by Joseph de Grasse.
CAST: Pauline Bush (Olga Brandt), William C. Dowlan (Rev. John Armstrong), Lon Chaney (Stephen Leslie)

STAR OF THE SEA
Rex/Universal, 2 reels. Released: January 10, 1915. Directed by Joseph de Grasse. Scenario by Phil Walsh.
CAST: Pauline Bush (The Fisher Girl), Laura Oakley (Janice), William C. Dowlan (Mario Brisoni), Lon Chaney (Tomasco)

THE MEASURE OF A MAN
Rex/Universal, 2 reels. Released: January 28, 1915. Directed by Joseph de Grasse.
CAST: Pauline Bush (Helen McDermott), William C. Dowlan (Bob Brandt), Lon Chaney (Mountie Lt. Stuart)

THREADS OF FATE
Rex/Universal, 2 reels. Released: February 21, 1915. Directed by Joseph de Grasse.
CAST: Pauline Bush (The Wife), William C. Dowlan (Her Lover), Lon Chaney (The Count)

WHEN THE GODS PLAYED A BADGER GAME
Rex/Universal, 2 reels. Released: February 28, 1915. (Working Title: *The Girl Who Couldn't Go Wrong*) Directed by Joseph de Grasse.
CAST: Pauline Bush (The Chorus Girl), Lon Chaney (The Property Man)

SUCH IS LIFE
Rex/Universal, 2 reels. Released: March 4, 1915. Directed by Joseph de Grasse.
CAST: Pauline Bush (Polly), William C. Dowlan (Will Deming), Lon Chaney (Tod Wilkes), Olive Golden (Olive Trent)

WHERE THE FOREST ENDS
Rex/Universal, 2 reels. Released: March 7, 1915. Directed by Joseph de Grasse.
CAST: Pauline Bush (Rose), William C. Dowlan (Jack Norton), Lon Chaney (Paul Rouchelle), Joseph de Grasse (Silent Jordan)

OUTSIDE THE GATES
Rex/Universal, 2 reels. Released: March 14, 1915. Directed by Joseph de Grasse.
CAST: Pauline Bush (Sister Ursula), William C. Dowlan (Manuel), Lon Chaney (Perez)

ALL FOR PEGGY
Rex/Universal, 1 reel. Released: March 18, 1915. Directed by Joseph de Grasse. Scenario by Ida May Park.
CAST: Pauline Bush (Peggy), William C. Dowlan (Will Jordan), Lon Chaney (The Stable Groom)

THE DESERT BREED
Rex/Universal, 2 reels. Released: March 28, 1915. Directed by Joseph de Grasse. Scenario by Tom Forman.
CAST: Pauline Bush (Pauline), Lon Chaney (Fred), William C. Dowlan (Fred's Partner)

MAID OF THE MIST
Rex/Universal, 1 reel. Released: April 1, 1915. Directed by Joseph de Grasse. Scenario by James Drayton.
CAST: Pauline Bush (The Girl), Ray Gallagher (The Boy), Lon Chaney (The Postmaster)

THE GIRL OF THE NIGHT
Rex/Universal, 2 reels. Released: April 8, 1915. Directed by Joseph de Grasse. Scenario by Ida May Park.
CAST: Pauline Bush, Hilda Slomen, Lon Chaney

THE STOOL PIGEON
Victor/Universal, 2 reels. Released: April 9, 1915. Directed by Lon Chaney. Scenario by L. G. Stafford.
CAST: J. Warren Kerrigan, Vera Sisson, George Periolat
(The first of six films Lon Chaney directed for Universal.)

THE GRIND
Rex/Universal, 3 reels. Released: April 11, 1915. Directed by Joseph de Grasse. Scenario: Ida May Park.
CAST: Pauline Bush, Queenie Rosson, and Helen Rosson (The Three Sisters), Lon Chaney (The Old Man)

FOR CASH
Victor/Universal, 2 reels. Released: May 3, 1915. Directed by Lon Chaney; scenario by W. M. Caldwell.
CAST: J. Warren Kerrigan, Vera Sisson

AN IDYLL OF THE HILLS
Rex/Universal, 2 reels. Released: May 3, 1915. Directed by Joseph de Grasse.
CAST: Pauline Bush (Kate Graham), Millard K. Wilson (Dick Massey) , Lon Chaney (A Mountaineer)

Lon Chaney

THE STRONGER MIND
United/Universal, 2 reels. Released: May 15, 1915. Directed by Joseph de
Grasse.
CAST: Murdock MacQuarrie (A Crook), Pauline Bush (The Girl), Lon
Chaney (The Crook's Pal)

THE OYSTER DREDGER
Victor/Universal, 2 reels. Released: June 7, 1915. Director and scenario:
Lon Chaney
CAST: J. Warren Kerrigan, Vera Sisson

STEADY COMPANY
Rex/Universal, 1 reel. Released: June 29, 1915. Directed by Joseph de
Grasse. Scenario by Ida May Park, from a story by Julius G. Furthman.
CAST: Pauline Bush (The Girl), Lon Chaney (Factory Worker)

THE VIOLIN MAKER
Victor/Universal, 1 reel. Released: July 1, 1915. Directed by Lon
Chaney. Scenario by Milton M. Moore.
CAST: Lon Chaney (A Violin Maker), Gretchen Lederer (His Wife)

THE TRUST
Victor/Universal 1 reel. Released: July 16, 1915. Directed by Lon
Chaney. Scenario by Katherine M. Kingsherry.
CAST: Vera Sisson and William Quinn (The Couple), Lon Chaney (The
Burglar)

BOUND ON THE WHEEL
Rex/Universal, 3 reels. Released: July 19, 1915. Directed by Joseph de
Grasse. Scenario by Ida May Park, from a story by Julius G. Furthman.
CAST: Elsie Jane Wilson, Lon Chaney, Lydia Yeamans Titus, Arthur
Shirley

MOUNTAIN JUSTICE
Rex/Universal, 2 reels. Released: August 6, 1915. Directed by Joseph de
Grasse. Scenario by Ida May Park, from a story by Julius G. Furthman.
CAST: Elsie Jane Wilson, Arthur Shirley, Lon Chaney, Grace Thompson

QUITS
Rex/Universal, 1 reel. Released: August 10, 1915. Directed by Joseph de Grasse. Scenario by Ida May Park, from the story "Sheriff of Long Butte" by Julius G. Furthman.
CAST: Arthur Shirley (The Sheriff), Lon Chaney (Frenchy)

THE CHIMNEY'S SECRET
Victor/Universal, 1 reel. Released: August 18, 1915. Director and scenario: Lon Chaney. Based on a story by Milton M. Moore.
CAST: Lon Chaney (The Robber), Gretchen Lederer (The Wife)

THE PINE'S REVENGE
Rex/Universal, 2 reels. Released: September 19, 1915. Directed by Joseph de Grasse. Scenario by Ida May Park, from her story "The King's Keeper."
CAST: Cleo Madison (The Girl), Lon Chaney, Arthur Shirley, Millard K. Wilson (The Rivals)

THE FASCINATION OF THE FLEUR DE LIS
Rex/Universal 3 reels. Released: September 26, 1915. Picture Code #: 1265. Directed by Joseph de Grasse; scenario by Bess Meredyth.
CAST: Cleo Madison (Lisette), Arthur Shirley (Antone Gerome), Millard K. Wilson (The King), Lon Chaney (Duke of Safoulrug)

ALAS AND ALACK *
Rex/Universal, 1 reel. Released: October 10, 1915. Picture Code #: 1346. Directed by Joseph de Grasse. Scenario by Ida May Park.
CAST: Cleo Madison and Arthur Shirley (The Lovers), Lon Chaney (The Husband)

A MOTHER'S ATONEMENT *
Rex/Universal, 3 reels. Released: October 17, 1915. Directed by Joseph de Grasse. Scenario by Ida May Park.
CAST: Cleo Madison (Alice -wife/Jen-daughter), Lon Chaney (Her Husband), Arthur Shirley (James Hilton), Wyndham Standing (Wilbur Kent), Millard K. Wilson (John Newton)

Lon Chaney

LON OF LONE MOUNTAIN
Rex/Universal, 1 reel. Released: October 19, 1915. Directed by Joseph de Grasse. Scenario by Ida May Park.
CAST: Marica Moore, Arthur Shirley, Lon Chaney, George Burrell

THE MILLIONAIRE PAUPERS *
Rex/Universal, 3 reels. Released: October 26, 1915. Directed by Joseph de Grasse. Scenario by Ida May Park.
CAST: Grace Thompson,Gretchen Lederer, Lon Chaney,Arthur Shirley, Marcia Moore, Millard K. Wilson

FATHER AND THE BOYS
Broadway/Universal, 5 reels. Released: December 20, 1915. Picture Code #: 1444. Directed by Joseph de Grasse. Scenario by Ida May Park, from the play of the same title by George Ade. Photographer: Edward Ullman.
CAST: Digby Bell (Lemuel Morewood), Louise Carbasse (Bessie Brayton), Harry Ham (William Rufus Morewood), Colin Chase (Thomas Jefferson Morewood), Yona Landowska (Emily Donelson) Mae Gaston (Frances Berkeley), Lon Chaney (Tuck Bartholomew), Hayward Mack (Major Bellamy) Didsworth H. Davenport (Tobias Ford)

UNDER A SHADOW
Rex/Universal, 2 reels. Released: December 5, 1915. Directed by Joseph de Grasse. Scenario by F. McGrew Willis, from his story "A Secret Service Affair."
CAST:Gretchen Lederer, Lon Chaney, Arthur Shirley, Millard K. Wilson

STRONGER THAN DEATH
Rex/Universal, 2 reels. Released: December 17, 1915. Directed by Joseph de Grasse. Scenario by Bess Meredyth.
CAST: Louise Carbasse, Lon Chaney, Arthur Shirley, Millard K. Wilson

DOLLY'S SCOOP *
Rex/Universal, 2 reels. Released: February 20, 1916. Picture Code #: 1557. Directed by Joseph de Grasse. Scenario by Ida May Park, from a story by Hugh Weir.
CAST: Louise Lovely (Dolly Clare), Lon Chaney (Don Fisher), Marjorie Ellison (Mrs. Fairfax), Mae Gaston (Helen), Laura Praether (Maid), Hayward Mack (James Fairfax), Millard K. Wilson (Philip), Edward Nes (Jap Boy)

THE GRIP OF JEALOUSY

Bluebird/Universal, 5 reels. Released: February 28, 1916. Picture Code #: 1499. (Working Title: *Love Thine Enemy*) Directed by Joseph de Grasse. Scenario by Ida May Park, from her story "Love Thine Enemy."

CAST: Louise Lovely (Virginia Grant), Lon Chaney (Silas Lacey), Grace Thompson (Beth Grant), Jay Belasco (Harry Grant), Hayward Mack (Philip Grant), Colin Chase (Hugh Morey), Harry Hamm (Jack Morey), Walter Belasco (Uncle Jeff), Marcia Moore (Lynda), Dixie Carr (Cora)

TANGLED HEARTS

Bluebird/Universal, 5 reels. Released: April 2, 1916. Picture Code #: 1592. Directed by Joseph de Grasse. Scenario by Ida May Park.

CAST: Louise Lovely (Vera Lane), Agnes Vernon (Lucille Seaton), Lon Chaney (John Hammond), Marjorie Ellison (Enid Hammond), Hayward Mack (Montgomery Seaton), Jay Belasco (Ernest Courtney), Georgia French (Child), Bud Chase (John Dalton)

THE GILDED SPIDER

Bluebird/Universal, 5 reels. Released: May 8, 1916. (Working Title: *The Full Cup*) Directed by Joseph de Grasse. Scenario by Ida May Park.

CAST: Louise Lovely (Leonita/Elisa), Lon Chaney (Giovanni), Lule Warrenton (Rosa), Gilmore Hammond (Cyrus Kirkham), Marjorie Ellison (Mrs. Kirkham), Hayward Mack (Burton Armitage), Jay Belasco (Paul Winston)

BOBBIE OF THE BALLET

Bluebird/Universal, 5 reels. Released: June 12, 1916. Picture Code #: 1705. Directed by Joseph de Grasse. Scenario by Ida May Park, from a story by Grant Carpenter. Photographer: George Kull

CAST: Louise Lovely (Bobbie Brent), Lon Chaney (Hook Hoover), Jay Belasco (Jack Stimson), Jean Hathaway (Mrs. Stimson), Gretchen Lederer (Velma Vrooman), Gilmore Hammond (Henry Fox), Lule Warrenton (Mrs. Hoover)

THE GRASP OF GREED

Bluebird/Universal, 5 reels. Released: July 17, 1916. Directed by Joseph de Grasse. Scenario by Ida May Park, from the novel *Mr. Meeson's Will* by H. Rider Haggard.

CAST: Louise Lovely (Alice Gordon), Lon Chaney (Jimmie), Jay Belasco (Eustace), C. N. Hammond (John Meeson), Gretchen Lederer (Lady Holmhurst)

MARK OF CAIN

Red Feather/Universal, 5 reels. Released: August 7, 1916. Picture Code #: 1790. (Working Title: *By Fate's Degree)* Directed by Joseph de Grasse. Scenario by Stuart Paton. Photographer: King Gray.

CAST: Lon Chaney (Dick Temple), Dorothy Phillips (Doris), Frank Whitson (John Graham), Gilmore Hammond (Jake), T. D. Crittenden (Mr. Wilson), Gretchen Lederer (Mrs. Wilson), Lydia Yeamans Titus (Dick's Mother), Mark Fenton (Dick's Father), Georgia French (Baby Wilson)

IF MY COUNTRY SHOULD CALL *

Red Feather/Universal, 5 reels. Released: September 25, 1916. Picture Code #: 1832. Directed by Joseph de Grasse. Scenario by Ida May Park, from a story by Virginia Terhune Van de Water. Photographer: King Gray.

CAST: Dorothy Phillips (Margaret Ardrath), Helen Leslie (Patricia Landon),, Frank Whitson (Robert Ogden), Lon Chaney (Dr. George Ardrath), Albert MacQuarrie (Col. Belden), Jack Nelson (Donald), Carl Von Schiller (Zuroff), Gretchen Lederer (Mrs. Ardrath)

PLACE BEYOND THE WINDS *

Red Feather/Universal, 5 reels. Released: November 6, 1916. Picture Code #: 1954. Directed by Joseph de Grasse. Scenario by Ida May Park, from the novel of the same title by Harriet T. Comstock. Photographer: King Gray.

CAST: Dorothy Phillips (Priscilla Glenn), Jack Mulhall (Dick Travers), Lon Chaney (Jerry Jo), Joseph de Grasse (Anton Farwell), C. Normand Hammond (Nathan Glenn), Alice May Youse (Mrs. Glenn), Grace Carlyle (Joan Moss), Countess Du Cello (Mrs. Travers)

FELIX ON THE JOB

Victor/Universal, 1 reel. Released: October 31, 1916. Directed by Joseph de Grasse. Scenario by Harry Wielze.

CAST: George Felix (Felix), Eva Loring (His Wife), Lon Chaney (Tod), Lydia Yeamans Titus (Tod's Wife)

ACCUSING EVIDENCE

Big U/Universal. Released: November 23, 1916.

CAST: Lon Chaney, Pauline Bush, Murdock MacQuarrie

(There is some evidence that this may have been a previously released film which was just retitled.)

PRICE OF SILENCE
Bluebird/Universal, 5 reels. Released: December 11, 1916. Picture Code #: 2066.Directed by Joseph de Grasse. Scenario by Ida May Park, from a short story by W. Carey Wonderly. Photographer: King Gray.
CAST: Dorothy Phillips (Helen Urmy), Jack Mulhall (Ralph Kelton), Lon Chaney (Edmond Stafford), Frank Whitson (Oliver Urmy), Evelyn Selbie (Jenny Cupps), Jay Belasco (Billy Cupps), Eddie Brown (Landlord)

THE PIPER'S PRICE
Bluebird/Universal, 5 reels. Released: January 8, 1917. Picture Code #: 2162. Directed by Joseph de Grasse. Scenario by Ida May Park, from the short story of the same title by Mrs. Wilson Woodrow. Photographer: King Gray.
CAST: Dorothy Phillips (Amy Hadley), William Stowell (Ralph Hadley), Lon Chaney (Billy Kilmartin), Maud George (Jessica Hadley), Claire Du Brey (Jessica's Maid)

HELL MORGAN'S GIRL
Bluebird/Universal, 5 reels. Released: March 5, 1917. Picture Code #: 2204. Directed by Joseph de Grasse. Scenario by Ida May Park, from the story "The Wrong Side of Paradise" by Harvey Gates. Photographer: King Gray. Cost of Production: $8,600; profit: $450,000.
CAST: Dorothy Phillips (Lola), William Stowell (Roger Curwell), Lon Chaney (Sleter Noble), Lilyan Rosine (Olga), Joseph Girard (Oliver Curwell), Alfred Allen ("Hell" Morgan)

THE MASK OF LOVE
Big U/Universal, 1 reel. Released: March 29, 1917. Directed by Joseph de Grasse.
CAST: Pauline Bush (The Girl), Lon Chaney (Marino)

THE GIRL IN THE CHECKERED COAT
Bluebird/Universal, 5 reels. Released: April 23, 1917. Picture Code #: 2280. Directed by Joseph de Grasse. Scenario by Ida May Park, from a story by E. M. Ingleton. Photographer: King Gray.
CAST: Dorothy Phillips (Mary Graham "Flash" Fan), William Stowell (David Norman), Lon Chaney (Hector Maitland), Mrs. A. E. Witting (Ann Maitland), David Kirby (Jim), Jane Bernoudy (Sally), Nellie Allen (Hector's lady friend), Countess Du Cello (Landlady)

Lon Chaney

THE FLASHLIGHT
Bluebird/Universal, 5 reels. Released: May 21, 1917. Picture Code #: 2355. (Working Title: *The Flashlight Girl*.) Director and Scenario: Ida May Park. Adapted from a short story "The Flash-Light" by Albert M. Treynore. Photographer: King Gray
CAST: Dorothy Phillips (Delice Brixton), William Stowell (Jack Lane), , Lon Chaney (Henry Norton and Porter Brixton), Alfred Allen (John Peterson), George Burrell (Barclay), Evelyn Selbie (Mrs. Barclay), Clyde Benson (Deputy), O. C. Jackson (Howard, Lane's servant) Mark Fenton (Judge)

A DOLL'S HOUSE
Bluebird/Universal, 5 reels. Released: June 11, 1917. Picture Code #: 2410. Director and Scenario: Joseph de Grasse, based on the play by Henrik Ibsen. Photographer: King Gray.
CAST: Dorothy Phillips (Nora Helmer), William Stowell (Torvald Helmer), Lon Chaney (Nils Krogstad), Sidney Dean (Dr. Rank), Miriam Shelby (Christina Linden), Helen Wright (Anna)

FIRES OF REBELLION
Bluebird/Universal, 5 reels. Released: July 2, 1917. Picture Code #: 2475. Director and Scenario: Ida May Park. Adapted from her own story. Photographer: King Gray
CAST: Dorothy Phillips (Madge Garvey), William Stowell (John Blake), Lon Chaney (Russell Hanlon), Belle Bennett (Helen Mallory), Golda Madden (Cora Hayes), Alice May Youse (Mrs. Garvey), Edward Brady (Dan Mallory), Richard La Reno (Joe Garvey)

THE RESCUE
Bluebird/Universal, 5 reels. Released: July 23, 1917. Picture Code #: 2499. Director and Scenario: Ida May Park. Adapted from a story by Hugh Kahler. Photographer: King Gray.
CAST: Dorothy Phillips (Anne Wetherall), William Stowell (Kent Wetherall), Lon Chaney (Thomas Holland), Gretchen Lederer (Nell Jerrold), Molly Malone (Betty Jerrold) , Claire Du Brey (Henriette), Gertrude Astor (Mrs. Hendricks)

TRIUMPH
Bluebird/Universal, 5 reels. Released: September 3, 1917. Picture Code #: 2540. Directed by Joseph de Grasse. Scenario by Fred Myton, from the story of the same title by Samuel Hopkins Adams.

CAST: Dorothy Phillips (Nell Baxter), Lon Chaney (Paul Neihoff), William Stowell (Dudley Weyman), William J. Dryer (David Montieth), Clair Du Brey (Lillian Du Pon), Clyde Benson (Rupert Vincent), Helen Wright (Character Woman), Ruth Elder (Second Woman)

PAY ME
Jewel/Universal, 5 reels. Released: September 1, 1917. Picture Code #: 2480. (Working Title: *The Vengeance of the West*). Directed by Joseph de Grasse. Scenario by Bess Meredyth, from a story by Joseph de Grasse; Photographer: King Gray.
CAST: Lon Chaney (Joe Lawson), Dorothy Phillips (Marta), William Stowell (Bill the Boss), Ed Brown (Martin), William Clifford (Hal Curtis) , Evelyn Selbie (Hilda Hendricks), Tom Wilson ("Mac" Jepson), Claire Du Brey (Nita), John George (Bar Patron)

THE EMPTY GUN
Gold Seal/Universal, 3 reels. Released: September 4, 1917. Directed by Joseph de Grasse. Scenario by J. Grubb Alexander and Fred Myton.
CAST: Lon Chaney, Claire McDowell, Sam de Grasse

BONDAGE
Bluebird/Universal, 5 reels. Released: October 17, 1917. Picture Code #: 2580. Director and Scenario: Ida May Park. Adapted from a story by Edna Kenton. Photographer: King Gray.
CAST: Dorothy Phillips (Elinor Crawford), William Stowell (Evan Kilvert), Lon Chaney (The Seducer), Gertrude Astor (Eugenia Darth), J. B. McLaughlin (Bertie Vawtry), Jean Porter (Jean), Eugene Owen (James)

ANYTHING ONCE
Bluebird/Universal, 5 reels. Released: October 8, 1917. (Working Title: *The Maverick.*) Directed by Joseph de Grasse. Scenario by William Parker, from a story by Izola Forrester and Mann Page. Photographer: Jack MacKenzie.
CAST: Franklyn Farnum (Theodore Crosby), Claire Du Brey (Senorita Dolores), Lon Chaney (Waught Mohr), Marjory Lawrence (Dorothy Stuart), Mary St. John (Mrs. Stuart), Sam de Grasse (Sir Mortimer Beggs), H. M. Thurston (Getting Mohr), Raymond Wells ("Horned Toad" Smith), William Dyer (Jethro Quail), Frank Tokunaga (Algeron)

Lon Chaney

THE SCARLET CAR *

Bluebird/Universal, 5 reels. Released: December 24, 1917. Picture Code #: 2760. Directed by Joseph de Grasse. Scenario by William Parker, from the novel by Richard Harding Davis. Photographer: King Gray.

CAST: Franklyn Farnum (Billy Winthrop), Al Filson (Samuel Winthrop), Lon Chaney (Paul Revere Forbes), Edith Johnson (Beatrice Forbes), Sam de Grasse (Ernest Peabody), Howard Crampton (Cyrus Peabody), William Lloyd (Jim Pettit)

BROADWAY LOVE

Bluebird/Universal, 5 reels. Released: January 21, 1918. Picture Code #: 2775. Director and Scenario: Ida May Park. Adapted from the novelette by W. Carey Wonderly. Photographer: King Gray.

CAST: Dorothy Phillips (Midge O'Hara), William Stowell (Henry Rockwell), Lon Chaney (Elmer Watkins), Juanita Hansen (Cherry Blow), Harry Von Meter (Jack Chalvey), Gladys Tennyson (Mrs. Watkins), Eve Southern (Drina)

THE GRAND PASSION

Jewel/Universal, 7 reels. Released: February 1, 1918. Picture Code #: 2640. (Working Title: *The Boss of Powderville.*) Director and Scenario: Ida May Park. Adapted from the novel *The Boss of Powderville* by Thomas Addison; Photographer: King Gray; Technical Directed by Milton Moore.

CAST: Dorothy Phillips (Viola Argos), Jack Mulhall (Jack Ripley), Lon Chaney (Paul Argos), William Stowell (Dick Evans), Bert Appling (Red Pete Jackson), Evelyn Selbie (Boston Kate), Alfred Allen (Ben Mackey)

THE KAISER, THE BEAST OF BERLIN

Jewel/Universal, 7 reels. Released: March 9, 1918. Picture Code #: 2812. Produced and Directed by Rupert Julian. Scenario by Elliott J. Clawson and Rupert Julian. Photographer: Edward Kull.

CAST: Rupert Julian (The Kaiser), Nigel de Brulier (Capt. Von Neigle), Lon Chaney (Bethmann-Hollweg), Harry Von Meter (Capt. Von Hancke), Harry Carter (General Von Kluck), Joseph Girard (Ambassador Gerard), H. Barrows (General Haig), Alfred Allen (General Pershing), Harry Holden (General Joffre), Elmo Lincoln (Marcas, the Blacksmith), Ruth Clifford (Gabrielle), Betty Carpenter (Bride), Ruby Lafayette (Grandmother Marcas), Zoe Rae (Gretel), Mark Fenton (Admiral Von Tirpitz), Jay Smith (Marshal Von

Hindenburg), Jack MacDonald (King Albert),Allan Sears (Capt. Von Wohlbold), W. H. Bainbridge (Col. Schmiedcke), Walter Belasco (Admiral Von Pliscott) Pedro Sose (General Diaz), Orlo Eastman (President Wilson, Georgie Hupp (Little Jean), Winter Hall (Dr. Von Gressler), Frank Lee (Hansel)

FAST COMPANY
Bluebird/Universal, 5 reels. Released: April 1, 1918. Directed by Lynn F. Reynolds. Scenario by Eugene B. Lewis and Waldemar Young, from a story by John McDermott. Photographer: Edward Ullman.
CAST: Franklyn Farnum (Lawrence Percival Van Huyler), Fred Montague (Peter Van Huyler), Katherine Griffith (Mrs. Van Huyler), Lon Chaney (Dan McCarty), Juanita Hansen (Alicia Vanderveldt), Edward Cecil (Richard Barnaby)

A BROADWAY SCANDAL
Bluebird/Universal, 5 reels, 4,400 ft. Released: June 1, 1918. Picture Code #: 2873. Directed by Joseph De Grasse. Story by Harvey Gates. Photographer: Edward Ullman.
CAST: Carmel Myers (Nenette Bisson), W. H. Bainbridge (Dr. Kendall), Edwin August (David Kendall), Lon Chaney ("Kink" Colby) , Andrew Robson (Armande Bisson), S. K. Shilling (Paul Caval), Frederick Gamble (Falkner)

RIDDLE GWANE
Paramount-Artcraft, 5 reels, 4,757 ft. Released: August 19, 1918. (Portions of this film were shot on location in Chatsworth, California.) Supervisor: Thomas H. Ince. Directed by Lambert Hillyer. Scenario by Charles Alden Seltzer, from his novel *The Vengeance of Jefferson Gwane*. Photographer: Joe August; art directed by G. Harold Percival.
CAST: William S. Hart (Jefferson "Riddle" Gwane), Katherine MacDonald (Kathleen Harkness), Lon Chaney (Hame Bozzam), Gretchen Lederer (Blanche Dillon), Gertrude Short (Jane Gwane), Leon Kent (Jess Cass), Milton Ross (Reb Butler), E. B. Tilton (Col. Harkness)

THAT DEVIL, BATEESE
Bluebird/Universal, 5 reels. Released: September 2, 1918. Picture Code #: 2949. Directed by William Wolbert. Scenario by Bernard McConville, from a story by Bess Meredyth. Photographer: Charles Seeling.
CAST: Monroe Salisbury (Bateese Latour), Ada Gleason (Katherine St. John), Lamar Johnstone (Martin Stuart), Lon Chaney (Louis Courteau), Andrew Robson (Father Pierre)

Lon Chaney

THE TALK OF THE TOWN
Bluebird/Universal, 6 reels. Released: September 28, 1918. Director and scenario: Allen Holubar. Adapted from the novelette *Discipline and Genevra* by Harold Vickers. Photographer: Fred Granville.

CAST: Dorothy Phillips (Genevra French), George Fawcett (Major French), Clarissa Selwynne (Aunt Harriet), William Stowell (Lawrence Tabor), Lon Chaney (Jack Langhorne), Gloria Jay (Genevra at age 5), Una Fleming (Dancer)

DANGER - GO SLOW
Universal Special/Universal, 6 reels. Released: December 16, 1918. Picture Code #: 2980. Directed by Robert Z. Leonard. Scenario by Robert Z. Leonard and Mae Murray. Photographer: Allan Siegler.

CAST: Mae Murray (Mugsy Mulane), Jack Mulhall (Jimmy, the Eel) Lon Chaney (Bud), Lydia Knott (Aunt Sarah), Joseph Girard (Judge Cotton)

THE WICKED DARLING
Universal, 6 reels. Released: February 3, 1919. Picture Code #: 3014. (Working Titles: *The Gutter Rose, The Rose of the Dark, The Rose of the Night.*) Directed by Tod Browning. Scenario by Harvey Gates, from a story by Evelyn Campbell. Photographer: Alfred Gosden.

CAST: Priscilla Dean (Mary Stevens), Wellington Playter (Kent Mortimer), Lon Chaney (Stoop Connors), Spottiswoode Aitken (Fadem), Gertrude Astor (Adele Hoyt), Kalla Pascha (Bartender)

THE FALSE FACES *
Paramount-Artcraft, 7 reels. 6,940 ft. Released: February 16, 1919. Presented by: Thomas H. Ince. Director and Scenario: Irvin V. Willat. Adapted from the novel by Louis Joseph Vance. Photographers: Edwin W. Willat and Paul Eagler.

CAST: Henry B. Walthall (Michael Lanyard, "The Lone Wolf"), Mary Anderson (Cecilia Brooke), Lon Chaney (Karl Ekstrom), Milton Ross (Ralph Crane), Thornton Edwards (Lt. Thackeray), William Bowman (Capt. Osborne), Garry McGarry (Submarine Lieutenant), Ernest Pasque (Blensop)

A MAN'S COUNTRY

Robertson-Cole Co., 5 reels. Released: July 13, 1919. Directed by Henry Kolker. Scenario by E. Richard Schayer, from a story by John Lynch. Photographer: Robert Newhard.

CAST: Alma Rubens (Kate Carewe), Albert Roscoe (Ralph Bowen), Lon Chaney ("Three Card" Duncan), Joseph Dowling (Marshall Leland), Edna May Wilson (Ruth Kemp), Alfred Hollingsworth (Oliver Kemp), Phil Gastrock (Connell)

PAID IN ADVANCE

Jewel/Universal, 6 reels, 5,565 ft. Released: July 7, 1919. Director and Scenario by Allen Holubar, based on a story by James Oliver Curwood. Photographer: King Gray; Film Editor: Grant Whytock.

CAST: Dorothy Phillips (Joan Gray), Joseph Girard (John Gray), Lon Chaney (Bateese Le Blanc), Priscilla Dean (Marie) , William Stowell (Jim Blood), Frank Brownlee (Gold Dust Barker), Bill Burress (Regan), Harry De More (Flapjack)

THE MIRACLE MAN *

Paramount-Artcraft, 8 reels. Released: August 31, 1919. Picture Code #: A 88. Producer, Director and Scenario: George Loane Tucker. Adapted from the novel by Frank L. Packard and the play by George M. Cohan. Photographer: Philip Rosen and Ernest Palmer. Assistant Director: Chester L. Roberts.

CAST: Thomas Meighan (Tom Burke), Betty Compson (Rose), Lon Chaney (The Frog), J. M. Dumont (The Dope), Joseph Dowling (The Patriarch), W. Lawson Butt (Richard King), Elinor Fair (Claire King), F. A. Turner (Mr. Higgins), Lucille Hutton (Ruth Higgins), Frankie Lee (Little Boy)

WHEN BEARCAT WENT DRY

C. R. Macauley Photoplays, 6 reels. Released: November 2, 1919. Directed by Ollie L. Sellers. Adapted from the novel by Charles Neville Buck. Photographer: Jack MacKenzie. Assistant Director: Justin McCloskey.

CAST: Vangie Valentine (Blossom Fulkerson), Walt Whitman (Joel Fulkerson), Bernard Durning (Turner Stacy, "Bearcat"), Winter Hall (Lone Stacy), Ed Brady (Rattler Webb), Millard K. Wilson (Jerry Henderson), Lon Chaney (Kindard Powers)

Lon Chaney

VICTORY * ✓
Paramount-Artcraft, 5 reels, 4,735 ft. Released: December 7, 1919.
Picture Code #: A 98. Presented and Directed by: Maurice Tourneur.
Scenario by Stephen Fox, from the novel by Joseph Conrad.
Photographer: René Guissart. Art Directors: Ben Carré and Floyd Mueller.
CAST: Jack Holt (Axel Heyst), Seena Owen (Alma), Lon Chaney
(Ricardo), Wallace Beery (Schomberg), Ben Deely (Mr. Jones), Laura
Winston (Mrs. Schomberg), Bull Montana (Pedro), George Nicholls
(Capt. Davidson)

DAREDEVIL JACK
Pathe Pictures (Serial 15 episodes). Directed by W. S. Van Dyke. Scenario
by Jack Cunningham, from a story by Frederic Chapin and Harry Hoyt.
CAST: Jack Dempsey, Josie Sedgewick, Lon Chaney, Spike Robinson,
        Ruth Langston, Hershall Mayall, Fred Starr, Frank Lanning, Albert
        Cody, Al Kaufman

TREASURE ISLAND
Paramount-Artcraft, 6 reels. Released: April 4, 1920. Picture Code #: A
97. Presented and Directed by Maurice Tourneur. Scenario by Stephen
Fox, from the novel by Robert Louis Stevenson. Photographer: René
Guissart. Art Director: Floyd Mueller
CAST: Shirley Mason (Jim Hawkins), Charles Ogle (Long John Silver),
       Sydney Dean (Squire Trelawney), Charles Hill Mailes (Dr. Livesey),
       Lon Chaney (Pew), Lon Chaney (Merry), Jose Melville (Mrs.
       Hawkins), Al Filson (Bill Bones), Wilton Taylor (Black Dog), Joseph
       Singleton (Israel Hands), Bull Montana (Morgan), Harry Holden
       (Capt. Smollet)

THE GIFT SUPREME * ✓
C. R. Macauley Productions, 6 reels. Released: May 9, 1920. Directed by
Ollie L. Sellers. Adapted from the novel by George Allan England.
Photographer: Jack MacKenzie. Assistant Director: Justin H. McCloskey.
CAST: Bernard Durning (Bradford Chandler Vinton), Seena Owen (Sylvia
Alden), Melbourne McDowell (Eliot Vinton), Tully Marshall (Irving
Stagg), Lon Chaney (Merney Stagg), Eugenie Besserer (Martha
Vinton), Jack Curtis (Rev. Ebenezer Crowley Boggs), Dick Morris
(Dopey Dan), Anna Dodge (Mrs. Wesson), Claire McDowell (Lalia
Graun)

NOMADS OF THE NORTH *

Associated First National, 6 reels. Released: October 11, 1920. Presented by: James Oliver Curwood. Directed by David M. Hartford. Scenario by David M. Hartford and James Oliver Curwood, from the novel by James Oliver Curwood. Photographer: Walter Griffin.

CAST: Lon Chaney (Raoul Challoner), Lewis S. Stone (Cpl. O'Connor), Melbourne MacDonald (Duncan McDougall), Spottiswoode Aitken (Old Roland), Francis MacDonald (Buck McDougall)

THE PENALTY *

Goldwyn Pictures, 7 reels. Released: November 21, 1920. In Production: February 7, 1920 to April 2, 1920, 49 Days. Picture Code #: 98. Portions of this film shot on location in San Francisco, California. The film was re-issued in 1926 by MGM. Presented by: Samuel Goldwyn and Rex Beach. Directed by Wallace Worsley. Scenario by Charles Kenyon and Philip Lonergan, from the novel by Gouverneur Morris. Photographer: Dan Short. Film Editors: Frank S. Hall and J. G. Hawks. Cost of Production: $88,868.

CAST: Lon Chaney (Blizzard), Ethel Grey Terry (Rose), Charles Clary (Dr. Ferris), Claire Adams (Barbara), Kenneth Harlan (Dr. Wilmont), James Mason (Frisco Pete), Edouard Trebaol (Bubbles), Milton Ross (Lichtenstein), Wilson Hummel (One of Blizzard's Men), Cesare Gravina (Sculpting Instructor)

OUTSIDE THE LAW *

Universal-Jewel 8 reels 7,754 ft. Released: January 6, 1921. Picture Code #: 3341. Portions of the film were shot on location in San Francisco's Nob Hill, waterfront and Chinatown areas. The film was re-released in 1926 by Universal. Presented by Carl Laemmle. Directed by Tod Browning. Scenario by Lucien Hubbard, from a story by Tod Browning. Titles: Lewis Lipton and Fred Archer. Photographer: William Fildew. Art Director: E. E. Sheeley. Assistant Director Leo McCarey.

CAST: Priscilla Dean(Molly Madden /Silky Moll), Wheeler Oakman (Dapper Bill Ballard), Lon Chaney (Black Mike Sylva), Ralph Lewis (Silent Madden), E. A. Warren (Chang Low), Lon Chaney (Ah Wing), Stanley Goethals (That Kid Across the Hall), Melbourne MacDowell (Morgan Spencer), Wilton Taylor (Inspector), John George (Humpy)

Lon Chaney

FOR THOSE WE LOVE
Goldwyn Pictures/Betty Compson Prods., 6 reels, 5,752 ft. Released: March 11, 1921. Producer: Betty Compson. Director and Scenario: Arthur Rosson. Adapted from a story by Perley Poore Sheehan.

CAST: Betty Compson (Bernice Arnold), Richard Rosson (Jimmy Arnold), Lon Chaney (Trix Ulner), Camille Astor (Vida), Bert Woodruff (Dr. Bailee), Harry Duffield (George Arnold), Walter Morosco (Johnny Fletcher), George Cooper (Bert), Frank Campeau (Frank)

BITS OF LIFE
Associated First National, 6 reels, 6,339 ft. Released: September 4, 1921. Presented and directed by Marshall Neilan. Scenario by Lucita Squier, additional story by Marshall Neilan. Photographer: David Kesson; Assistant Directors: James Flood and William Scully.

CAST: Wesley Barry (Tom Levitt, as a boy), Rockliffe Fellowes (Tom Levitt), Lon Chaney (Chin Gow), Noah Beery (Hindoo), Anna May Wong (Chin Gow's wife) John Bowers (Reginald Vanderbrook). Others in the cast included Dorothy Mackaill, Edythe Chapman, Frederick Burton, James Bradbury, Jr., Teddy Sampson, Tammany Young, Harriet Hammond, James Neil, and Scott Welsh.

ACE OF HEARTS *
Goldwyn Pictures 6 reels 5,883 ft. Released: November 21, 1921. Picture Code #: 151. Directed by Wallace Worsley. Scenario by Ruth Wightman, from the novel by Gouverneur Morris; Photographer: Don Short.

CAST: Leatrice Joy (Lilith), John Bowers (Forrest), Lon Chaney (Farralone), Hardee Kirkland (Morgridge), Raymond Hatton (The Menace), Roy Laidlaw (Doorkeeper), Edwin Wallock (Chemist)

THE TRAP *
Universal-Jewel, 6 reels, 5,481 ft. Released: May 9, 1922. (The film was re-released in 1926 by Universal.) Picture Code #: 3678. (Working Title: *Wolfbreed, The Heart Of A Wolf.*) Directed by Robert Thornby. Scenario by George C. Hull, from a story by Lon Chaney, Lucien Hubbard, Robert Thornby and Irving Thalberg. Photographer: Virgil Miller. (Portions of this film were shot on location in Yosemite, California.)

CAST: Lon Chaney (Gaspard), Alan Hale (Benson), Dagmar Godowsky (Thalie), Stanley Goethals (The Boy), Irene Rich (The Teacher), Spottiswoode Aitken (The Factor), Herbert Standing (The Priest), Frank Campeau (The Police Sergeant)

VOICES OF THE CITY
Goldwyn Pictures, 6 reels, 5,630 ft. Released: August 20, 1922. Picture Code # 143. Working Titles: *The Night Rose, Flowers of Darkness.* Directed by Wallace Worsley. Scenario by Arthur F. Statter, from the novel by Leroy Scott.
CAST: Leatrice Joy (Georgia Rodman), Lon Chaney (O'Rourke), John Bowers (Graham), Cullen Landis (Jimmy), Richard Tucker (Clancy), Mary Warren (Mary Rodman), Edythe Chapman (Mrs. Rodman), Betty Schade (Sally), Maurice B. Flynn (Pierson), Milton Ross (Courey), John Cossar (Garrison)

FLESH AND BLOOD *
Western Pictures Exploitation, 6 reels, 5,300 ft. Released: August 27, 1922. Presented and directed by Irving Cummings. Scenario by Louis Duryea Lighton.
CAST: Lon Chaney (David Webster), Edith Roberts (The Angel Lady), Noah Beery (Li Fang), DeWitt Jennings (Detective Doyle), Ralph Lewis (Fletcher Burton), Jack Mulhall (Ted Burton), Togo Yamamoto (The Prince), Kate Price (The Landlady), Wilfred Lucas (The Policeman)

THE LIGHT IN THE DARK *
Associated First National, 7 reels, 5,600 ft. Released: September 3, 1922. Directed by Clarence Brown. Scenario by William Dudley Pelley and Clarence Brown. Photographer: Alfred Ortlieb. (Filmed on location in New York City.)
CAST: Hope Hampton (Bessie MacGregor), E. K. Lincoln (J. Warburton Ashe), Lon Chaney (Tony Pantelli), Theresa Maxwell Conover (Mrs. Templeton Orrin), Dorothy Walters (Mrs. Callerty), Charles Mused (Detective Braenders), Edgar Norton (Peters), Dore Davidson (Jerusalem Mike)

SHADOWS *
Preferred Pictures, 7 reels, 7,040 ft. Released: November 5, 1922. Picture Code #: F 1. (Working Title: *Ching, Ching, Chinaman*). Presented by: B. P. Schulberg. Directed by Tom Forman. Scenario by Eve Unsell and Hope Loring, from the story "Ching, Ching, Chinaman" by Wilbur Daniel Steele. Photographer: Harry Perry. (Portions of this film shot on location in Balboa, California and at the Louis B. Mayer Studios.)
CAST: Lon Chaney (Yen Sin), Marguerite De La Motte (Sympathy Gibbs), Harrison Ford (John Malden), John Sainpolis (Nate Snow), Walter Long (Daniel Gibbs), Buddy Messenger ("Mister Bad Boy"), Priscilla Bonner (Mary Brent), Frances Raymond (Emsy Nickerson)

Lon Chaney

OLIVER TWIST *

Associated First National/Jackie Coogan Prods., 8 reels, 7,761 ft. Released: November 5, 1922. Presented by Sol Lesser; Supervisor: Jack Coogan, Sr. Directed by Frank Lloyd. Scenario by Frank Lloyd and Harry Weil, from the novel by Charles Dickens. Photographers: Glen McWilliams and Robert Martin. Titles: Walter Anthony; Art Director: Stephen Goosson. Film Editor: Irene Morra. Costumes: Walter J. Israel.

CAST: Jackie Coogan (Oliver Twist), Lon Chaney (Fagin), Gladys Brockwell (Nancy Sikes), George Siegmann (Bill Sikes), James Marcus (Mr. Bumble), Aggie Herring (The Widow Corney), Lionel Belmore (Mr. Brownlow), Edouard Trebaol (Artful Dodger), Taylor Graves (Charley Bates), Carl Stockdale (Mr. Monks), Lewis Sargent (Noah Claypool), Joan Standing (Charlotte), Nelson McDowell (Mr. Sowerberry), Joseph H. Hazelton (Mr. Grimwig), Eddie Boland (Toby Crackitt), Florence Hale (Mrs. Bedwin), Esther Ralston (Rose Maylie), Gertrude Claire (Mrs. Maylie)

QUINCY ADAMS SAWYER

Metro Pictures, 8 reels, 7,895 ft. Released: December 4, 1922. Picture Code #: 136. Directed by Clarence Badger. Scenario by Bernard McConville, from the novel by Charles Felton Pidgin. Photographer: Rudolph Berquist.

CAST: John Bowers (Quincy Adams Sawyer), Blanche Sweet (Alice Pettengill), Lon Chaney (Obadiah Strout), Barbara La Marr (Lindy Putnam), Elmo Lincoln (Abner Stiles), Louise Fazenda (Mandy Skinner), Joseph Dowling (Nathaniel Sawyer), Claire McDowell (Mrs. Putnam), Edward Connelly (Deacon Pettengill), June Elvidge (Betsy Ann Ross), Victor Potel (Hiram Maxwell), Gale Henry (Samanthy), Hank Mann (Ben Bates), Kate Lester (Mrs. Sawyer), Billy Franey (Bob Wood), Harry Depp and Taylor Graves (The Cobb Twins)

A BLIND BARGAIN

Goldwyn Pictures, 5 reels, 4,473 ft. Released: December 10, 1922. Picture Code #: 165. Directed by Wallace Worsley. Scenario by J. G. Hawks, from the novel *Octave Of Claudius* by Barry Pain. Photographer: Norbert Brodin.

CAST: Lon Chaney (Dr. Lamb/Ape-Man), Raymond McKee (Robert), Jacqueline Logan (Angela), Virginia True Boardman (Mrs. Sandell), Fontaine La Rue (Mrs. Lamb), Aggie Herring (Bessie), Virginia Madison (Angela's Mother)

ALL THE BROTHERS WERE VALIANT

Metro Pictures, 7 reels, 6,265 ft. Released: January 15, 1923. Picture Code #: 140. Directed by Irvin V. Willat. Scenario by Julien Josephson, from the novel by Ben Ames Williams. Photographer: Robert Kurrle.

CAST: Malcolm McGregor (Joel Shore), Billie Dove (Priscilla Holt), Lon Chaney (Mark Shore), William H. Orlamond (Aaron Burnham), Robert McKim (Finch), Robert Kortman (Varde), Otto Brower (Morrell), Curt Rehfeld (Hooper), William V. Mong (Cook), Leo Willis (Tom), Shannon Day (The Brown Girl)

WHILE PARIS SLEEPS

W. W. Hodkinson Corp./Maurice Tourneur Prods., 6 reels, 4,850 ft. Released: January 21, 1923. Picture Code #: H-134. (Working Title: *The Glory of Love;* made in 1920.) Directed by Maurice Tourneur. Based on the story "The Glory of Love" by Pan. Photographer: René Guissart. Scenic Effects: Floyd Mueller.

CAST: Lon Chaney (Henri Santodos), Mildred Manning (Bebe Larvache), John Gilbert (Dennis O'Keefe), Hardee Kirkland (His Father), Jack MacDonald (Father Marionette), J. Farrell MacDonald (George Morier)

THE SHOCK *

Universal-Jewel. 7 reels. 6,738 ft. Released: June 10, 1923. Picture Code #: 3817. (Working Title: *Bittersweet.)* Directed by Lambert Hillyer. Scenario by Arthur Statter and Charles Kenyon, from a story by William Dudley Pelley. Photographer: Dwight Warren.

CAST: Lon Chaney (Wilse Dilling), Virginia Valli (Gertrude Hadley), Jack Mower (Jack Cooper), William Welsh (Mischa Hadley), Henry Barrows (John Cooper, Sr.), Christine Mayo (Anne Vincent), Harry Devere (Olaf Wismer), John Beck (Bill), Walter Long (The Captain), Robert Kortman (Henchman), Togo Yamamoto (Messenger at restaurant)

HUNCHBACK OF NOTRE DAME *

Universal-Super Jewel, 12 reels, 12,000 ft. Released: September 6, 1923. Picture Code #: 3874. In Production: December 16, 1922 to June 3, 1923, 146 Days. Presented by Carl Laemmle. Directed by Wallace Worsley. Scenario by Edward T. Lowe, Jr. Adapted from the novel by Victor Hugo by Perley Poore Sheehan. Photographers: Robert Newhard and Tony Kornman. Additional Photographers: Virgil Miller, Charles Stumar and Stephen S. Norton. Film Editors: Sidney Singerman, Maurice Pivar and Edward Curtiss. Art Directors: Elmer E. Sheeley and Sidney

Ullman. Costume Supervision: Col. Gordon McGee. Assistant Directors: Jack Sullivan, James Dugan and William Wyler. Cost of Production: $1,250,000.

CAST: Lon Chaney (Quasimodo), Ernest Torrance (Clopin), Patsy Ruth Miller (Esmeralda), Norman Kerry (Phoebus), Kate Lester (Madame de Gondelaurier), Brandon Hurst (Jehan), Raymond Hatton (Gringoire), Tully Marshall (Louis XI), Nigel De Brulier (Dom Claude), Harry Van Meter (Monsieur Neufchatel), Gladys Brockwell (Godule), Eulalie Jensen (Marie), Winifred Bryson (Fleur de Lis), Nick De Ruiz (Monsieur le Torteru), Edwin Wallock (King's Chamberlain), Ray Meyers (Charmolou's Assistant), John Cossar (Judge of Court), William Parke, Sr. (Josephus), Roy Laidlaw (Charmolu), Robert Kortman (Hook-Hand), Harry Holman (Fat Man), Joe Bonomo and Harvey Perry (Stunt Doubles for Lon Chaney)

THE NEXT CORNER
Paramount Pictures, 7 reels, 7,081 ft. Released: February 18, 1924. Picture Code #: 628. Presented by Adolph Zukor and Jesse L. Lasky. Directed by Sam Wood. Scenario by Monte Katterjohn, from the novel and play by Kate Jordan. Photographer: Alfred Gilks.

CAST: Conway Tearle (Robert Maury), Lon Chaney (Juan Serafin), Dorothy Mackaill (Elsie Maury), Ricardo Cortez (Don Arturo), Louise Dresser (Nina Race), Remea Radzina (Countess Longueval), Dorothy Cumming (Paula Vrain), Mrs. Bertha Feducha (Julie), Bernard Seigel (The Stranger)

HE WHO GETS SLAPPED * ∨
Metro-Goldwyn, 7 reels, 6,614 ft. Released: November 2, 1924. Picture Code #: 192. In Production: June 17, 1924 to July 28, 1924, 37 Days. Presented by Louis B. Mayer. Produced by Irving G. Thalberg. Directed by Victor Seastrom. Scenario by Victor Seastrom and Carey Wilson, from the play by Leonid Andreyev. Photographer: Milton Moore. Sets: Cedric Gibbons. Film Editor: Hugh Wynn. Costumes: Sophie Wachner. Assistant Director: M. K. Wilson. Production Manager. David Howard. Cost of Production: $172,000; Profit: $349,000.

CAST: Lon Chaney (HE), Norma Shearer (Consuelo), John Gilbert (Bezano), Tully Marshall (Count Mancini), Marc MacDermott (Baron Regnard), Ford Sterling (Tricaud), Harvey Clark (Briquet), Paulette Duval (Zinida), Ruth King (HE's Wife), Clyde Cook, Brandon Hurst, and George Davis (Clowns), Erik Stocklassa (Ringmaster). Billy Bletcher's appearance as a Clown was cut from the final release print.

THE MONSTER *

Metro-Goldwyn, 7 reels, 6,425 ft. Released: February 22, 1925. Directed by Roland West. Scenario by Willard Mack and Albert Kenyon, from the play by Crane Wilbur. Titles: C. Gardner Sullivan. Photographer: Hal Mohr. Film Editor: A. Carle Palm. Production Manager: W. L. Heywood.

CAST: Lon Chaney (Dr. Ziska), Gertrude Olmsted (Betty Watson), Hallam Cooley (Watson's Head Clerk), Johnny Arthur (The Under Clerk), Charles A. Sellon (The Constable), Walter James (Caliban), Knute Erickson (Daffy Dan), George Austin (Rigo), Edward McWade (Luke Watson), Ethel Wales (Mrs. Watson)

THE UNHOLY THREE *

Metro-Goldwyn-Mayer, 7 reels, 6,948 ft. Released: August 16, 1925. Picture Code #: 217. In Production: December 20, 1924 to January 17, 1925, 25 Days. Presented by Louis B. Mayer. Produced by Irving G. Thalberg. Directed by Tod Browning. Scenario by Waldemar Young, from the novel by Clarence A. Robbins. Photographer: David Kesson; Sets: Cedric Gibbons and Joseph Wright. Film Editor: Daniel J. Gray; Cost of Production: $114,00; Profit: $328,000.

CAST: Lon Chaney (Echo), Mae Busch (Rosie), Matt Moore (Hector McDonald), Victor McLaglen (Hercules), Harry Earles (Tweedledee), Matthew Betz (Regan), Edward Connelly (Judge), William Humphreys (Defense Attorney), A. E. Warren (Prosecuting Attorney), John Merkyl (Jeweler), Charles Wellesley (John Arlington), Percy Williams (Butler), Lou Morrison (Commissioner of Police). Violet Crane's appearance as the Arlington Baby and Marjorie Morton as Mrs. Arlington were cut from the release print.

PHANTOM OF THE OPERA *

Universal-Jewel, 10 reels, 8,464 ft. Released: September 6, 1925. Picture Code #: 4159. In Production: October 29, 1924 to early January 1925. Originally released with Technicolor sequences. Re-issued with sound effects, musical score and talking sequences on February 21, 1929. Presented by Carl Laemmle. Directed by Rupert Julian; supplemental Direction by Edward Sedgwick. Scenario by Elliott Clawson, from the novel by Gaston Leroux. Titles: Walter Anthony. Photographers: Charles Van Enger, A.S.C. and Milton Bridenbecker. Art Director: Charles D. Hall. Film Editor: Maurice Pivar. Ballet Master: Ernest Belcher; Cost of Production: $632,357; Profit: $539,682.

CAST: Lon Chaney (The Phantom), Mary Philbin (Christine Daae), Norman Kerry (Raoul de Chagny), Snitz Edwards (Florine Papillon),

Gibson Gowland (Simon), John Sainpolis (Phillippe de Chagny), Virginia Pearson (Carlotta), Arthur Edmund Carewe (Ledoux), Edith Yorke (Mama Valerius), Anton Vaverka (The Prompter), Bernard Seigel (Joseph Buquet), Olive Ann Alcorn (La Sorelli), Edward Cecil (Faust), Alexander Bevani (Mephistopheles), John Miljan (Valentine), Grace Marvin (Martha), George B. Williams (M. Richard, Manager), Bruce Covington (M. Moncharmin, Manager), Cesare Gravina (Retiring Manager), Ward Crane (Count Ruboff), Chester Conklin (Orderly), William Tryoler (Director of Orchestra), George Davis (Man at Christine's Dressing Room)

TOWER OF LIES
Metro-Goldwyn-Mayer 7 reels 6,753 ft.
Released: October 11, 1925
Picture Code #: 235
In production: May 5, 1925 to July 2, 1925, 53 Days. Working Title: *The Emperor of Portugallia.* Producer: Irving G. Thalberg; Directed by Victor Seastrom. Scenario by Agnes Christine Johnson, from the novel *The Emperor of Portugallia* by Selma Lagerlof. Titles: Marian Ainslee, Ruth Cummings. Photographer: Percy Hilburn. Sets: Cedric Gibbons, James Basevi. (Portions of the film shot on location in the Sacramento River Delta area of California.) Cost of Production: $185,000; Profit: $271,000.
CAST: Norma Shearer (Goldie), Lon Chaney (Jan), Ian Keith (Lars), Claire McDowell (Katrina), William Haines (August), David Torrence (Eric), Anne Schaffer (Helma), Leo White (Peddler), Bodil Rosing (Midwife), Mary Jane Irving (Little Girl), Adele Watson (Farmer's wife), Edward Connelly (Curate)

THE BLACKBIRD * √
Metro-Goldwyn-Mayer, 7 reels, 5,437 ft. Released: January 11, 1926. Picture Code #: 249. In Production: 26 Days. (Working Title: *The Mockingbird*) Produced by Irving G. Thalberg. Directed by Tod Browning. Scenario by Waldemar Young; adapted from "The Mockingbird" story by Tod Browning. Titles: Joseph Farnham. Photographer: Percy Hilburn. Film Editor: Errol Taggart. Sets: Cedric Gibbons, Arnold Gillespie. Wardrobe: Kathleen Kay, Maude Marsh and André-Ani. Cost of Production: $166,000; Profit: $263,000.

CAST: Lon Chaney (The Blackbird/The Bishop), Renee Adoree (Fifi), Owen Moore (West End Bertie), Doris Lloyd (Limehouse Polly), Andy MacLennon (The Shadow), William Weston (Red), Eric Mayne (A Sightseer), Sidney Bracy (Bertie's No. 1 Man), Ernie S. Adams (Bertie's No. 2 Man), Cecil Holland (Man at the Mission), Eddie Sturgis (The Bartender), Mrs. Louise Emmons (Old Lady at Mission)

THE ROAD TO MANDALAY * √

Metro-Goldwyn-Mayer, 7 reels, 6,641 ft. Released: June 28, 1926. Picture Code #: 275. In Production: March 29, 1926 to April 29, 1926, 28 Days. Produced by Irving G. Thalberg. Directed by Tod Browning. Scenario by Elliott Clawson, from a story by Tod Browning and Herman Mankiewicz. Titles: Joseph Farnham. Photographer: Merritt Gerstad. Art Directors: Cedric Gibbons, Arnold Gillespie. Film Editor: Errol Taggart. Cost of Production: $209,000. Profit: $267,000.
CAST: Lon Chaney (Singapore Joe), Henry B. Walthall (Father James), Owen Moore (The Admiral), Lois Moran (Joe's Daughter), Kamiyama Sojin (English Charlie Wing), Rose Langdon (Pansy), John George (Servant), Willie Fung (Man in Bar), Eddie Sturgis (Bartender)

TELL IT TO THE MARINES * √

Metro-Goldwyn-Mayer, 10 reels, 8,748 ft. Released: January 29, 1927. Picture Code #: 266. In Production: June 7, 1926 to August 3, 1926, 57 Days. Portions of the film were shot on location at the U. S. Marine Corps Recruit Depot, San Diego, California; aboard the battleship USS California and at Iverson's Ranch, Chatsworth, California. Produced by Irving G. Thalberg. Directed by George Hill. Story and Scenario by E. Richard Schayer. Titles: Joseph Farnham. Photographer: Ira Morgan. Sets: Cedric Gibbons and Arnold Gillespie. Film Editor: Blance Sewell. Wardrobe: Kathleen Kay and Maude Marsh. Assistant Director: M. K. Wilson. Cost of Production: $433,000; Profit: $664,000.
CAST: Lon Chaney (Sgt. O'Hara), William Haines (Pvt. "Skeet" Burns), Eleanor Boardman (Norma Dale), Eddie Gribbon (Cpl. Madden), Carmel Myers (Zaya), Warner Oland (Chinese Bandit Leader), Mitchell Lewis (Native), Frank Currier (General Wilcox), Maurice Kains (Harry), Sgt. H. H. Hopple (USMC Marine), Daniel G. Tomlinson (The Major), Willie Fung (Chinese Man at Mission). Sgt. Jiggs, U.S.M.C. Mascot played himself.

Lon Chaney

MR. WU *

Metro-Goldwyn-Mayer, 8 reels, 7,460 ft. Released: May 16, 1927. Picture Code #: 301. In Production: November 30, 1926 to January 22, 1927, 41 Days. Produced by Harry Rapf. Directed by William Nigh. Scenario by Lorna Moon, from the play by Maurice Vernon and Harold Owen. Titles: Lotta Wood. Photographer: John Arnold. Sets: Cedric Gibbons and Richard Day. Film Editor: Ben Lewis. Wardrobe: Lucia Coulter. Cost of Production: $267,000; Profit: $439,000.

CAST: Lon Chaney (Mr. Wu/Wu's Grandfather), Renee Adoree (Nang Ping), Louise Dresser (Mrs. Gregory), Holmes Herbert (Mr. Gregory), Ralph Forbes (Basil Gregory), Gertrude Olmsted (Hilda Gregory), Mrs. Wong Wing (Ah Wong), Anna May Wong (Loo Song), Sonny Lu (Little Wu), Claude King (Mr. Muir)

THE UNKNOWN *

Metro-Goldwyn-Mayer, 7 reels, 5,521 ft. Released: June 13, 1927. Picture Code #: 305. In Production: February 7, 1927 to March 18, 1927, 35 Days. (Working Title: *Alonzo the Armless*.) Producd by Irving G. Thalberg. Directed by Tod Browning. Scenario by Waldemar Young, from a story by Tod Browning. Titles: Joseph Farnham. Photographer: Merritt Gerstad. Art Directors: Cedric Gibbons and Richard Day. Film Editors: Harry Reynolds and Errol Taggart. Wardrobe: Lucia Coulter. Cost of Production: $217,000; Profit: $362,000.

CAST: Lon Chaney (Alonzo), Joan Crawford (Nanon), Norman Kerry (Malabar), John George (Cojo), Nick de Ruiz (Zanzi), Frank Lanning (Costra). Polly Moran as the landlady and Bobbie Mack as the gypsy were cut from the release print.

MOCKERY *

Metro-Goldwyn-Mayer, 7 reels, 5,956 ft. Released: August 13, 1927. Picture Code #: 320. In Production: May 19, 1927 to June 27, 1927, 33 Days. (Working Title: *Terror*.) Produced by Erich Pommer. Directed by Benjamin Christensen. Scenario by Bradley King, from a story by Benjamin Christensen. Titles: Joseph Farnham. Photographer: Merritt Gerstad. Sets: Cedric Gibbons and Alexander Toluboff. Film Editor: John W. English. Wardrobe: Gilbert Clark. Cost of Production: $187,000; Profit: $318,000.

CAST: Lon Chaney (Sergei), Barbara Bedford (Tatiana), Ricardo Cortez (Dimitri), Mack Swain (Mr. Gaidaroff), Emily Fitzroy (Mrs. Gaidaroff), Charles Puffy (Ivan), Kai Schmidt (Butler), Johnny Mack Brown (Officer at table)

√ **LONDON AFTER MIDNIGHT**
Metro-Goldwyn-Mayer, 7 reels, 5,692 ft. Released: December 17, 1927.
Picture Code #: 330. In Production: July 25, 1927 to August 20, 1927, 24
Days. (Working Title: *The Hypnotist.*) Produced by Irving G. Thalberg.
Directed by Tod Browning. Scenario by Waldemar Young, from a story
by Tod Browning. Titles: Joseph Farnham. Photographer: Merritt B.
Gerstad. Set Design: Cedric Gibbons and Arnold Gillespie. Film Editor:
Harry Reynolds. Wardrobe: Lucia Coulter. Cost of Production: $152,000;
Profit: $540,000.

CAST: Lon Chaney (Burke), Marceline Day (Lucille Balfour), Henry B.
Walthall (Sir James Hamlin), Percy Williams (Butler), Conrad Nagel
(Arthur Hibbs), Polly Moran (Miss Smithson), Edna Tichenor (Bat
Girl), Claude King (The Stranger), Andy MacLennon (Bat Girl's
Assistant)

THE BIG CITY
Metro-Goldwyn-Mayer, 8 reels, 7,277 ft. Released: March 24, 1928.
Picture Code #: 346. In Production: October 27, 1927 to November 19,
1927, 30 Days. Produced by Irving G. Thalberg. Directed by Tod
Browning. Scenario by Waldemar Young, from a story by Tod Browning.
Titles: Joseph Farnham. Photographer: Henry Sharp. Art Director:
Cedric Gibbons. Film Editor: Harry Reynolds. Wardrobe: Lucia Coulter.
Cost of Production: $172,000; Profit: $387,000.

CAST: Lon Chaney (Chuck Collins), Marceline Day (Sunshine), James
Murray (Curly), Betty Compson (Helen), Matthew Betz (Red), John
George (The Arab), Virginia Pearson (Tennessee), Walter Percival
(Grogan), Lew Short (O'Hara), Eddie Sturgis (Blinkie), Clinton Lyle
(Mobster), Alfred Allen (Policeman)

√ **LAUGH, CLOWN, LAUGH** *
Metro-Goldwyn-Mayer, 8 reels, 7,064 ft. Released: April 14, 1928.
Picture Code #: 352. In Production: December 19, 1927 to February 2,
1928, 36 Days. Produced by Irving G. Thalberg. Directed by Herbert
Brenon. Scenario by Elizabeth Meehan, from the play by David Belasco
and Tom Cushing, based on the Italian play *Ridi Pagliacci* by Gausto
Martino. Titles: Joseph Farnham. Photographer: James Wong Howe. Set
Design: Cedric Gibbons. Film Editor: Marie Halvey. Wardrobe: Gilbert
Clark. Assistant Director: Ray Lissner. Cost of Production: $293,000;
Profit: $450,000.

CAST: Lon Chaney (Tito), Bernard Seigel (Simon), Loretta Young
(Simonetta), Cissy Fitzgerald (Giancinta), Nils Asther (Luigi), Gwen
Lee Lucretia (Diane)

Lon Chaney

WHILE THE CITY SLEEPS * V
Metro-Goldwyn-Mayer, 9 reels, 7,227 ft. Released: October 20, 1928.
Picture Code #: 370. In production: April 13, 1928 to May 19, 1928, 32
Days. (Working Title: *Easy Money.*) Portions of the film were shot in
downtown Los Angeles. Released with sound effects and musical score
(Movietone). Produced by Bernard Hyman. Directed by Jack Conway.
Story and scenario by A. P. Younger. Titles: Joseph Farnham.
Photographer: Henry Sharp. Sets: Cedric Gibbons. Film Editor: Sam S.
Zimbalist. Wardrobe: Gilbert Clark. Assistant Director: M. K. Wilson.
Cost of Production: $259,000; Profit: $399,000.
CAST: Lon Chaney (Dan), Anita Page (Myrtle), Carroll Nye (Marty),
    Wheeler Oakman (Skeeter), Mae Busch (Bessie), Polly Moran (Mrs.
    McGinnis), Lydia Yeamans Titus (Mrs. Sullivan), William Orlamond
    (Dwiggins), Richard Carle (Wally), Eddie Sturgis (Skeeter's Driver),
    Fred Kelsey (Detective in Shadow Box), Joseph W. Girard (Capt. of
    Detectives), L. J. O'Connor (Police Officer in Hallway), Sidney Bracy
    (Short Order Cook), Sam Feinberg (Man On Street), Clinton Lyle,
    Eddie Kane and Angelo Rossito (Skeeter's Gang)

WEST OF ZANZIBAR * V
Metro-Goldwyn-Mayer 7 reels 6,198 ft. Released: December 24, 1928
Picture Code #: 378. In production: June 25, 1928 to July 31, 1928.
(Working Title: *Kongo.*) Released with sound effects and musical score
(Movietone). Produced by Irving G. Thalberg. Directed by Tod
Browning. Scenario by Elliott Clawson, from the play *Kongo* by Charles
de Vonde & Kilbourn Gordon. Titles: Joseph Farnham. Photographer:
Percy Hilburn. Sets: Cedric Gibbons. Film Editor: Harry Reynolds.
Wardrobe: David Cox. Cost of Production: $249,000; Profit: $337,000.
CAST: Lon Chaney (Phroso), Lionel Barrymore (Crane), Warner Baxter
    (Doc), Mary Nolan (Maizie), Jacqueline Daly (Anna), Roscoe Ward
    (Tiny), Kalla Pasha (Babe), Curtis Nero (Bumbu), Chaz Chase (Music
    Hall Performer), Mrs. Louise Emmons (Old Woman on Street)

WHERE EAST IS EAST * V
Metro-Goldwyn-Mayer, 7 reels, 6,185 ft. Released: May 4, 1929. Picture
Code #: 415. In Production: 33 Days. Released with sound effects and
musical score (Movietone). Producer: Irving G. Thalberg. Directed by
Tod Browning. Scenario by Richard Schayer, from a story by Tod
Browning and Harry Sinclair Drago, adapted by Waldemar Young.

Photographer: Henry Sharp. Art Director: Cedric Gibbons. Film Editor: Harry Reynolds. Wardrobe: David Cox. Cost of Production: $295,000; Profit: $283,000.

CAST: Lon Chaney (Tiger Haynes), Lupe Velez (Toyo), Estelle Taylor (Mme. de Silva), Lloyd Hughes (Bobby), Louis Stern (Father Angelo), Mrs. Wong Wing (Ming), Willie Fung (Servant)

THUNDER
Metro-Goldwyn-Mayer, 9 reels, 7,872 ft. Released: July 8, 1929. Picture Code #: 425. In production March 3 to April 30, 1929; production halted on April 30 due to Lon's illness. Resumed on May 13, 1929 and finished May 23, 1929; retakes on May 28, 1929 and June 1, 1929, 56 Days. Portions of the film shot on location at the Chicago-Northwestern Railroad yards, Green Bay, Wisconsin. Released with sound effects and musical score (Movietone). Produced by Hunt Stromberg. Directed by William Nigh. Scenario by Byron Morgan and Ann Price, from a story by Byron Morgan. Titles: Joseph Farnham. Photographer: Henry Sharp. Film Editor: Ben Lewis. Cost of Production: $352,000; Profit: $272,000.

CAST: Lon Chaney (Grumpy Anderson), Phyllis Haver (Zella), James Murray (Tommy), George Duryea (Jim), Frances Norris (Molly), Wally Albright, Jr. (Davey), John MacIntosh (Railroad Man)

THE UNHOLY THREE * V
Metro-Goldwyn-Mayer, 8 reels, 6,662 ft. Released: July 3, 1930. Picture Code #: 494. In production: March 26, 1930 to April 24, 1930, 27 Days. Retake on April 30, 1930. Produced by Irving G. Thalberg. Directed by Jack Conway. Scenario by J. C. Nugent and Elliott Nugent, from the novel by Clarence A. Robbins. Photographer: Percy Hilburn. Art Director: Cedric Gibbons. Film Editor: Frank Sullivan. Recording Engineer: Anstruther MacDonald and Douglas Shearer. Wardrobe: David Cox. Cost of Production: $279,000; Profit: $375,000.

CAST: Lon Chaney (Echo), Lila Lee (Rosie), Elliott Nugent (Hector), Harry Earles (Tweedledee), Ivan Linow (Hercules), John Miljan (Prosecuting Attorney), Clarence Burton (Regan), Crawford Kent (Defense Attorney), Richard Carle (Barker), Fred Kelsey (Cop at Train), Ray Cooke (Sailor at Sideshow), Joseph W. Girard (The Judge), Trixie Friganza (Lady Customer), Charlie Gamora (Gorilla), Sylvester (Sword Swallower), De Garo (Fire Eater), Birdie Thompson (Fat Lady)

Lon Chaney

MGM FILMS PLANNED FOR CHANEY
BUT NEVER MATERIALIZED

SPAN OF LIFE - announced for 1926 release; based on the play by Sutton Vane with William Haines and Pauline Starke to co-star.

HATE - announced for 1927-28 release; based on the novel *The Four Stragglers* by Frank Packard, author of *The Miracle Man*; Tod Browning was once reported to be assigned to direct the project.

SEVEN SEAS - announced for 1927-28 release; based on the character "Cheri-Bibi" created by Gaston Leroux, author of *Phantom of the Opera*.

ORDEAL - announced for 1927-28 release; based on the novel by Dale Collins; production was scheduled to begin after completion of *London After Midnight*, with scenario by Josephine Lovett.

THE WANDERING JEW - announced for 1927-28 release; based on the novel by Eugene Sue.

THE BUGLE SOUNDS - announced in June, 1929; based on the novel by Major Linovi Pechkoff of the French Foreign Legion; was originally planned as a silent film and then re-written to be made as a talking picture. George Hill was set as director, not to be confused with the 1941 MGM film of the same title starring Wallace Berry.

BROTHER OFFICERS - announced as a silent film in June, 1929; written by Lt. Commander Frank "Spig" Wead; Fred Niblo was assigned to direct.

SGT. BULL - was announced as a silent film in January 1930; written by Hans Kraly and Dale Van Every; Jack Conway was assigned to direct.

CHERI-BIBI - announced as Chaney's second talking picture in July 1930; based on the novel by Gaston Leroux, it was eventually made in 1932 under the title *Phantom of Paris* by MGM, starring John Gilbert.

MAN OF A THOUSAND FACES *

Universal-International. Released: August 14, 1957. Picture Code #: 1844. The film was re-released in 1964. Produced by Robert Arthur. Directed by Joseph Pevney. Scenario by R. Wright Campbell, Ivan Goff and Ben Roberts, from a story by Ralph Wheelwright. Photographer: Russell Metty. Art Directors: Alexander Golitzen and Eric Orbom. Sound: Leslie I. Carey and Robert Pritchard. Film Editor: Ted J. Kent. Musical Score: Frank Skinner. Orchestrator: Joseph Gershenson. Costumes: Bill Thomas. Mr. Cagney's Wardrobe: Marilyn Sotto. Make-Up Artists: Bud Westmore and Jack Kevan. Special Effects: Clifford Stine. Assistant Director: Phil Bowles. Sign Language Technical Advisor: Marjorie Ramsey. Running Time: 122 minutes. Filmed in Cinemascope.

CAST: James Cagney (Lon Chaney), Dorothy Malone (Cleva Creighton Chaney), Jane Greer (Hazel Bennett Chaney), Marjorie Rambeau (Gert), Jim Backus (Clarence Locan), Robert J. Evans (Irving Thalberg), Celia Lovsky (Mrs. Chaney), Jeanne Cagney (Carrie Chaney), Jack Albertson (Dr. J. Wilson Shields), Nolan Leary (Pa Chaney), Roger Smith (Creighton Chaney At 21), Robert Lyden (Creighton Chaney At 13), Rickie Sorensen (Creighton Chaney At 8), Dennis Rush (Creighton Chaney At 4), Simon Scott (Carl Hastings), Danny Beck (Max Dill), Phil Van Zandt (George Loane Tucker), Hank Mann and Snub Pollard (Comedy Waiters), Larry J. Blake (David T. Stone), Hank Patterson (Stage Door Man), Marjorie Bennett (Vera), Leo Needham (John Chaney), Hugh Lawrence (George Chaney), Elizabeth Flournoy (Thalberg's Secretary), George Mather (Bullpen Assistant Director), John George (Extra in Bullpen), Sammee Tong (Oriental Extra), Billy Curtis (*Unholy Three* Midget), Robert Brubaker (*Unholy Three* Director), Harry Antrim (Cleva's Birth Doctor), Peter Adams (Reporter, *Miracle Man* set), Russ Bender (Divorce Judge), Tom Kennedy (Man in Audience at Eulogy). Clarence Kolb played himself.

Endnotes

1. "The Man Behind The Mask," *Screen Secrets*, June, 1929.
2. "A Martyr To The Movies?" *Motion Picture*, December, 1930.
3. "Motion Picture Roll of Honor," *Good Housekeeping*, August, 1932.
4. "Lon Chaney," *Vanity Fair*, February, 1928.
5. "Lon Chaney Recognized In Taxi," *New York Times*, June 3, 1928.
6. William N. Dunphy to the author, February, 1992.
7. George Wagner to the author, March 1984.
8. "Discoveries About Myself," *Motion Picture*, July, 1930.
9. *Dark Star: The Untold Story of the Meteoric Rise and Fall of the Legendary John Gilbert*, St. Martin's Press, 1985.
10. Ibid.
11. "It Might Be Pagliacci," *Motion Picture Classic*, May, 1928.
12. *Colorado Springs Telegraph*, January 1, 1922.
13. Loren Harbert to the author, March 1985.
14. George Chaney to the author, October, 1973.
15. "A Miracle Man Of Make-Up," *Picture Play*, March, 1920.
16. Lon Chaney File, Pioneer's Museum, Colorado Springs, Colorado.
17. George Johnson collection, UCLA Special Collections Department.
18. *Oklahoma City Times*, August 27, 1930.
19. "The Lon Chaney I Knew," *Photoplay*, November, 1930.
20. "Lon Chaney, A Portrait of the Man Behind a Thousand Faces," *Liberty Magazine*, May 2, 1931.
21. Anita Page to the author, October, 1992.
22. "The Lon Chaney I Knew," *Photoplay*, November, 1930.
23. "The True Life Story Of Lon Chaney," *Photoplay*, December, 1927.
24. August 26, 1930.
25. *Colorado Springs Gazette*, April 20, 1902.

26. *Colorado Springs Gazette,* December 19, 1902.

27. Loren Harbert to the author, March, 1985.

28. "The True Life Story Of Lon Chaney," *Photoplay Magazine,* January, 1928.

29. Ibid.

30. *Oklahoma City Times,* Aug. 26, 1930.

31. Lon Ralph Chaney to the author, August, 1983; Stella George to the author, January 1984.

32. *Oklahoma City Times,* August 26, 1930.

33. Betty Felch-Griffin to the author, January, 1993.

34. Stella George to the author, January, 1984.

35. "The Lon Chaney I Knew," *Photoplay,* November, 1930.

36. According to her daughter, Cleva swallowed the bichloride of mercury in the wings of the theatre, not in a dressing room. Stella George to the author, January, 1984.

37. Lon and Cleva's divorce papers, December 19, 1913.

38. *Colorado Springs Evening Telegraph,* June 9, 1914.

39. Lon Ralph Chaney to the author, August, 1983.

40. Stella George to the author, January, 1984.

41. Lon Ralph Chaney to the author, August, 1983.

42. Ibid.

43. "Lon Chaney, A Portrait Of A Man Behind A Thousand Faces," *Liberty Magazine,* May 23, 1931.

44. Lon Ralph Chaney to the author, August, 1983.

45. Ibid.

46. "The True Life Story Of Lon Chaney," *Photoplay,* February, 1928.

47. "Lon Chaney, A Portrait Of A Man Behind A Thousand Faces," *Liberty Magazine,* May 23, 1931.

48. William N. Dunphy to the author, February, 1992.

49. Jackie Coogan to the author, June, 1983.

50. James Crabe, A.S.C. to the author, November, 1984.

51. Ron Borst to the author, Aug. 1980.

52. *The Big U*, A. S. Barnes & Co., 1977, New York.
53. *Allan Dwan, the Last Pioneer*, Praeger Publishers, Inc., 1971
54. "My Own Story," *Movie Magazine*, October, 1925.
55. *Colorado Springs Gazette*, May 8, 1915.
56. "Lon Chaney, A Portrait Of A Man Behind A Thousand Faces," *Liberty Magazine*, May 16, 1931.
57. Ibid.
58. Jack Mulhall to the author, July, 1973.
59. Bob Birchard to the author, August, 1988.
60. Takashi Teshigawara to the author, February, 1992.
61. Loren Harbert to the author, March, 1985.
62. "The True Life Story Of Lon Chaney," *Photoplay*, February, 1928.
63. Ibid.
64. Bob Birchard to the author, August, 1988.
65. "Motion Picture Roll Of Honor," *Good Housekeeping*, August, 1932.
66. Carroll Nye to the author, May, 1970.
67. Priscilla Dean to the author, September, 1987.
68. "The True Life Story Of Lon Chaney," *Photoplay*, February, 1928.
69. Ibid.
70. George Chaney to the author, January, 1974.
71. In the 1913 film, *The Sea Urchin*, he played a hunchbacked fisherman.
72. Bob Birchard to the author, February, 1989.
73. "The True Life Story Of Lon Chaney," *Photoplay*, February, 1928.
74. Ron Chaney, Jr. to the author, March, 1990.
75. Lon Ralph Chaney to the author, August, 1983.
76. "Laugh Lon Laugh," *Motion Picture*, May, 1929.
77. Ann Wright to the author, March, 1985.
78. George Wagner to the author, June, 1992.
79. Ibid.
80. Ibid.

81. Priscilla Bonner to James Curtis, August, 1992.

82. "Acting Is Masquerade," *Motion Picture*, December, 1922.

83. Esther Ralston to the author, October, 1983.

84. Patsy Ruth Miller to the author, July, 1988.

85. Ibid.

86. *Faces, Forms, Films — The Artistry of Lon Chaney*, A. S. Barnes & Co., 1971.

87. Patsy Ruth Miller to the author, July, 1988.

88. Ibid.

89. George Chaney to the author, January, 1974.

90. *Light Your Torches and Pull Up Your Tights*, Arlington House, New Rochelle, NY 1973.

91. Patsy Ruth Miller to the author, July, 1988.

92. *The Strong Man*, Bonomo Studios, New York, 1968.

93. Harvey Perry to the author, July, 1974.

94. *American Cinematographer*, February, 1940.

95. *Light Your Torches and Pull Up Your Tights*, Arlington House, New Rochelle, NY 1973

96. The home Lon was building when he wrote this letter was located at 7166 Sunset Boulevard, just a few feet from where he was living at the time. The hair tonic Hugh Harbert was marketing, which reputedly restored natural hair color, sold regionally in the Pacific Northwest for over 40 years. Loren Harbert to the author, March, 1985.

97. *Thalberg — Life and Legend*, Doubleday & Co., 1969.

98. *American Cinematographer*, June, 1985.

99. Ibid.

100. Burt Lancaster to the author, March, 1986.

101. Mike Ragan to the author, October, 1991.

102. Charles Van Enger to the author, March, 1973.

103. Philip J. Riley to the author, April, 1990.

104. Charles Van Enger to the author, March, 1973.

105. Philip J. Riley to the author, April, 1990.

106. Eddie Quillan to the author, September, 1988.

107. Lamar D. Tabb to the author, July, 1987.

108. Ibid.

109. George Chaney to the author, January, 1974.

110. Philip J. Riley to the author, April, 1990.

111. Harry Earles to the author, February, 1985.

112. Loren Harbert to the author, March, 1985.

113. "Lon Chaney A Portrait Of A Man Behind A Thousand Faces," *Liberty Magazine,* May 23, 1931.

114. George Chaney to the author, January, 1974.

115. Hazel Chaney probate papers.

116. *Philadelphia Bulletin*, August 27, 1930.

117. Thomas Butler to the author, March, 1991.

118. Col. Carl K. Mahakian, USMC, (Ret.) to the author, May, 1992.

119. Ibid.

120. Hal K. Dawson to the author, July, 1973.

121. Fred Phillips to the author, July, 1988.

122. Harvey Perry to the author, July, 1974.

123. Fred Phillips to the author, July 1988.

124. "Why I Prefer Grotesque Characters," *Theatre Magazine,* October, 1927.

125. George Chaney to the author, Jan. 1974.

126. "His Faces Are His Fortune," *Collier's Weekly*, May 8, 1926.

127. *The Faces of Hollywood*, A. S. Barnes & Co., 1968, N.Y.

128. *Tim McCoy Remembers The West*, Bison Books, 1988.

129. *Portrait Of Joan,* Doubleday & Co., 1962.

130. Lamar D. Tabb to the author, July, 1987.

131. Burt Lancaster to the author, March, 1986.

132. "The True Life Story Of Lon Chaney," *Photoplay,* February, 1928.

133 .Lamar D. Tabb to the author, July, 1987.

134. Takashi Teshigawara to the author, March, 1992.

135. Harry Earles to the author, February, 1985.

136. George Chaney to the author, January, 1974.

137. The Lon Chaney I Knew," *Photoplay,* November, 1930.

138. *Karloff,* Drake Publishers, 1972.

139. "Lon Chaney Recognized In Taxi," *New York Times,* June 3, 1928.

140. "Lon Chaney, A Portrait Of A Man Behind A Thousand Faces," *Liberty Magazine,* May 23, 1931.

141. Harry Earles to the author, February, 1985.

142. George Chaney to the author, January, 1974.

143. Lon Ralph Chaney to the author, August, 1983.

144. Sam Gill to the author, August, 1992.

145. "The True Life Story Of Lon Chaney," *Photoplay,* February, 1928.

146. "Lon Chaney, A Portrait Of A Man Behind A Thousand Faces," *Liberty Magazine,* May 30, 1931.

147. "Discoveries About Myself," *Motion Picture,* July, 1930.

148. "The Last Of Mr. Chaney," Picture Play, September, 1930.

149. "Acting Is Masquerade," Motion Picture, December, 1922.

150. "Lon Chaney, A Portrait Of A Man Behind A Thousand Faces," *Liberty Magazine,* May 30, 1931.

151. Lamar D. Tabb to the author, July, 1987.

152. "The True Life Story Of Lon Chaney," *Photoplay,* February,1928.

153. Eddie Quillan to the author, September, 1988.

154. "Lon Chaney, A Portrait Of A Man Behind A Thousand Faces," *Liberty Magazine,* May 30, 1931.

155. James Curtis to the author, May, 1992.

156. "Lon Chaney, A Portrait Of A Man Behind A Thousand Faces," *Liberty Magazine,* May 23, 1931.

157. James Wong Howe to the author, March, 1974.

158. George Chaney to the author, January, 1974.

159. Anita Page to the author, October, 1992.

160. Carroll Nye to the author, March, 1970.

161. The Last of Mr. Chaney," *Picture Play*, Sept. 1930.

162. Herbert Voight to the author, July, 1985.

163. *American Cinematographer*, January, 1930.

164. *Rocky Mountain News*, June 12, 1928.

165. George Chaney to the author, January, 1974.

166. Anita Page to the author, October, 1992.

167. *Los Angeles Examiner*, May 2, 1929.

168. Philip J. Riley to the author, April, 1990.

169. Lamar D. Tabb to the author, July, 1987.

170. *London After Midnight,* Cornwall Books, 1985.

171. *The MGM Story*, Crown Publishers, 1975.

172. Anita Page to the author, October, 1992.

173. George Chaney to the author, January, 1974.

174. William N. Dunphy to the author, February, 1992.

175. "Lon Chaney, A Portrait Of A Man Behind A Thousand Faces," *Liberty Magazine*, May 30, 1931.

176. George Chaney to the author, January, 1974.

177. Ibid.

178. Ibid.

179. "The True Life Story of Lon Chaney," *Photoplay,* Feb. 1928.

180. "Chaney Comes Back," *Screenland,* May 1930.

181. George Chaney to the author, January, 1974.

182. Ibid.

183. Ibid.

184. Ibid.

185. There is no evidence of any *Unholy Three* foreign versions having been filmed. This may have been due in part to Lon's failing health.

186. George Chaney to the author, January, 1974.

187. Leonard Maltin to the author, March, 1988.

188. Harry Earles to the author, February, 1985.

189. George Wagner to the author, October, 1987.

190. *The Unholy Three Pressbook.*

191. Ibid.

192. Philip J. Riley to the author, April, 1990.

193. "The Lon Chaney I Knew," *Photoplay*, November, 1930.

194. Philip J. Riley to the author, April, 1990.

195. Henry Kurth to the author, June, 1988.

196. Jim Nikolaus to the author, June 1988.

197. Lawson Brainard to the author, July, 1988.

198. Henry Kurth to the author, June, 1988.

199. Kenneth Partridge to the author, June, 1988.

200. "It Might Be Pagliacci," *Motion Picture Classic*, May, 1928.

201. "The True Life Story Of Lon Chaney," *Photoplay*, February, 1928.

202. "Lon Chaney Recognized In A Taxi," *New York Times*, June 3, 1928.

203. "Lon Chaney, A Portrait Of A Man Behind A Thousand Faces," *Liberty Magazine*, May 2, 1931.

204. George Chaney to the author, January, 1974.

205. *Variety*, August 28, 1930.

206. Thomas Butler to the author, May, 1991.

207. Lamar D. Tabb to the author, July, 1987.

208. "Discoveries About Myself," *Motion Picture*, July, 1930.

209. *Glendale News Press,* August 29, 1930.

210. Ibid.

211. *Motion Picture Magazine*, December, 1930.

212. *The Pasadena Star News,* August 29, 1930.

213. *Photoplay*, December, 1930.

214. Lon Chaney Will and probate papers.

215. Ibid.

216. Philip J. Riley to the author, April, 1990.

217. Lon Chaney probate papers.

218. Lon Chaney Cabin File, U.S. Forest Service, Bishop, CA.

219. George Chaney to the author, January, 1974.

220. Hazel Chaney Will and probate papers.

221. *Los Angeles Times*, September 15, 1934.

222. Lon Ralph Chaney to the author, August, 1983.

223. Fred Phillips to the author, July, 1988.

224. Joseph Pevney to the author, July, 1974.

225. Philip J. Riley to the author, October, 1987.

226. George Chaney to the author, October, 1973.

227. Lon Ralph Chaney to the author, August, 1983.

228. Patsy Ruth Miller to the author, July, 1988.

229. Patrick Wood to the author, March, 1985.

Make-up Glossary

Acetone   A clear liquid solvent for removing non-flexible collodion pieces, spirit gum, etc. Can be abrasive to the skin.

Aluminum Powder   Formerly used to whiten or gray the hair. Very difficult to wash out,and if any powder got on the face, it would darken the make-up and could not be brushed off. This item is no longer used. Today a liquid in various shades is combed into the hair for the proper effect.

Appliances   A current term for any number of foam rubber or plastic pieces (noses, cheeks, necks, etc.) that are glued onto the face to change its shape and appearance.

Bandoline   .A thick hair-setting liquid. Was also applied to false mustaches, beards, etc. to hold their shape during filming. This item has been replaced by a fixative spray.

Base Make-Up   The primary make-up color that is applied to the actor's face.

Blindness   An actor could roll his eyes up into his head (as Lon did in *Treasure Island*), or he could take the thin white skin from the inside of an egg shell and place it in the eye. This is uncomfortable, but not dangerous. Lon had an optician make a glass lens for him to wear over his eye (like a contact lens) for *Road To Mandalay*. Contact lenses are now used to achieve this effect.

Brilliantine   A hair styling gel. Sometimes was used in place of water to apply Masque (a hair whitener in cake form).

Cold Cream   Used before applying grease paint and also for removing make-up. No longer in use; numerous creme or liquid removers have replaced it.

Collodion   (1) **Rigid** (also known as common or non-flexible) is a liquid used to make scars, pock marks, etc. When applied, it draws and puckers the skin. It is still used in motion picture make-up.

(2) **Flexible** is a liquid plastic skin adhesive used to provide a protective coating for various make-up constructions.

Cotton and Collodion Method   An old carry-over from the stage. A coat of spirit gum was painted on the desired areaof the face. Cotton was then placed over the spirit gum. Additional coats of flexible collodion or spirit gum could be painted over the cotton, with additional pieces of cotton placed on top of the collodion/spirit gum until the desired effect is achieved. Lon used this method to achieve the prominent cheek bones in *Hunchback of Notre Dame*, *Phantom of the Opera* and *Mr. Wu*. This method has been replaced by the use of foam rubber or plastic appliances.

Crepe-wool Hair   Used to make beards, sideburns and mustaches. It comes in braids of assorted colors. Crepe-wool is a common item found in the make-up case of today's make-up artist as well as those of Lon's day.

Curling Iron   Hair styling iron that, when heated by a small stove or over a can of sterno, is used to style false beards, mustaches, etc. These irons should not be confused with electric curling irons.

Eyebrow Pencils   Wooden pencils with soft grease lead used for lining eyes, penciling in or darkening eyebrows, emphasizing wrinkles, etc. They are still in use today.

False Teeth   See **Gutta-percha**.

Fishskin   A thin, tough, transparent material made from the stomach lining of animals. Lon used it to simulate Oriental eyes, and in *Phantom of the Opera*, for the up-tilting of his nose. Fishskin is rarely used today.

Foam Rubber   A three or four part combination of chemicals which is used to produce foam latex appliances. The chemicals are mixed together and poured into a negative mold of the appliance. It is then joined together with the positive mold and baked. When properly cured, the foam rubber pieces are ready to be glued onto the actor's face.

Greasepaint   Traditional foundation paint used to give the skin its basic coloring. Made in various shades, it came in stick form or in a soft consistency (it first came in a jar and later in a collapsible tube). By the early 1940's it was replaced by Max Factor's Pan-Stik™ (a cream stick base) and Pancake™ (a greaseless, water-soluble foundation applied with a wet sponge). Pan-Stik™ and Pancake™, along with other creme and liquid make-up bases, are still used today.

Grotesque Whiteface   Circus-clown term for an elaborate whiteface clown make-up. Lon's make-up in *Laugh, Clown, Laugh* is an example.

Gutta-percha   A hard dental rubber used by dentists for temporary fillings. In films, the material was used to make false teeth. When molded to the shape of the mouth, either individual false teeth could be placed into the rubber or teeth could be carved out of the rubber and painted. The latter method looked less realistic. Today false teeth are made out of acrylic and snap over the actor's own teeth.

Highlights and Shadows   Term for using a light color (highlight) to accentuate the prominent areas of the face or using a darker color (shadow) to hollow or recede areas of the face. Highlights and shadows are used in every aspect of make-up from beauty to character.

Laying the Hair   Make-up term for applying crepe wool or real hair onto the face to create a beard, mustache or sideburns.

Lining Colors   Old make-up term for colors to be used for eyes, character make-ups and shadows.

Masque   A hair whitener that came in cake form and was applied with a tooth brush moistened with either water or brilliantine. Today a liquid in various shades is combed into the hair for the proper effect.

Mortician's Wax   Also known as Plasto Wax. Though rarely used today, it is a soft wax used to remodel or build up features of the face like noses and cheekbones.

Lon Chaney

Muslin   A very fine-woven cloth used with wigs to create a bald head.

Neat Whiteface   A circus-clown term for a clown face whose make-up is not elaborate. Lon's make-up in *He Who Gets Slapped* is an example.

Nose Putty   A clay-like composition used to build up the bony parts of the face, like noses, cheekbones, etc. It is no longer used today n make-up for motion pictures.

Orthochromatic Film Stock   The original film stock used by filmmakers. This stock made a person's normal skin color photograph very dark, so make-up was used to "lighten up" the face. This is why actors and actresses in most silent pictures appeared so "white-faced."

Panchromatic Film   This film produced a photographic image of colors in more true relationship to each other compared to Orthochromatic film. Studios started using this stock by 1927.

Panchromatic Make-Up   Max Factor developed a line of make-up in 1927 to be used with the new film stock which allowed performers to look more natural and less "white-faced."

Plastic Appliances   Appliance pieces made from a plastic-based material, sometimes used in place of foam rubber appliance pieces.

Powder   Originally when powder was applied to the make-up for film, it had to be at least a shade lighter than the base make-up because the powder darkened when dry.With the use of Panchromatic film and subsequent Panchromatic make-up,powder needed to match the make-up base exactly. Today a translucent powder is used.

Rubber Cigar Holders   Cigars used to be packaged in a rubber holder. The ends of the holders could be cut off and inserted into the nostrils to broaden the nose; Lon used this method in a number of his films, including the ape-man make-up for *A Blind Bargain*. Clear plastic tubing is now used.

Spirit Gum   A liquid gum adhesive used to attach crepe-wool hair, nose putty, etc. to the skin. In addition to spirit gum, several new adhesives are used today for the same effect.

Stipple   Small, short touches or dabs with a sponge that together make an even or softly graded shadow.

Straight Make-up   Term used for a basic, corrective make-up applied to an actor's face. Straight make-up does not involve character make-up of any kind.

Textured Look Make-up   Term for the skin having a certain texture and age so it does not appear smooth or flat to the camera.

Tooth Enamel   An enamel that is used to whiten or darken teeth. Could also be used to paint false teeth made from gutta-percha.

Wrinkled Skin   In Lon's time the entire face could be covered with a mixture of nose putty or plasto wax and greasepaint. Then a pointed instrument was used to make a series of very fine lines cut into the paint, cris-crossing them to resemble very old, dried skin. Another method was to paint the face with a thin solution of white glue mixed with warm water to a creamy consistency. Then sheets of Fishskin were applied and wrinkled to the desired effect. Greasepaint was then applied. Today, liquid latex is stippled onto the face in sections. That area of the skin is then stretched and when dry, wrinkles form. Extra coats will further deepen the wrinkles and the entire area is covered with a castor-oil-base make-up. This process is called "stretch rubber."

Bibliography

BOOKS AND MAGAZINE ARTICLES

American Film Institute. *Feature Films 1911-1920.* University of California Press,1988.

American Film Institute. *Feature Films 1921-1930.* New York: R. R. Bowker Co., 1971.

Anderson, Robert G. *Faces, Forms, Films: The Artistry of Lon Chaney,* New York: A. S. Barnes & Co., 1971.

Balch, David A. "I Never Forget That I Was Once Poor." *Movie Weekly* (September 29, 1923): 10-11.

Biery, Ruth. "The Man Behind The Mask." *Screen Secrets* (June 1929): 72-73, 109-110.

Biery, Ruth. "Lon Chaney Goes Talkie." *New Movie* (December 1929).

Biery, Ruth. "Lon Chaney's Reward." *Screen Play Secrets* (November 1930): 28-29, 93.

Bodeen, DeWitt. "Lon Chaney: Man of a Thousand Faces." *Focus On Film* (May-August 1970): 21-39.

Braff, Richard E. "A Lon Chaney Index." *Films In Review* (April 1970): 217-228.

Bull, Clarence S. (as told to Raymond Lee). "Face 1001," *The Faces Of Hollywood.* New York: A. S. Barnes & Co., 1968.

Chaney, Creighton. "My Father — Lon Chaney." *Screen Book* (May 1934).

Chaney, Lon. "Effects of Make-up Under Incandescent Lights." *Academy Digest* of the Academy of Motion Pictures Arts & Sciences (April 1928): 25-26.

Chaney, Lon. "Wanted: New Medicine." *The Island Lantern*, U.S. Penitentiary, McNeil Island, Washington (January 1930): 31-36.

Chaney, Lon. "The Art of Make for Stage and Screen." (Preface only.) Hollywood, CA: Cinematex Publishing Co., 1927.

Chaney, Lon. "Why I Prefer Grotesque Characters." *Theatre*

Magazine (October 1927).

Chaney, Lon (as told to Gladys Hall). "Discoveries About Myself." *Motion Picture* (July 1930): 59, 106.

Chaney, Lon (as told to Maude Cheatham). "The Darkest Hour." *Motion Picture Classic* (September 1922): 38, 81-82.

Chaney, Lon (possibly ghostwritten). "My Own Story," *Movie Magazine*. Part I (September 1925): 42-44, 108-110. Part II (October 1925): 55-57, 86-89. Part III (November 1925): 55-56, 74-75.

Cheatham, Maude S.. "Meet The Frog." *Motion Picture Classic* (March 1920): 38, 81-82.

Chrisman, J. Eugene. "Another Lon Chaney." *Motion Picture Classic* (October 1930): 41, 94, 97.

Collins, Frederick L. "A Motion Picture Roll of Honor." *Good Housekeeping* (August 1932): 63, 156-157.

Cruikshank, Herbert. "There's Always Carpet Laying." *Motion Picture Classic* (March 1929): 43, 70.

Currie, Homer. "The Uncanny Mr. Chaney." *Motion Picture* (September 1925): 44, 102.

Denbo, Doris. "The Phantom of Hollywood." *Picture Play* (April 1925): 88-89, 100.

Donnell, Dorothy. "A Martyr to the Movies ?" *Motion Picture*, (December 1930): 34-35, 90-92.

I.G. Edmonds. *The Big U.* New York: A. S. Barnes & Co., 1977.

Gerhart, Myrtle. "Would You Know Lon Chaney ?" *Picture Play* (May 1923): 58-59, 84.

Gerhart, Myrtle. "The Last of Mr. Chaney." *Picture Play* (September 1930): 46-48, 112.

Goldbeck, Willis. "The Star Sinister." *Motion Picture Classic* (November 1923): 62-63, 90.

Gordon, Leonard. "Some Part of the World Is Thrilled Every Day By a Barber's Son." *The Film Weekly* (June 14, 1930): 25.

Haley, Alex. "The Man of a Thousand Faces." *Coronet* (December 1955).

Howard, Marjorie. "Lon Chaney, A Master of Make-up." *Movie Picture Weekly* (September 16, 1916).

Howe, Herbert. "A Miracle Man of Make-up." *Picture Play* (March 1920): 37–39, 96–97.

Howe, Milton. "The Man Who Made Homeliness Pay." *Motion Picture Classic* (March 1926): 34–35, 80.

Hyland, Dick. "The Face of a Thousand Memories." *New Movie*, (November 1930): 44–45, 90, 104.

Kennedy, John B. "His Faces Are His Fortune." *Colliers' Weekly* (May 8, 1926): 21, 43.

Kingsley, Grace. "The Better I Get, the Worse I Look." *Movie Weekly* (April 21, 1923): 21, 30.

Kuttner, Alfred B. "Lon Chaney." *The National Board of Review Magazine* (September 1930): 7–8.

Lang, Harry. "Chaney Talks." *Photoplay* (May 1930): 75, 141.

"Lights Out For Lon Chaney." *The Literary Digest* (September 13, 1930).

Locan, Clarence A. "Lon Chaney Speaks For The Criminals Whom He Understands." *Photoplay* (1928).

Locan, Clarence A. "The Lon Chaney I Knew." *Photoplay* (November 1930): 58–60, 106, 108.

Mayer, Edwin Justice. "The Portrait of an Artist." *Moving Pictures Stories* (February 11, 1921): 21.

McCoy, Tim, with Ronald McCoy. *Tim McCoy Remembers The West.* Bison Books, University of Nebraska Press, 1988.

Mitchell, George. "Lon Chaney." *Films In Review.* (December 1953): 497–510.

"Good-bye Lon." *Modern Screen.* (November 1930): 38–39, 125.

Mackinnon, B. A. "Lon Chaney." *Screen Book* (November 1930): 78–80.

Nelson, Bradford. "Chaney Comes Back." *Screenland* (May 1930): 32-33, 116-117.

Nyvelt, Eleanor Beach. "Lon Chaney." *World Today* (February 1929): 265-267.

"Rich Man, Poor Man, Beggarman, Thief — Lon Chaney." *Photoplay Journal* (November 1917).

Ussher, Kathleen. "Chaney The Chameleon," *Picturegoers* (March 1926).

Riley, Philip J. *London After Midnight*. New York: Cornwall Books, 1985.

St. Johns, Adela Rogers. "Lon Chaney, A Portrait of the Man Behind a Thousand Faces." *Liberty*. Part I (May 2, 1931): 16-20, 22, 24-25. Part II (May 9, 1931): 28-36. Part III (May 16, 1931): 28-34. Part IV (May 23, 1931): 36-37, 40-44. Part V (May 30, 1931): 39-44.

St, Johns, Ivan. "Mr. Nobody." *Photoplay* (February 1927).

Schallert, Elza. "Behind Lon Chaney's Mask.", *Picture Play* (July 1927): 16-18, 108.

Stanley, L. "Lon Chaney As I Knew Him." *Film Weekly* (1930).

Steele, Joseph Henry. "It Might Be Pagliacci." *Motion Picture Classic* (May 1928).

Spensley, Dorothy. "Laugh, Lon, Laugh." *Motion Picture* (May 1929): 67, 113.

Stull, William, A.S.C. "Professional Amateurs." *American Cinematographer* (January 1930).

Tully, Jim. "Lon Chaney." *Vanity Fair* (February 1928): 55, 100.

Turner, George. "A Silent Giant: *The Hunchback of Notre Dame*." *American Cinematographer* (June 1985).

Waterbury, Ruth. "The True Life Story of Lon Chaney." *Photoplay*. Part I (December 1927): 32-33, 110-114. Part II (January 1928): 36-37, 119-121. Part III (February 1928): 56-57, 94, 112-113.

Waterbury, Ruth. "In Memoriam: Lon Chaney." *Silver Screen* (November 1930): 51.

NEWSPAPER ARTICLES

"Lon Chaney Had New Home Under Way Here." *Beverly Hills Citizen* (August 28, 1930).

"Lon Chaney, Film Star, Reported Dying In West." *Chicago Times* (August 24, 1930).

"Mrs. Frank H. Chaney Dies." *Colorado Springs Evening Telegraph* (April 9, 1914).

"Lon Chaney Visitor Here; Rests From Filming Hunchback." *Colorado Springs Evening Telegraph* (June 20, 1923).

"Lon Chaney Visits Boyhood Scenes on Visit to Springs." *Colorado Springs Evening Telegraph* (June 12, 1928).

"Chaney Must Keep His Face Unknown; Movie Star Back To Boyhood Scenes." *Colorado Springs Evening Telegraph* (January 1, 1922).

"Lon Chaney, City's Great Film Actor, Passes Away.", *Colorado Springs Evening Telegraph* (August 26, 1930).

"J.O. Chaney Got Rough Treatment." *Colorado Springs Gazette* (January 25, 1900).

"Stage Employees to Essay the Role of Thespians." *Colorado Springs Gazette* (December 19, 1902).

"The Little Tycoon" (Stage Review). *Colorado Springs Gazette* (April 20, 1902).

"Said Pasha Given Splendid Presentation By Good Company" (Stage Review). *Colorado Springs Gazette* (June 9, 1903).

"Local Entertainers Who Will Contribute to Summer Gaiety." *Colorado Springs Gazette* (July 12, 1903).

"Frank H. Chaney Forced To Give Up Work As Barber." *Colorado Springs Gazette* (June 9, 1914).

"Universal City Marvel in Design Says Earl Cox." *Colorado Springs Gazette* (May 8, 1915).

"Used To Shift Scenes Here In The Long Ago At The Opera House; Now Noted As One Of The Best Character Actors In The Movies." *Colorado Springs Gazette*, January 9, 1921.

Lon Chaney

"Chaney Comes To Colorado To Restore Broken Health." *Colorado Springs Gazette* (June 20, 1923).

"Lon Chaney's Father Dies At Los Angeles." *Colorado Springs Gazette* (April 14, 1927).

"Lon Chaney, Noted Actor, Visits Here." *Colorado Springs Gazette* (June 12, 1928).

"Lon Chaney Dies In Los Angeles Hospital." *Colorado Springs Gazette* (August 26, 1930).

"Little Theatre May Borrow Actor's Name." *Colorado Springs Gazette-Telegraph* (October 12, 1985).

"Little Theatre Re-named in Honor of Lon Chaney." *Colorado Springs Gazette-Telegraph* (May 30, 1986).

"Lon Chaney's Star Rising in Hometown." *Colorado Springs Sun* (November 24, 1985).

"The Royal Chef" (Stage Review). *The Denver Post* (October 24, 1909).

"Theatre Shares Lon Chaney Fame." *The Denver Post* (June 1, 1986).

"Hold Last Rites For Lon Chaney." *Glendale News-Press* (August 28, 1930).

"Throngs Mourn At Chaney Rites." *Glendale News-Press* (August 29, 1930).

"Critical Illness Grips Lon Chaney." *Hollywood Daily Citizen* (August 23, 1930).

"Rambling Reporter." (Column). *Hollywood Reporter* (August 4, 1983).

"Make-Up Award to Honor Lon Chaney II." *Hollywood Reporter* (August 22, 1983).

"Cleva Creighton, Famous Singing Soubrette Sings At Brink's." *Los Angeles Evening Herald* (April 29, 1913).

"Cabaret Singer Near Death From Poison." *Los Angeles Evening Herald* (May 1, 1913).

"Lon Chaney Better After Flu Attack." *Los Angeles Examiner* (May 2,

1929).

"Return Engagement Of Popular Singer." *Los Angeles Express* (April 29, 1913).

"Stage Manager's Wife Tries To End Life." *Los Angeles Express* (May 1, 1913).

"The Hen Pecks" (Stage Review). *Los Angeles Daily Times* (April 8, 1912).

"From The Mason To The Majestic" (Column). *Los Angeles Daily Times* (April 11, 1912).

"From The Mason To The Majestic" (Column). Los Angeles Daily Times, April 17, 1912.

"In The Big Play World" (Column). *Los Angeles Daily Times* (April 24, 1912).

"Tillie's Nightmare" (Stage Review). *Los Angeles Daily Times* (May 6, 1912).

"From The Mason To The Majestic" (Column), Los Angeles Daily Times, May 9, 1912.

"The Man Who Owns Broadway" (Stage Review). *Los Angeles Daily Times* (June 17, 1912).

"From The Mason To The Majestic" (Column). *Los Angeles Daily Times* (June 20, 1912).

"The Chaperones" (Stage Review). *Los Angeles Daily Times* (June 24, 1912).

"The Yankee Prince" (Stage Review). *Los Angeles Daily Times* (July 1, 1912).

"An American Idea" (Stage Review). *Los Angeles Daily Times*. (July 22, 1912).

"Summer Flirts" (Stage Review). *Los Angeles Daily Times* (August 12, 1912).

"Adolph and Oscar" (Stage Review). *Los Angeles Daily Times* (August 18, 1912).

"A New Ragtime Singer to Make her Debut at Brink's is Cleva

Creighton." *Los Angeles Daily Times* (August 28, 1912).

"Drinks Poison Behind Scenes." *Los Angeles Daily Times* (May 1, 1913).

"Lon Chaney in New York to See Specialist." *Los Angeles Times* (July 4, 1930).

"Lon Chaney Given Blood." *Los Angeles Times* (August 24, 1930).

"A Gallery of Grotesques." *Los Angeles Times* (June 26, 1983).

"Lon Chaney Tribute Set." *Los Angeles Times* (August 11, 1983).

"A Face-to-Face Look at Lon Chaney Sr." *Los Angeles Times* (February 28, 1985).

"Revenue Sought." *New York Times* (April 17, 1926).

"Lon Chaney Recognized In Taxi." *New York Times* (June 3, 1928).

"Lon Chaney Dead of a Lung Aliment, Was Screenland's Man of a Thousand Faces." *Oklahoma City Times* (August 26, 1930).

"Lon Chaney Visits Springs First Time In Several Years." *Rocky Mountain News* (June 12, 1928).

"Hometown Will Honor Lon Chaney." *Rocky Mountain News* (October 28, 1985).

"Springs To Pay Homage to Chaney." *Rocky Mountain News* (May 21, 1986).

"Man Behind 1,000 Faces." *Rocky Mountain News* (June 1, 1986).

Index

Lon Chaney

Index

Names of films are in bold italic; newspapers and magazines are in regular italic.

About the Author

Michael F. Blake is a make-up artist in motion pictures and television, working on such productions as *Star Trek VI, Soapdish, Back To The Future II* and *III, Tough Guys, Magnum P.I., Happy Days,* and *The Disney Sunday Night Movie*. His first-hand knowledge of motion picture make-up, as well as his personal interviews with pioneer make-up artists, have given him a great advantage in understanding and describing the make-ups Lon Chaney used.

At the age of ten, Michael watched his father, character actor Larry J. Blake, in the Chaney film biography *Man Of A Thousand Faces*. His interest in Chaney grew from that point and with his father's professional connections, he was able to meet and interview actors and technical staff who knew Chaney. As a result of his six-year research, he has been able to document six films that have never before been credited to Chaney in any published film list.

Owning the foremost collection of movie memorabilia on Lon Chaney (10 posters, 120 lobby cards, over 1900 photos, 4 autographed pictures and a hand-written letter by Chaney to name just a few of the items), Michael is regarded by film buffs and collectors as the leading authority on Lon Chaney. He has lectured at colleges and for historical groups across the country about the actor and his films. In 1982, while working at Universal Studios, Michael advised the studio tours department on Chaney's biographical and career information.

Michael Blake started his career in the motion picture business as a child actor working on television shows such as *Adam-12, Bonanza, Marcus Welby M.D., The Munsters, The Lucy Show, Kung Fu*, and *The Red Skelton Show*, to name a few. At the age of twenty-one, he started working as a make-up artist at Universal Studios — the same studio where Lon Chaney began his motion picture career.

Michael resides with his wife, Linda, and dog, Tara, in Los Angeles, California.

Lon Chaney

Endleaves Identification

Row 1
1. *Pay Me* (1917)
2. *London After Midnight* (1927)
3. *Tower of Lies* (1925)
4. *The Miracle Man* (1919)
5. *Where East is East* (1929)
6. circa 1916
7. On the Goldwyn lot (1921)

Row 2
1. On the *He Who Gets Slapped* set (1924)
2. Fisher's Follies (1912)
3. *The Scarlet Car* (1917)
4. *Tell It to the Marines* (1926)
5. Between Scenes, *A Blind Bargain* (1922)
6. On *Where East Is East* set (1929)
7. *Father and the Boys* set (1915)

Row 3
1. *The Road to Mandalay* (1926)
2. As Pew in *Treasure Island* (1920)
3. *Mr. Wu* (1927)
4. On *He Who Gets Slapped* set (1924)
5. Candid photo (1923)
6. *The Unholy Three* (1925)
7. *Thunder* (1929)

Row 4
1. On *The Unknown* set (1927)
2. On *Tell It To The Marines* Set (1926)
3. *The Fascination of the Fleur de Lis* (1915)
4. On *All the Brothers Were Valient* set (1923)
5. Merry in *Treasure Island* (1920)
6. On vacation (1923)
7. Candid (1922)

Row 5
1. On *Laugh, Clown, Laugh* set (1928)
2. *The Big City* (1928)
3. *Thunder* (1929)
4. On *West of Zanzibar* set (1928)
5. On vacation (1923)
6. On *West of Zanzibar* set (1928)
7. On *The Next Corner* set (1924)

Row 6
1. Opening of *Tell It to the Marines* (1927)
2. Pew in *Treasure Island* (1920)
3. *Riddle Gwane* (1918)
4. On *London After Midnight* (1927)
5. *The Penalty* (1920)
6. Appearing in *Shadows* (1922)
7. On location, *Tell It to the Marines* (1926)

Row 7
1. *While Paris Sleeps* (1920)
2. Wax Model
3. *Mr. Wu* (1927)
4. *Mockery* (1927)
5. Ah Wing in *Outside the Law* (1921)
6. About 22 years old
7. On the set of *The Penalty* (1920)

Row 8
1. *West of Zanzibar* (1928)
2. On *The Unknown* set (1927)
3. Early version of the ape-man in *A Blind Bargain* (1922)
4. *The Hunchback of Notre Dame* (1923)
5. *Victory* (1919)
6. *Tower of Lies* (1925)
7. *Tower of Lies* (1925)

Row 9
1. *London After Midnight* (1927)
2. *The Penalty* (1920)
3. *He Who Gets Slapped* (1924)
4. *Hell Morgan's Girl* (1917)
5. *Phantom of the Opera* (1925)
6. Candid (1923)
7. "Black Mike" in *Outside the Law* (1921)

Row 10
1. On *Tell It to the Marines* set (1926)
2. *Mr. Wu* (1927)
3. *While the City Sleeps* (1928)
4. On *The Big City* set (1928)
5. *The Road to Mandalay* (1926)
6. *The Blackbird* (1926)
7. As Fagin in *Oliver Twist* (1922)

Row 11
1. *The Grip of Jealousy* (1916)
2. *The Unholy Three* (1925)
3. On Goldwyn Lot (1922)
4. On Goldwyn Lot (1921)
5. On vacation fly fishing
6. *Almost An Actress* (1913)
7. *Laugh, Clown, Laugh* (1928)

Row 12
1. *The Big City* (1928)
2. *Where East Is East* (1929)
3. *The Road to Mandalay* (1926)
4. *Mr. Wu* (1927)
5. *London After Midnight* (1927)
6. *Tragedy of Whispering Creek* (1914)
7. The Doctor in *A Blind Bargain* (1922)

Row 13
1. On *Shadows* set (1922)
2. *Thunder* (1929)
3. Fischer's Follies (1912)
4. Arrival in LA (1928)
5. Ape-man in *Blind Bargain* (1922)
6. *The Unknown* (1927)
7. *The Road to Mandalay* (1926)

Row 14
1. Candid, *Hunchback* filming (1923)
2. *The Monster* (1925)
3. *The Unholy Three* (1930)
4. On *Tell It to the Marines* set (1926)
5. *Mockery* (1927)
6. *Tell It to the Marines* (1926)
7. Merry in *Treasure Island* (1920)